PRICE WARS

PRICE WARS

How the Commodities Markets Made Our Chaotic World

Rupert Russell

DOUBLEDAY
New York

Library of Congress Cataloging-in-Publication Data
Names: Russell, Rupert, author.
Title: Price wars : how the commodities markets made our chaotic world / Rupert Russell.
Description: New York : Doubleday, [2022] | Includes index.
Identifiers: LCCN 2021031111 (print) | LCCN 2021031112 (ebook) |
ISBN 9780385545853 (hardcover) | ISBN 9780385545860 (ebook)
Subjects: LCSH: Commodity exchanges. | International finance. | Pricing.
Classification: LCC HG6046 .R94 2022 (print) |
LCC HG6046 (ebook) | DDC 332.64/4—dc23
LC record available at https://lccn.loc.gov/2021031111
LC ebook record available at https://lccn.loc.gov/2021031112

To Mum

Contents

PART IV—IMAGININGS

PRICE
WARS

Introduction

Monsters and Mazes

I crawl into a tent. Arabic chatter bounces between a dozen teenage boys as they pass around a bottle of wine. Some are sitting in a circle, others are lying on stretcher-like beds against canvas walls. A few speak English. One tells me they're from Iraq. He tells me how he travelled with his girlfriend through Turkey to the shores of the Mediterranean. "I was standing on the beach," he says, gesturing eastwards towards the Turkish coast seven miles away. "I was just wearing my shorts. No wallet, nothing. I walked into the water. Then—"

"He is gay!" someone shouts behind me. I flinch. Is he talking about me? I am gay.

I turn around. One of the teenagers has stood up. He's holding the bottle of wine and pointing at someone lying on a bed. The drunkard is short, skinny and young—maybe sixteen years old.

He catches my eye. "He is gay!" He pauses to wait for my response.

My awkwardness peaks. I freeze. Maybe if I don't move, I'll become invisible somehow.

He persists. "He is gay!"

I change tactics and ignore him. "What happened next?" I shout to the swimmer.

"I started to swi—" he begins.

"Where are you from?" the drunkard asks me.

I surrender. "I'm from Britain."

"Brittany! Brittany!" he chants.

I turn back to the swimmer. "What did you do?" I say louder still.

"I got into the water," he shouts back, "started to swim."

"Brittany! Brittany!"

"I was in the water for two hours and the—"

"He is gay!"

"—and then the helicopter saw me. A boat came."

"He is gay!" he says as he jumps into the middle of the circle and pulls his trousers down. He stands for a moment expecting a reaction. Silence. Heads down, we all pretend not to notice. He twists, trips and collapses into a disorderly heap.

Strangely, this is what I've come looking for: chaos.

It's the summer of 2018 and I'm sitting in the Moria refugee camp. Tucked into a mountainside on Lesvos, the Greek island closest to Turkey, it's the gateway from East to West and the epicentre of the global refugee crisis. Wars, famines, recessions, persecutions thousands of miles from each other converge here through the one thing they all create: people searching for safety. From these few acres an invisible web of connections radiates out across the Mediterranean, the Sahara, the Euphrates and the Caucasus, linking disparate episodes of chaos large and small. Moria is the node.

I've come here in the hope of unscrambling my brain. It hasn't been at ease since 24 June 2016. It was the day after the British public voted to leave the European Union (EU) and I had just returned to the UK after a decade living in America. When my plane landed, I fired up my phone to discover that Prime Minister David Cameron had resigned. No one seemed to have any idea what was going on, least of all me, who had missed the whole thing. I was confused. I grew up with Princess Diana and the Spice Girls and movies where Hugh Grant struggles to find love. I didn't recognise this hermit kingdom. I was now a stranger in a strange land.

It was a topsy-turvy time, but at least, I reassured myself, parochial. Like our culinary delights "toad in the hole" and "bubble and squeak," foreigners saw our political tastes as similarly eccentric and not for them. But before long, there was a movement to import this British delicacy. "At the ballot box on November 8th we are going to do something so special," presidential candidate Donald J. Trump told a crowd of supporters in Raleigh, North Carolina. "It will be an amazing day, it will be called 'Brexit plus plus plus.'"

The weirdness was just beginning. Brexit plus Brexit plus plus plus were soon subsumed by an avalanche of horrors. The relentless Feed of tweets and posts and headlines and memes and viral videos plunged me into a digital vertigo, a kaleidoscope of tear gas, beheadings, black flags, floating bodies, burning rainforests, caged children and a new breed of monsters at the centre of it all. Nigel Farage, Donald Trump, Viktor Orbán, Matteo Salvini, Jair Bolsonaro, Rodrigo Duterte, Nicolás Maduro, Narendra Modi, Vladimir Putin, Xi Jinping, Kim Jong-un, Boko Haram and ISIS towered over everything, Godzilla-like. Everywhere they went destruction followed. Each calamity fed The Feed, a real-time conveyer belt of anxiety and outrage delivered directly into my brain. Equal parts Hollywood disaster movie and reality TV show, the spectacle was horrifying and captivating—a global-scale car crash I struggled to look away from.

I felt ill equipped to deal with this monstrous world. Born in 1985, I had grown up in London during the peaceful and prosperous 1990s. History was supposed to be over. It wasn't until I was sixteen that I saw my first real monsters when planes flew into the Pentagon and the World Trade Center on live TV. These monsters were, reassuringly, outsiders. They came from distant caves in faraway lands. Now, the monsters came from inside the bubble I called home. The familiar turned alien. My brain scrambled.

I had to know: where had the monsters come from?

To map their origins, I'd have to make sense of the chaos they had created. I'd somehow have to bring order to sprawling histories, endless variables and ever-growing datasets. Fortunately, mathematicians in the 1970s developed the tools for just such a task. These legendary "chaos theorists" discovered that what looks like irreducible randomness can, in fact, have a logic. And this logic need not be complicated. It can be devilishly simple.

Imagine mapping the extinction of the dinosaurs. You could describe in detail every single micro event, every tsunami, hurricane and alteration to the ecosystem that, over thousands of years, led to their demise. Or you could point to one macro moment: when an asteroid struck the earth. It was this moment that triggered a cascade: a chain reaction that grew and grew and grew. Chaos theory teaches us that such moments need not be big. Triggering events can be very small, as small as the flap of a butterfly's wings. Perhaps my cartography of chaos just needed to discover one thing. I just needed to spot the butterfly.

I wondered if the chaos of the 2010s had been triggered by a singular disturbance, large or small. On the surface, it appeared that each of The Feed's modern-day horrors arose from circumstances that were profoundly unique. Trump locking children in cages, Putin invading Ukraine, ISIS beheading apostates and Farage's Brexit victory all felt like independent events. Each could exist without the other. But their simultaneous eruption points to another possibility: that these episodes are not free-floating snowflakes but bound together in an avalanche. A cascade of crises with a shared beginning.

I spent 2017 gathering clues. I made use of my sociology doctorate I had earned from Harvard to survey the social-science literature. But much of the tumult was too recent to have made it into academic publications. So I decided to undertake an investigation of my own. The Franco-German broadcaster ARTE agreed to finance such a journey as a documentary film, and by the spring of 2018 I was finally ready. I stepped through the digital black mirror and descended the circles of the twenty-first-century Inferno.

I went to Mosul, Iraq, with a United Nations Mine Action Service (UNMAS) bomb-disposal unit to witness the post-apocalyptic wasteland left by perhaps the world's greatest monster of all, the Islamic State. In what was once Eastern Ukraine, I hid from sniper fire with Russian-backed separatist fighters in snow-covered trenches to understand Putin's postmodern warfare. In Maduro's Venezuela, I encountered an economic catastrophe so brutal that young women sought sterilisation and kids formed gangs to fight over garbage in a kind of absurdist Hobbesian nightmare where the struggle to eat is a war of all against all. I went to northern Kenya in search of the chaos that climate change will bring and found cattle herders in a

Martian landscape guarding their goats with AK-47s. I embedded with the UN peacekeeping force AMISOM in Somalia to see how Al-Shabaab were exploiting the climate crisis by weaponising hunger itself. By 2019, the US border was in chaos as Trump subjected hundreds of thousands of migrants to a militarised festival of cruelty. I retraced the migrants' journey through the cartel-controlled corridors up into the mountains of Guatemala to see what had sent so many so suddenly to America's border.

Each stop surprised me, and surprised me in the same way. The closer I came to the monsters, the smaller they became. They were unimpressive: not even "mini-me's" to the Pol Pots and Hitlers and Genghis Khans. I realised that, in our telling of monster stories, we had overlooked an archetypal feature. Monsters confront man not on an open plain but always in an elaborate maze. Whether in Ancient Greek myths or Hollywood movies, the labyrinth is as essential to the story as the creature itself. Think of winding hotel corridors in *The Shining*, the spaceship in *Alien* or the mall in *Dawn of the Dead*. It is precisely these enclosures that make the chase exciting. It's not, however, the feature we remember. Instead, we are captivated by what is unusual and grotesque. As The Feed has adopted the tropes of the horror genre, it has incorporated its archetypal distortions. The monster is the star, inflated into an awesome physical creature whose destruction is understood through his monstrous biology, psychology or ideology. But real-life monsters are not superhuman; they are *Homo sapiens* made of flesh and bone. Their power comes from the architecture they inhabit. It enables as well as constrains. And during the 2010s, the walls had crumbled. The cages were unlocked.

I discovered that this architecture was neither mysterious nor unimaginably complex. It is built out of something specifically designed to make chaos simple. A social engine that condenses billions of human interactions down to a single number. The maze was built with prices.

Consider the millions of human interactions that make an ordinary pencil: the forest cutters, graphite miners, rubber growers, factory workers, warehouse packers, truck drivers and shopkeepers. They do not speak the same language, nor even know of each other's existence. But by looking to those Arabic numerals fronted by peculiar symbols—£ $ €—they know what they each need to do to make that pencil. The price has simplified the sum of those millions of trades between buyers and sellers into a single digit. It tells them whether the world wants more or less of what it is they are providing. These prices harmonise the global supply chain that criss-crosses cultures and continents without any central authority dispensing orders to anyone.

Prices are like the air we breathe. We have integrated them so deeply into our lives that we barely recognise them as human inventions. We take it for granted that they appear on everything because they define the value of everything. A value created by the constant negotiation of the world's buyers and sellers. These trades "price in" the impact of climate shocks, political revolutions and demographic shifts before they've even happened. But they do more than just describe the world and simplify it down to a few digits. They are the coordinating engines that move food and fuel and manufactured goods and savings and equities and debt across the globe.

Prices create a spontaneous order all around us. They tell us what to do. Prices govern which jobs we take, which neighbourhoods we live in, how many children we can have and what medical treatment we can seek. Prices do this to us so frequently that it's easy to forget this invisible force is ordering so much of our day-to-day lives. And this is true for nations as well as households, for prime ministers and presidents, terrorists and insurgents. We are all living in a world ruled by prices.

What I found was that when prices suddenly change, order fractures and chaos erupts. Things that we thought were solid melt into air. Price can create a tsunami of hunger, an exodus of refugees and an entirely new class of oligarchs. Price can spark riots, revolutions and war. Prices can bankroll palaces, police states and foreign invasions. Prices unlock cages and release monsters.

In price, I found my butterfly: the singular trigger that launches a cascade of crises. I found not just one instance but many beats of the butterfly's wing over the chaotic decade. These beats took place in the commodities markets each time the price of essential commodities—basic goods such as food and oil—changed sharply and dramatically. There were multiple price shocks, each causing a wave of chaos and each one linked to the next. Each wave was its own kind of war, a rupture that tore through the social fabric: starving and displacing, killing and maiming. Each of these wars was rooted in prices. They are price wars.

To find out why prices were swinging so wildly during the tumultuous 2010s, I went on another journey, to the world's financial capitals: New York and London. I met with hedge-fund managers, bankers and commodity traders who, like me, were trying to get to the bottom of what a "price" really was. They told me that much was hidden inside this deceptively simple number, and great fortunes were being built on figuring it out—if only for a moment. They spoke of how commodity prices had begun to change at the turn of the twenty-first century, and how this change accelerated at the start of its second decade. Prices swung wildly, and these swings defied the so-called economic fundamentals of real-world supply and demand. They believed that these swings were due to a silent war taking place between financial speculators—be they banks, hedge funds, or any other entity with a towering portfolio. This war, like all wars, was an ever-escalating arms race: each year would bring new innovations, new tactics and new strategies. Yet their effect was always the same: chaotic prices.

As I traced the butterfly's path, I found that it didn't fly in a straight line. Its path was circular. Price spikes in food and oil triggered crises, and these crises were then "priced" back into the markets, only to create yet another spike and another crisis. Chaos in the commodities markets and chaos in the real world fed off each other. This feedback loop had grown into an engine of chaos: mutating it, amplifying it, spreading it. It is what connects the Arab Spring, the rise of ISIS, the Brexit vote, the war in Ukraine, the collapse of Venezuela and the US border crisis into a singular butterfly's path, a path that starts and ends in the West. Along the way, shocks from climate change and Covid-19 would multiply the chaos as speculative finance "priced in" their imagined effects, causing the butterfly's wings to beat again and again.

This is a story about global finance capitalism—how the power of price connects disparate regions of the world and how a small disturbance in one region can cause chaos in another. It is a story about how economic freedom is undermining political freedom; how the madness of markets is connected to the madness of war; how rational systems have irrational outcomes; how monsters are unleashed from their cages. It is a story about how chaotic markets are creating a chaotic world.

PART I

PRICES

1

Chaos: Why Societies Boil at 210

As the dust settled and the "I Survived 2016" T-shirts sold out, I realised that the populist explosion was far bigger than Donald Trump and Nigel Farage. They were just the English-speaking insurrectionists of a reactionary revolution that had already swept across Europe. Starting in 2015, populist parties racked up double-digit gains throughout the continent, came in close seconds in France and Austria, and won power in Poland and Italy. Something had rocked the Western world all at once. It had transcended language barriers, political peculiarities and currency unions. But what was it? Some blamed the economic collapse in 2008, but the Financial Crisis was nearly a decade old. It seemed to me that there must be a more immediate reason why voters from Rome to Raleigh to Rzeszów pushed the button marked "detonate."

"For me, the problem is the thousands of illegal immigrants stealing, raping and dealing drugs," said Matteo Salvini, the leader of Italy's Northern League, at a rally in Rome. It was 2015, in the midst of the global refugee crisis that saw over a million migrants come to Europe. Right-wing populists declared it an invasion of "barbaric, Muslim, rapist hordes of men" (AfD, Germany), "young barbarians" (Golden Dawn, Greece), "criminals, terrorists and idlers!" (National Alliance, Latvia), and "masses of young men in their twenties, with beards singing 'Allahu Akbar'" (Party of Freedom, Holland). On the campaign trail, Trump promised to extend his wall with Mexico to the Middle East, with "a total and complete shutdown of Muslims entering the United States." The Vote Leave campaign distributed leaflets showing Iraq, Syria and Turkey joining the EU, with a threatening arrow indicating their impending migrant invasion of Britain. In case the message wasn't clear enough, Nigel Farage personally launched a poster campaign depicting thousands of brown-skinned people with the all-caps warning: "BREAKING POINT." The barbarians were no longer at the gates, they had broken through. "Give us back France, damn it!" Marine Le Pen demanded. "We drink wine whenever we want!"

I'm sitting in the heart of this "barbarian invasion." Nearly half of the refugees who travelled to Europe since 2015 have passed through the Moria camp and slept in tents just like the one I'm in now. These Iraqi teenagers are the "rapist hordes" incarnate, the monsters of the populist imagination. But they aren't singing "Allahu Akbar." They don't have beards. They have hip, undercut haircuts. They're smoking, drinking wine and bragging about their secret girlfriends. *What could be more French than that?* I wonder.

Scenes like this didn't make it into The Feed. Instead, images of migrants—packed in boats, dead on beaches, camped in tent cities—dominated. The accompanying headlines framed migrants as a "security threat," lending false credibility to the populists' alleged "invasion." It is why the right-wing firebrands, many of whom had decades-long careers at the margins of politics, were suddenly propelled towards power. Their xenophobic message finally resonated with just enough voters to shake the foundations of the Western liberal order.

I step outside. I walk through the "jungle," the hastily constructed overflow camp housing 6,000 refugees. I walk up a hill that was once an olive grove. UN-branded tents are scattered haphazardly among piles of plastic bottles, torn clothes and used nappies. Kids leap over the garbage and hide behind tents, firing bows and arrows made from olive-tree branches. Three women have cleared out a space between piles of garbage to light a makeshift fire to boil rice. A man leans over a bucket of water as another shaves off his hair. They say there's a scalp fungus going around. Behind them I see the main camp they would be in, if it wasn't already over-capacity. Built to house 3,000, it is a fortress of watchtowers and barbed-wire fences. Greek soldiers patrol the perimeter.

This camp may well be what the populists fear, but it's also a mirror image of themselves. It's a kind of authoritarian disorder, a militarised messiness. Trump deployed the army at the US–Mexico border, but the migration crisis surged. Johnson wants to "take back control" from the EU, but he's losing his grip on Northern Ireland and Scotland, on secure food and medical supplies. Salvini closed down refugee camps in Italy, only to create an epidemic of home-lessness as migrants were forced onto the streets. Their attempts to impose order created a new kind of chaos. Perhaps this is because they never dealt with the cause of the migrant crisis, the very crisis that had propelled them to power. Indeed, why did the number of refugees surge so suddenly in 2015 and 2016 after two decades of declining?

Another tent. One young man sits cross-legged on his stretcher-bed fiddling with his phone. He's got a striking, John Lennon look: narrow face, circular glasses and long, curly hair. He turns the screen to me and shows me pictures of his home in Raqqa, Syria. He shows me the street, the houses, the cars—it's all ordinary. He tells me life was peaceful growing up. But then, when he was nine years old, protests started. Assad responded with force. Protestors were shot and killed. Militias sprang up. A civil war erupted. ISIS took over his hometown. Then the Kurdish Peshmerga forces came. He shows me another photograph. The street is barely recognisable. He points to one pile of bricks: "That was my home." The Peshmerga forced him out of the city, he says. He fled Syria, travelled through Turkey, crossed the Mediterranean to this Greek island. For him, chaos was a seven-year journey. It started with those protests in March 2011. It started with the Arab Spring. But he doesn't want to talk about what happened afterwards. He's worried about discussing ISIS or the Peshmerga. He's got family still in Syria. He's worried about other people in the camp, whom they might be connected to, and what they might do.

I hop from tent to tent. I meet young men from Iraq, Syria and Yemen. Each of them is fleeing a civil war, each started in the aftermath of the Arab Spring. The protests in Yemen began a revolution which, in 2014, escalated into a civil war. Syria's civil war spread into Iraq in 2014 when ISIS captured Mosul. But most were too young to remember the protests. Nor were they interested. They didn't want to talk about the chaos nearly a decade ago. They want to talk about the chaos they're living in now.

Hakar is an Iraqi Kurd. He was imprisoned by ISIS when they took Mosul. "Every day, we were in pain, we were tortured," he says as he shows me scars on his arms and legs. He was there for nine months until the Peshmerga captured the prison and freed him. He visited his old home for the first time with a friend. When they got there, something exploded. Perhaps it was a booby trap, perhaps they triggered a dormant bomb buried in the rubble. His friend died instantly. "My face was destroyed," he says. He parts his hair and shows me where the doctors inserted bolts to keep his skull altogether. When the hospital discharged him, he knew he had to leave Iraq. Maybe he could get a second—or third—shot at life somewhere else.

He says we have to find a different tent to film his interview. Someone here is making him feel uneasy. Mohammed's tent seemed friendly, so I take Hakar there. Mohammed is sitting on his bed sipping a plastic cup of coffee. He offers us a sip. Hakar gestures no thank you.

"Where are you from?" Mohammed asks him.

"Kurdi," Hakar replies.

Silence. It dawns on me that maybe this wasn't such a great idea. Mohammed had been exiled by the Kurdish army. Hakar had been imprisoned by ISIS, a Sunni Muslim group. He probably suspected that Mohammed was a Sunni Muslim too, and could have been a member of ISIS or supported them. We make a quick exit.

After an hour of searching, we find an empty tent. The camera is finally rolling and Hakar wants to talk about what just happened. "Fights happen here, because of food, religion, anything," he says. For him the conflict isn't something old or faraway. The very people they were fleeing from were right here in the camp, sometimes in the same tent. Like a cruel psychology experiment from the 1950s, it was as if the camp administrators were trying to see what happened if you mixed together Sunni and Shia, Christian and Muslim, Syrian and Iraqi, Arab and Kurd. Hakar shows me the results on his phone. I see faces erupt with blood as masked men beat them with metal bars. Hakar says the victims were Kurdish and their crime was not fasting during Ramadan. That first flap of the butterfly's wings may have been nearly seven years earlier and thousands of miles away, but the chaos continued to spread, to upend lives and end them.

Hakar says that an online community of Kurds have been trying to identify the masked men. They've managed to match the faces in the videos with Facebook profiles. The men are dressed up in jihadi garb, brandishing automatic weapons, with ISIS-style "Abu" prefixes to their names. Hakar believes the attackers are ISIS. "There is not any difference between here and an ISIS jail. I can't go outside because I see them with their beards and moustaches. I'm afraid, really. I'm terrified." He went to one of the camp guards. He hoped the attackers would be arrested or at least he'd be moved to another part of the camp. "I showed him the pictures. I told him that ISIS was in the camp."

"What did the guard say?" I ask.

"He said he'd give me twenty euros for a blow job."

A chain of events was coming into view: the Arab Spring revolutions, the outbreak of civil wars, the rise of ISIS, the global refugee crisis and the populist explosion. This all seemed like a butterfly effect. But when I looked into the science behind this famous metaphor, I discovered that it is far more than the mere linking of disparate events. It's a powerful mathematical theory that describes not just their connection, but their explosiveness too.

The theory began on a routine winter day in 1961 at the Massachusetts Institute of Technology (MIT). A climatology professor named Edward Lorenz stood by his Royal McBee as the 113 vacuum tubes inside whirred and rattled. Enormous, slow and noisy, it was one of the first factory-made computers and Lorenz had programmed one of the first climate simulations. He watched a mechanical type-writer print line after line of numbers. Each line predicted how the elements—pressure, temperature, rain, etc.—would combine to produce the weather. Looking at the printout, he wondered what would happen a few more months into the future. But rather than start the program over from the beginning, he entered numbers from a line in the middle of the printout. He set the Royal McBee to work and left it to get himself a fresh cup of coffee. When he returned an hour later, he thought the computer had malfunctioned. The results didn't make any sense. "The numbers being printed were nothing like the old ones," he later wrote. "I immediately suspected a weak vacuum tube or some other computer trouble."

The Royal McBee wasn't broken. The vacuum tubes were working just fine. Lorenz found there was a tiny difference in how each one started. When he restarted the simulation, he had rounded the original number 0.506127 down to 0.506. "The initial round-off errors were the culprits," he discovered. "They were steadily amplifying until they dominated the solution." A thousandth of a degree Celsius should have had no impact. Satellites couldn't even measure a difference that small. Ever since Isaac Newton, physicists had assumed that cause and effect were proportional. Small forces had small effects. Measurements only needed to be approximate. But Lorenz's printouts suggested something different. Small forces could have big effects. But how?

There was something unusual about the equations that Lorenz was using. He was trying to capture how the weather today could impact the weather tomorrow, and how tomorrow's weather would impact the day after tomorrow's weather, and so forth. His equations had to capture this feedback. He had to use a "non-linear" function to do so. Before computers, non-linear functions were hard to calculate. Each new day would require a new set of calculations that would have to be done by hand. It was cumbersome and impractical. So the world of feedback was largely ignored, and its scientific importance dismissed. Computers made this world of feedback suddenly accessible. And almost as soon as the first computers began processing these non-linear equations, discoveries were made.

Lorenz's was one of the first. He found that systems filled with feedback are highly *sensitive*. Small changes in temperature or pressure could be amplified over time. A gust of wind could become turbulence, the turbulence could gather into a storm and a storm could grow into a hurricane. Feedback amplifies, it turns something small into something big. Lorenz called the power of these small starting points the "sensitivity to initial conditions." He described it with a metaphor: a seagull flapping its wings in Brazil causing a tornado in Texas.

In 1972, he was ready to present his big idea to an academic conference in Washington, D.C. But before giving the talk, he received a suggestion from the conference organiser, Philip Merilees. Why not swap the seagull for a butterfly? Lorenz doesn't know why Merilees made this suggestion. He thought he might have been inspired by Ray Bradbury's short story "A Sound of Thunder," where the death of a prehistoric butterfly sets in motion a series of events that alters the result of a presidential election. But Merilees said he'd never heard of it. "[T]he butterfly, with its seeming frailty and lack of power," Lorenz later reasoned, "is a natural choice for a symbol of the small that can produce the great." His talk, "Does the Flap of a Butterfly's Wings in Brazil Set Off a Tornado in Texas?," sparked a revolution that spread through meteorology, mathematics, the natural sciences and even philosophy and popular culture. The chance change to the title of his talk—swapping out a seagull for a butterfly—was a testament to the power of sensitivity that he had discovered. Without it the revolution may never have occurred.

The popular telling of the butterfly effect emphasises the importance of chance encounters in sparking a chain reaction. But Lorenz's point was quite different. Sensitivity is not a universal feature of the world with its own causal power. It is instead a feature of a system, a system that at its heart is an amplifying engine: something which grows small things into big things.

As I looked into the events of my own causal chain, I found a constellation of amplifying engines all working together. In Syria, it was the regime's violence. By oppressing the initial Arab Spring protests so violently they encouraged more protests, which they also violently oppressed, which encouraged the formation of militias to defend the protestors who, when the regime attacked them as well, grew into small armies fighting what was fast becoming a civil war. As the fighting reduced cities to rubble, refugees first fled to Lebanon and Turkey and then later to Europe. Populists held rallies denouncing their arrival, which the media covered and the algorithms powering Facebook and Twitter promoted, fuelling yet more rallies. It was a feedback loop of escalating outrage, an engine that turned the arrival of refugees into overwhelming "invasions."

As powerful as the engines of state oppression, media coverage and algorithmic engagement are, none started the chaos. They had amplified what was already there. I still had to find the first flap of the butterfly's wings. It had happened in a place I had been to. The place where the Arab Spring began.

An egg whistled past my head and smashed near my shoes. The crowd was bored. Behind me was an enormous poster of Mohamed Bouazizi stretching across a building. I was standing on the spot where he had doused himself with gasoline, lit a match and ignited the Arab Spring. It was here in Sidi Bouzid, a small rural town in Tunisia, that the butterfly's wings first flapped. Bouazizi's self-immolation sparked the protests, the revolutions, the civil wars, the refugee crisis and Europe's populist explosion. His act was the "initial condition."

I had gone to Sidi Bouzid years before I began thinking about chaos and where it all began. I was there for a different reason: to find out what happened after the revolution for my first documentary film, *Freedom for the Wolf*. It was 17 December 2014, the four-year anniversary of Bouazizi's protest, and local dignitaries were giving speeches. After fifteen minutes, the crowd stopped listening. They broke down the barricade and marched down the street. They held signs with symbols of Islam and the Salafist parties. My translator and two producers had fled, but black flags shimmered in the winter light through my lens so I stayed put and filmed. Three kids passed me chanting, "*Daesh, Daesh*" ("Isis, Isis").

"The Libyan people rose against their dictators after the events of Sidi Bouzid, so did the Egyptians, Yemenis and the Syrians," said President Moncef Marzouki an hour later at a rally. He was the first revolutionary president and the election was less than two weeks away. He told a familiar story, a story that we liked to tell in the West as well. He spoke of a single hero who stood up against Ben Ali's dictatorship and inspired not just a nation but the world. "People knew from that moment that they had to fight for their freedoms."

The more time I spent in Tunisia, the more holes I found in this "freedom" narrative. True, there were plenty of people—especially devout Muslims and Islamists—who sought freedom from the old dictatorship's religious oppression. "Life under Ben Ali was hell, I spent five years in his prisons," Rached Ghannouchi, the leader of Tunisia's foremost Islamist party, Ennahda, told me. But even among the devout there were other grievances. El Général, the rapper who produced the revolution's anthem "Rais Lebled," told me he wanted Tunisia to enact Sharia Law in order to get "rid of joblessness." Everywhere people spoke of everyday necessities, not abstract ideals. "People want to afford their basic needs: food and clothes," a man told me in a café. His friend chimed in, "When the change came, we thought that our lives were going to be better especially in 'bad' neighbourhoods where the revolution galvanised. They were the heart of the revolution. However, nothing really happened after the revolution."

On the eve of the election, I interviewed Marzouki. I asked him if he had overlooked bread-and-butter issues for lofty rhetoric about freedom. "I prefer to talk about our earthquake, because, in fact, it was an earthquake and the old regime was destroyed and now we are trying to build a new political regime," he began, "and I must confess that it's a tough issue. It's not so easy. I have been many times to Sidi Bouzid and their people were expecting more from the revolution. They were expecting better living conditions and so forth. Unfortunately, we have just given them freedom of expression, freedom of association, and so forth. And even this is not enough. People are expecting more."

Marzouki went on to lose that evening to Beji Caid Essebsi. Essebsi had run on a nationalist platform. He promised to bring economic security to Tunisia. He had also been the interior minister under the dictatorship, before Ben Ali, of Habib Bourguiba. As a man who had run the police state, he was hardly a symbol of freedom. But Marzouki had, like most of us in the West, misjudged the revolution. The "earthquake" was not triggered by a sudden yearning for freedom brought about by the sacrifice of a single individual. Something else had shifted, suddenly, violently and not just in Tunisia. A tectonic plate had shaken the Arab world.

Perhaps the origin of chaos I was looking for wasn't best pictured in the graceful motion of a butterfly. Perhaps the origin was, as Marzouki suggested, seismic: pent-up, sudden, violent. Perhaps there was a mathematical model that could illuminate the logic of this sort of chaos, one that could predict when earthquakes would strike.

This question was first posed in 1983. Kurt Wiesenfeld had graduated from Berkeley with a doctorate that delved into the new world of non-linear mathematics. His first job was as a post-doctoral researcher for the noted Dutch physicist Per Bak at the Brookhaven Lab on Long Island, New York. "[Bak] had tackled a series of very hot problems," Wiesenfeld tells me. "His taste was to go where the controversy was." He had done important work on the theoretically impossible five-sided quasi-crystal. Now he wanted to get into the revolutionary field of chaos.

Lorenz's meteorological models had revealed how chaotic systems are highly sensitive and powered by feedback. But weather is hard to study. There are so many moving parts, so many different variables all interacting with each other. You can't put the weather in a lab and run experiments on it. So physicists began searching for simpler things, things that could be controlled, manipulated and isolated in a laboratory. Bak, Wiesenfeld and another post-doc, Chao Tang, settled on exploring chaos in "phase transitions."

An everyday phase transition is the boiling of water. At a certain pressure and temperature, water transitions from liquid to steam. But what does this have to do with the butterfly effect? "If you change the temperature a little bit the system only changes a little bit," Wiesenfeld explains. "If you're at 98 degrees centigrade, nothing special happens. But if you're at 100 degrees, you get these amazing, miraculous changes." In other words, the butterfly effect didn't have to be a gathering storm. Chaos can erupt all at once.

Per Bak's breakthrough, however, came not with water but with sand. "Imagine you have a level pile of sand and you drop a grain, drop a grain, drop a grain," Wiesenfeld says. "At the beginning, probably nothing will happen. It will just nestle in a tiny hole somewhere, or a gap between grains of sand. If you keep dropping it on the same place, you build up a pile vertically. But once that angle is too sheer, the tension won't be enough to stop gravity from pulling it down." That last grain of sand triggers an avalanche. Order breaks down.

Like Edward Lorenz's weather simulation, the sandpile is highly sensitive. If a grain of sand lands just one millimetre to the right, perhaps nothing happens. But just one millimetre to the left and the grains of sand begin to tumble. But while the sandpile is sensitive, it operates with different rules than the butterfly. "It wasn't wildly chaotic or random," Wiesenfeld says. "If it had a more chaotic behaviour, it wouldn't sustain itself day to day." It has the regularity of a stable system of dropping grains of sand on a single point. But this regular behaviour was driving what looks like an orderly mound towards chaos. And the tension that gives the mound its apparent solidity is brittle. It is highly sensitive to the smallest of disturbances. Bak, Wiesenfeld and Chang called this phenomenon "self-organised criticality." Their paper became one of the most cited in physics. As its popularity spread, it acquired a metaphorical name: the edge of chaos.

One of the most productive applications of their theory was on earthquakes. Earthquakes, it turns out, do not happen randomly. They happen at a frequency predicted by the sandpile. Tectonic plates are in tension with each other. They move by themselves. And every once in a while, the tension breaks and the ground shakes beneath our feet. To live on top of this self-organised system is also—as any resident of Tokyo or San Francisco can attest—to live on the edge of chaos. This conception of chaos fuses a psychological metaphor with a mathematical prediction. It captures both the human and the physical sides of earthquakes. It also describes, I came to discover, a social one as well.

Post-docs and graduate students from Harvard and MIT mill about the open-plan office chit-chatting about chaos and complexity. They take Edward Lorenz's and Per Bak's ideas about the physical world to understand the social world in all its glorious messiness. I've come to New England Complex Systems Institute in Cambridge, Massachusetts, to talk to its founder and president, Yaneer Bar-Yam. "It turns out that the mathematics that has been developed in physics," he tells me, "describes not just chaos, but also how collective behaviours arise." These mathematical models "can be used effectively for understanding social systems, particularly for understanding these cascading effects that are propagating around the world." He, like me, was trying to understand how chaos had spread and how one crisis was linked to the next. But, unlike me, he had predicted much of it. He had seen the chaos I'd witnessed in Tunisia and Greece before it erupted.

In 2010, Bar-Yam and his team were looking into a crisis that had convulsed across the world two years earlier. Not the headline-grabbing Financial Crisis, but the perhaps equally grave "Global Food Crisis" of 2008. Between 2005 and 2008, global food prices had risen by 83 per cent as the price of wheat more than doubled. As the prices surged, over 155 million people were pushed into poverty and 80 million into hunger in 2008 alone. Riots broke out in forty-eight countries from India to Egypt to Argentina. Even Italy was rocked by "pasta protests."

Bar-Yam wondered if just one number—the global price of food—could predict riots breaking out spontaneously on every inhabited continent. Perhaps the unique messiness of each of these forty-eight countries—their histories, cultures and political systems—was, in fact, irrelevant. Perhaps it didn't matter which religion dominated, who their president was, or what climate they had. Perhaps all the incredible complexity of the world could be reduced to something simple, something elemental: sustenance.

The theory was a straightforward hypothesis: it could be tested and used to predict the future. But first Bar-Yam and his team needed to figure out how expensive food had to get before people took to the streets. "The methods that were developed in physics enable us to understand the transition from water to steam. The boiling of water," Bar-Yam explains, can also be used to model "the transition between peaceful and disrupted societies." Societies, like water, have a boiling point. A number that tips them over the edge of chaos. Chaos isn't just a metaphor: it's a way of modelling behaviour. And it doesn't matter if the elements involved are people, grains of sand or water molecules.

Yet the metaphor helps us to understand how these social avalanches work. A food-price spike may start a riot, but it isn't the *only* cause of the riot. It is the proverbial straw that breaks the camel's back. It is the extra grain of sand that triggers an avalanche. Many grains of sand are already there, such as corruption, extreme poverty, high unemployment or ethnic persecution. The regime was able to contain them, to hold them together with a stable façade. But despite its orderly appearance, the regime teeters on the edge of chaos.

A sudden rise in food prices is that final grain of sand. When it drops, it hits the others, it dislodges them, breaks them free, and as they fall they tumble and gather more grains—more resentments, more complaints, more grievances—until a small disturbance becomes a full-blown avalanche. By the time the avalanche is under way, that original grain of sand—the food prices—may be lost and forgotten. Other grains of sand, buried deeper and for longer, may come to the foreground. In a riot or revolution, it may be these long-lasting grievances that we notice, but they were not what triggered the cascade and ignited the protests.

But in 2010, while Bar-Yam and his team were building their model, something strange was happening. The price of food was escalating rapidly just as it had done in 2008. Bar-Yam was alarmed. The Financial Crisis had precipitated a global recession, unemployment was soaring and governments were broke. The money wasn't there to absorb the costs of rising prices. The pain would be magnified. "In December of 2010 we sent a report to the US government warning that high food prices could lead to social unrest and political instability," Bar-Yam says. "And that was four days before Mohamed Bouazizi started things in Tunisia."

"Corruption in Tunisia is getting worse," the US Embassy in Tunis reported to Washington in a leaked diplomatic cable. A Tunisian blog had found it among the WikiLeaks trove, just three weeks before Yaneer Bar-Yam submitted his report. "Whether it's cash, services, land, property, or yes, even your yacht, President Ben Ali's family is rumoured to covet it and reportedly gets what it wants," the cable continued. The corruption is "keeping domestic investment rates low and unemployment high." Another cable revealed just what this corruption looked like. It described a dinner the US Ambassador attended with Sakher El Materi, Ben Ali's brother-in-law:

> The dinner included perhaps a dozen dishes, including fish, steak, turkey, octopus, fish couscous and much more. The quantity was sufficient for a very large number of guests. Before dinner a wide array of small dishes were served, along with three different juices (including Kiwi juice, not normally available here). After dinner, he served ice cream and frozen yoghurt he brought in by plane from Saint Tropez, along with blueberries and raspberries and fresh fruit and chocolate cake . . . El Materi has a large tiger ("Pasha") on his compound, living in a cage. He acquired it when it was a few weeks old. The tiger consumes four chickens a day.

These cables lit up Tunisia's burgeoning blogosphere just as food prices were skyrocketing. Youth unemployment was already over 30 per cent. More and more people were going hungry. The country was teetering on the edge of chaos. Then, three weeks later, Mohamed Bouazizi set himself on fire.

Protests erupted all over the country. Waving baguettes in the air, people chanted, "Water and bread, yes! Ben Ali, no!" The police responded with live ammunition and, on 8 January 2011, shot and killed thirty protestors. Outraged, even more took to the streets. Ben

Ali changed tactics. He announced new subsidies for bread, milk and sugar. But it was too little, too late; the avalanche had begun. "We don't want bread or anything else, we just want him to leave," the protestors chanted. "After that we will eat whatever we have to." A viral Facebook post showed the body of a dead protestor with the caption, "Too bad he won't be able to enjoy the new low prices." The food-price spike had been the trigger, but it was no longer the cause. It was the final grain of sand that dislodged all the grievances that had built up year after year. Decades of corruption, surveillance, torture and religious persecution were now out in the open. What was first called the *thwart el-Khobz* ("Bread Revolution") became the all-encompassing "Jasmine Revolution." On 14 January Ben Ali fled the country. The dictatorship collapsed.

The grains continued to tumble. The global food-price spike was pushing the entire Middle East—which imports much of its grain—to the edge of chaos. Another self-immolation, this time in Egypt. The owner of a Cairo restaurant set himself on fire because he didn't qualify for the government-subsidised bread. A week later, 15,000 protestors filled Tahrir Square singing, "Bread, freedom and dignity." In Jordan, the "day of rage" saw protestors display bread on their placards as they chanted, "Bread is not only for the rich. Bread is a red line. Beware of our starvation and fury." King Abdullah announced a $125 million package to reduce prices and boost salaries, but the protestors—demanding "bread and freedom"—now wanted more. Yemenis took to the streets with signs saying: "Our stomachs ache. There is no bread." Their government tried to appease them with food subsidies, but the protests continued. In Syria, protestors brandished bread above their heads and, when Assad announced his own food subsidies, ignored him, as the crowds had done elsewhere. Even Kuwaitis, who had never struggled to afford bread, staged protests demanding an end to corruption. The tension that had been building in Middle Eastern dictatorships was finally released. The food-price spike had pushed them over the edge of chaos.

Seeing the Arab Spring this way was a revelation. It showed how something simple—food prices—could be the engine of chaos across an entire region. It explained why the revolutions all took place

within the same few months, why so many civil wars raged, and why
so many people were forced to flee their homes. It's why there was an
unprecedented migrant surge, a surge that overwhelmed The Feed
and fed the populist-media-algorithm outrage machine. On the one
hand, it was a feverishly complex story stretching from Tunis and
Damascus to Lesvos and Berlin, encompassing dozens of countries,
hundreds of militias and tens of millions of migrants. But on the
other hand, it was simple—a chain of events set into motion by a
single number: the price of food.

Bar-Yam and his colleagues built a model of the phase transition
from social order to chaos. They mapped out the twin eruptions of
2008 and 2010–11 and found there was indeed a boiling point. They
used the UN's Food Price Index, a monthly average of the price
of food commodities, such as wheat, rice and corn, trading on the
international markets. "We found that a Food Price Index value of
about 210," where prices were more than double what they were
in the early 2000s, was the "tipping point, above which food-price
increases appear to cause social unrest around the world." Just as 100
degrees Celsius is the boiling point for water, 210 on the Food Price
Index "is the boiling point for societies." Bar-Yam says, "It's when
riots are triggered."

The Tunisian dictator Ben Ali should have known better. His path
to power was paved by the food riots that struck his predecessor,
Habib Bourguiba. In 1984 Bourguiba raised the price of bread by
slashing state subsidies. Riots erupted. The police killed 150 protestors. Bourguiba hastily restored the subsidies and the unrest came to
an end, but his regime had suffered a critical blow. The ambitious
government minister Ben Ali seized on Bourguiba's weakness and
came to power in a *coup d'état* three years later.

Bread isn't just bread. It is the cornerstone of the social contract
between the rulers and the ruled across the Middle East. When the
colonial empires collapsed, the revolutionary leaders promised a new
kind of "Arab socialism" or "Arab nationalism" that would provide
economic security for all. Subsidies ensured that food was cheap,
and job guarantees meant people could always afford it. This social

RIOTS &
FOOD PRICES

1. Burundi
2. Somalia
3. India
4. Mauritania
5. Mozambique
6. Cameroon, Yemen
7. Haiti, Egypt,
Côte d'Ivoire, Sudan
8. Somalia
9. Tunisia
10. India, Sudan
11. Mozambique

12. Tunisia
13. Egypt, Libya
14. Yemen
15. Algeria, Saudi Arabia,
Mauritania, Sudan, Jordan
16. Oman, Morocco, Iraq,
Bahrain
17. Syria
18. Uganda, Iran, Georgia
19. Kenya, Malawi
20. Somalia

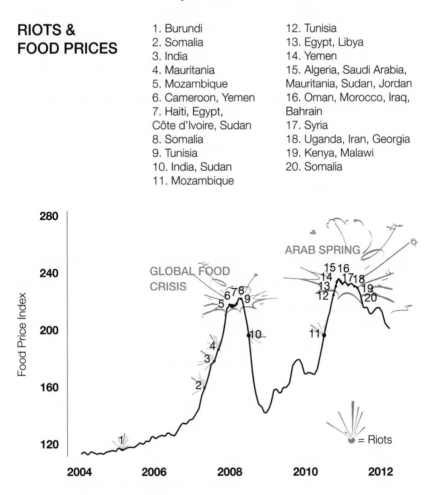

Adapted from Lagi et al. (2011)

contract was part of an authoritarian bargain, whereby security was traded for freedom and people enjoyed the "democracy of bread" rather than the "democracy of the vote."

But bread is also bread. It's the source of 35 per cent of daily caloric intake for people living in the Middle East and North Africa. This bread is made by acquiring wheat from the global supply chain. The region imports more wheat than any other, with Egypt the world's largest importer. The price of these imports is set by the international commodity exchanges in Chicago, Atlanta and London. Even with the government subsidies, people in Egypt, Tunisia, Syria, Algeria and Morocco spend between 35 and 55 per cent of their income on food. They're living on the edge: small price rises bring poverty and hunger.

This combination of symbol and sustenance is what makes rising food prices so combustible. Bourguiba's troubles in 1984 were not unique. From the late 1970s through to the mid-1980s, the International Monetary Fund (IMF) forced Middle Eastern countries to slash food subsidies in exchange for much-needed debt relief. A wave of riots rocked Egypt, Algeria, Turkey, Morocco and Jordan. Thousands were killed in clashes with police. The Sudanese government was overthrown. The incumbent dictators got the message and rolled back the IMF-mandated cuts as far as they could. But government food subsidies had shrunk nevertheless, and would continue to shrink over the decades to come.

By 2010, unemployment was soaring and the food-subsidy system was corrupt and badly administered. Bakers in Cairo were reselling flour on the black market for five times the official subsidised price. When prices rose and riots broke out, dictator after dictator tried to reinstate and upgrade the social contract by announcing new subsidies and government jobs. Only those regimes that offered the most generous packages survived, and this generosity was dependent upon another commodity: oil.

The most lavish packages were offered by the oil juggernauts Kuwait and Saudi Arabia. Kuwaitis got free food for thirteen months and a cheque for $3,600. Saudi Arabia offered tens of thousands of jobs, half a million houses and generous unemployment benefits. Both regimes survived without political concessions. The oil-poor nations—Tunisia, Yemen and Egypt—were unable to roll back the revolutionary tide with a financial tide of their own. All three regimes were overthrown. Syria, with only marginally more oil, could have suffered their fate had it not been for the swift support from Iran and Russia in the early months of 2011. Libya, with abundant oil, appears to be the outlier. Gaddafi was able to use his oil wealth to fund a private mercenary army after the official military abandoned him. He would have been successful in crushing the

2011	Country	Oil revenues per person**
Regime Survives	Qatar	$38,160
	Kuwait	$29,840
	UAE	$21,570
	Oman	$12,160
	Saudi Arabia	$11,930
	Bahrain	$5,690
	Algeria	$2,950
Civil War	Libya	$9,820
	Syria	$690
Revolution	Yemen*	$410
	Egypt	$400
	Tunisia	$380

Adapted from: Leif Wenar, *Blood Oil: Tyrants, Violence, and the Rules That Run the World* (Oxford: Oxford University Press, 2015), p. 32. *Conflict began in 2014. **On eve of Arab Spring; also, this is not oil revenue allocated to individuals, but the total national oil revenue divided by the population.

revolution if it were not for NATO's bombing campaign against his forces. In Yemen, it would likewise be foreign interventions that created the civil war in 2014.

These dictators were monsters. They oversaw vast police states that employed systematic torture and rape. They enriched themselves through orgies of corruption as millions struggled to afford to eat. They squashed any form of free expression—religious or secular—as a threat to their own cult of personality. Yet their grip on power was brittle. It depended on forces that were often outside of their control. It depended on the price of food set in the commodity exchanges many thousands of miles away, and whether they had oil revenues to offset any rise in prices. This was the international maze, the structure of opportunity and constraint, the social source of their political power. In 2010 and 2011, the maze changed shape. The walls that had protected the monsters crumbled. Some fled, some were killed, and some managed to cling on to power.

This change in the architecture of the maze didn't just kill monsters, it also unleashed new ones. These new monsters took many forms. Some were formed in the image of the old regime. Egypt saw the return of the military dictatorship. Tunisia slid into an illiberal democracy with the former head of the police state as president. The civil wars in Libya, Syria and Yemen brought a world of horrors: cities reduced to rubble, hundreds of thousands of dead, over 10 million forced from their homes, and tens of millions pushed into extreme poverty and starvation. At the heart of this Inferno would be perhaps the greatest modern monster of all: ISIS. Once caged in Iraq, they were now free to grow in Libya and Syria.

As images of these horrors dominate The Feed it is easy to forget where it all began. The populist explosion, the global refugee crisis, the civil wars, the Arab Spring are presented as disconnected events. Each is a discrete tragedy the size of a headline. Their simultaneous appearance, however, is no coincidence. They all tumble together in one avalanche. An avalanche that started with something simple and singular: prices.

There was something about this story that still didn't quite make sense to me. The notion that the second decade of the twenty-first century would be plunged into chaos through a global eruption of bread riots was bizarre. I thought bread riots were ancient history. I had seen multiple actresses in extravagant royal garb utter Marie Antoinette's famous quip "Let them eat cake" when told that the peasants were starving because they had no bread. Were we really living in a global remake of this period drama?

Marie Antoinette's legendary retort allegedly took place during the infamous "October days" of the French Revolution. On 1 October 1789, King Louis XVI threw a banquet for the Royal Flanders Regiment at the Palace of Versailles. They drank and ate and sang and laughed, but outside the palace walls the mood was different. The previous year's harvest was poor. Grain prices had shot up to their highest point in a century. Peasants normally spent half their income on bread; now it was 88 per cent. Riots had broken out in Nantes, Amiens, Rouen, Rheims, Grenoble and Marseilles. The king had been forced to recognise the Constituent Assembly. The rioting had subsided, but the hunger continued.

News of the banquet scandalised Paris. The press described an "orgy" where the king and queen were plotting to starve the French people into submission as soldiers trampled upon the Revolutionary tricolour flag. Anger swelled. On 5 October, some 7,000 women marched to Versailles. They dragged cannons, brandished knives and chanted: "Kill! Kill! We want to cut off her head, cut out her heart, and fry her liver!" On their arrival, the king promised them cheap bread. But that night, the mob stormed the palace. They raided Marie Antoinette's empty chamber and killed her two guards. By the morning, the crowd had swelled to 60,000. They brought the king and queen to Paris together with carts filled with wheat and flour. Mockingly, they sang, "The baker, the baker's wife, and the baker's boy!" Out of her carriage window Marie Antoinette could see the heads of her guards stuck on spikes paraded beside her. These "October days" were a turning point in the Revolution: the king was now a prisoner of the mob.

The Revolutionary pamphleteers turned Marie Antoinette into a monster. Their descriptions were no less vile than the meme-makers of the twenty-first-century Feed. "More often than not the queen appeared as a wild beast of rapacious appetites—a panther, hyena, or tigress who fed on the French people," writes the historian Nancy Barker. Marie Antoinette killed her parents, bathed in their blood and communed with Satan. Even prison could not contain her debauchery. She kept a harem of lesbian lovers whose sexual depravity shocked even their jailers. An aristocrat, a woman, a foreigner: Marie Antoinette was the perfect scapegoat for France's ills. Soon her neck met the guillotine.

Yet the slaying of this monster didn't bring down the price of bread. The Revolutionaries scrambled to find a remedy. Maximilien Robespierre tried imposing a "maximum" price of bread. The policy failed, and he looked for a new scapegoat. "Conspirators," he pleaded on the eve of his downfall, "have plunged the Republic into the most frightful famine." His audience was unconvinced. As he was marched to the guillotine, the crowd cheered: "Down with Mr. Maximum!"

France's bread problem was larger than any of these personalities. High bread prices existed long before and after each of them. In the eighty years before the Revolution, twenty-one were rocked by bread riots. Throughout the eighteenth century, kings and peasants had found themselves trapped in a maze of failed harvests, famines and high prices. Their dilemma dated back to Charlemagne, who had struck a social contract with his people: he was duty-bound to ensure they had affordable bread, to be the "baker of last resort." Over the centuries, this social contract evolved into an elaborate system of state interventions and regulations. Should famine strike, the king's administrators would search for stores of grain and ensure fair distribution. They would stop speculators hoarding grain to push up prices even further and force the peasants to pay exorbitant prices. However, the administrators were usually disorganised and incompetent and failed to bring down prices. Riots would erupt. Crowds would enforce the social contract themselves. Speculators were lynched. Granaries were raided. The grain wasn't stolen, but sold at a "fair price"—usually half the going rate. The bread riots that sparked the French Revolution were routine. They were merely the biggest among many.

I saw in this episode the anthropomorphisation of hunger: how the suffering of a population could become projected onto a single human body. This projection was shone through the prism of the social contract—the agreement between ruler and ruled. Yet this contract was political in nature. It had little to say about how bread

should be made, how wheat should be grown, provisions distributed, and weather shocks ameliorated. This economic architecture
was overshadowed by the ruler's towering presence. And when this
maze failed to feed ordinary people, their anger twisted her human
body into the distorted shape of an all-powerful monster. Questions
of economic production become moral questions of greed and glut-
tony. The result was misdirection. The true cause was missed, and
the problem remained unsolved.

FOOD PRODUCTION & FOOD PRICES

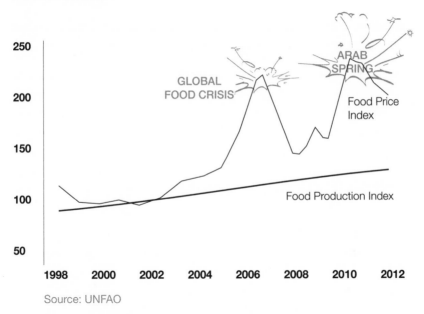

Source: UNFAO

It seemed to me that we had made the same mistake in 2011. The
Arab Spring was a revolt against a host of monstrous people. Ben
Ali's greed, his banquets, his family's pet tiger and trips to Saint-
Tropez were exposed for all to see. But when I visited Tunisia in
2014, people still complained about unemployment, high prices and
the lack of opportunity. We had misunderstood the Arab Spring as
a morality tale, of good against evil, of freedom against dictatorship, of dignity against corruption. This tale obscured the economic

foundations that these regimes were built upon—the democracy of bread—and the international market forces that could reduce them to rubble.

I also discovered, however, a disturbing difference between the two historical episodes. The high bread prices that triggered the French Revolution were the result of a poor harvest. There was less grain, so prices rose. However, during the Arab Spring, and the Global Food Crisis before it, there was plenty of food. In fact, both years had seen the most food produced in history. So why did prices soar at a time of abundance? What was the trigger behind the trigger?

2

Magic: Fairy Tales, Financial Alchemy
and the Business of Cargo Cults

"We have got someone that is morbidly overweight," a hedge-fund manager named Michael Masters told the US House Committee on Energy and Commerce on 23 June 2008. "He probably needs to diet. He probably needs to exercise. There's a lot of things that he needs to do. But right now he's having a heart attack." Commodity prices were skyrocketing as the escalating Financial Crisis was plunging the global economy into recession. Oil was an eye-watering $130 a barrel and wheat prices had reached historic highs. The UN had declared a "Global Food Crisis" as 100 million starved and riots broke out in Egypt, Haiti and the Côte d'Ivoire. These spikes hadn't been seen since the oil shocks of the 1970s. But there was no oil embargo. No revolution in Iran.

Some blamed growing demand from China's industrial revolution, others believed oil supplies had "peaked." But food and oil production was up from the previous years, and the recession was depressing demand. And it wasn't just food and oil: the prices of all commodities were moving upwards together for the first time. There was no reason why the supply of American wheat, Indian cotton, Guatemalan coffee, Russian oil, Chilean nickel or Qatari natural gas should be connected. It was unprecedented.

Michael Masters had a theory. "Index speculators have bought more commodities futures contracts in the last five years than any other group," he told the committee. These "index speculators" were investors who had purchased a complex derivative product called a "commodity index fund." Sold by Goldman Sachs, AIG and other financial institutions, they allowed investors to park their money in a mixture of around two dozen commodities. Masters put up a graph to show the committee how investments into commodity index funds had grown from $13 billion in 2003 to $260 billion in the middle of March 2006. "If they had been the largest buyer of futures contracts," he asked, "is it not reasonable that they would have had one of the largest impacts on futures prices?"

Masters quoted Goldman Sachs' answer. "Without question increased fund flow into commodities has boosted prices," the bank's own analysts had concluded just a month earlier. Indeed, Masters had found that China was spending less money buying commodities than Wall Street was spending through commodity index funds. And it was because commodity index funds purchased commodities as a bundle that all commodity prices were moving upwards together. This onslaught of financial capital was pushing prices away from their "fundamental" real-world values. It was a classic speculative bubble. All bubbles eventually pop, and by the end of 2008 commodity prices had crashed. But for the hundreds of millions caught up in the Global Food Crisis the market "correction" had come too late. "Keynes had a great expression," Masters had warned the committee at the peak of the bubble: "In the long run we're all dead."

"After my testimony it was sort of like kicking over an anthill," Masters tells me at his home in the Atlanta suburbs. "There was a visceral reaction from the financial industry. They were very upset that someone from the financial industry would actually come out and say, 'Hey, this is a problem.' And there were a lot of attacks on me, *ad hominem* attacks. There was disbelief that I was doing this." The Wall Street "Masters of the Universe" treated him as a traitor and a heretic. He'd be out at dinners with hedge-fund managers and bankers, and they all wanted to know the same thing: why was he doing this? He was a fellow Master of the Universe, how could he betray the financial world so publicly, and in Congress of all places? There were rumours that it was a calculated move, that it would somehow help his own speculative bets. After all, what other motivation could he possibly have? The idea that one of their own would call out the irrationality of commodity prices was beyond reason.

The more I learnt about this episode, the more disturbed I became. I thought I knew what prices were. Ever since I can remember, I've counted pounds and pennies—and later dollars and cents—to pay for things. Prices are simply how much things cost. But as I looked closer, I found that prices were so much more than that. And, like peering down a microscope, a hidden alien world revealed itself. I saw new features of prices, new structures and powers I didn't know existed. There was a secret world made of ones and zeros, a world that lives in a state of constant revolution—a revolution that dramatically affects the global distribution of the essential goods we all need to survive. To understand this hidden transformation, I had to start at the beginning: what is a "price" supposed to be?

"Look at this lead pencil," Milton Friedman says as he holds up an unassuming black and yellow striped pencil. I'm watching him talk in his PBS documentary *Free to Choose* on YouTube. "There's not a single person in the world who could make this pencil." The "eraser" probably "comes from Malaysia." The "wood," he supposes, was "cut down in the state of Washington." The "graphite," he believes, comes from "some mines in South America." And as for the yellow and black paint or the brass ferrule, he admits with a chuckle that he has "no idea" where it came from. "Literally thousands of people cooperated to make this pencil. People who don't speak the same language, who practice different religions, who might hate one another if they ever met! . . . What brought them together and induced them to cooperate to make this pencil? There was no commissar sending out orders from some central office. It was the magic of the price system: the impersonal operation of prices that brought them together and got them to cooperate, to make this pencil, so you could have it for a trifling sum."

But how do prices perform this "magic"?

Friedman argued that every time something is bought the buyer is "voting" for its worthiness. These "votes" tell us what is valued and what we need to make more of. Take his pencil. Imagine that, for whatever reason, the world's supply of rubber is diminishing. Perhaps there's a freak weather event or a revolution in the country exporting most of the world's rubber. Whatever the reason— you don't even need to know why—the price of rubber will start to rise. There are too many buyers chasing too little rubber. The information—"there's not enough rubber"—is incorporated into the price, or rather, the rising price communicates the information "there is not enough rubber." Suppose you own land in Malaysia. Now that the price of rubber is rising, you can make a profit by planting rubber trees and take advantage of the higher prices. It's not just you either, it's all these other people with land for rubber trees. Without anybody being given an order, the resources—land, seeds, fertiliser—are brought together to fix the problem of too little rubber. Thousands and thousands of suppliers across a global supply chain can coordinate their production just by looking at a single number: the price.

Friedman was illustrating an idea articulated by his friend and colleague Friedrich Hayek. He viewed prices as information-gathering machines. It is this information that gives prices their magical power. *Prices coordinate.* "The function of prices," Hayek said, "is to tell people what they ought to do." This function made state planning unnecessary: no "commissar" was needed to tell people how much to produce of what. Instead, prices could coordinate through a decentralised network that Hayek called a "spontaneous order." Economists soon pushed this idea a step further: prices are better at gathering and synthesising information than anything else. No technocrat, government regulator, hedge-fund manager or supercomputer has better information than what is already contained in the price. This is because, they believed, prices derive from the collective wisdom of the crowd. They are the result of votes cast by people with their own money. This crowd can draw on local knowledge and instantly incorporate it into the price. So-called experts— often hundreds or thousands of miles away—would always be a step behind. Economists would come to call this information-gathering function of prices "efficiency." And the idea that prices would always be more efficient than anything else human beings could come up with was formulated in 1970 as the Efficient Market Hypothesis. Only it didn't remain a mere "hypothesis" for long: it soon became the taken-for-granted orthodoxy of the economics profession.

For Friedman, the consequences of this idea were not just economic but political. "A political system, in which you decide by a vote," Friedman said of democracy, "is a system of highly weighted voting in which special interests have far greater roles to play than does the general interest." This is because, according to Friedman, special-interest groups will always fight harder for what's important to them; they'll also know more about it and have the upper hand in getting what they want from feckless politicians. So, although a democracy allegedly works by one man, one vote, in practice it is governed not by the majority but by a highly motivated minority. "Consider, by contrast with this, the characteristic of the economic market, where voting is by dollars. It also is a system of unequal voting with one dollar worth one vote, because some people have more dollars than other people; but it is no more unequal than one man one vote, in the political system, where, as I have shown, you also have unequal voting; and the great virtue of the economic method of voting is that each person gets what he votes for." Think about the pencils—you get the pencils you vote for with your purchasing power as a consumer. If I only want pink pencils, pink pencils are all I will get. This market democracy where people vote with dollars is, according to Friedman, a far more effective democracy than the actual democracy of voting with ballots. "The existence of a free market does not of course eliminate the need for government," Friedman clarified. "[G]overnment is essential both as a forum for determining the 'rules of the game' and as an umpire to interpret and enforce the rules decided on."

Friedman was optimistic that once the rules of the game were established, once people across the world were free to "vote" for things that they wanted, then conflicts of all kinds would disappear. "That is why the operation of the free market is so essential," Friedman said as he concluded his discussion of the pencil and the magical price system. "Not only to promote productive efficiency, but even more to foster harmony and peace among the peoples of the world."

In 2008, this uplifting story of magical prices was exposed as a fairy tale. Prices were not synthesising information across the global supply chains as they were supposed to. Instead, prices reached record highs right as supply was peaking—more food had been produced in 2008 than at any point in human history—and demand was falling as the global economy cratered. Nor were prices bringing in an era of "harmony" and "peace": riots had broken out in forty-eight countries, 100 million were starving and two governments had been deposed. Something had gone deeply wrong with the "magic" of the price system.

"There were many things that led this to happen," Masters tells me. "First of all, you had the Commodities Futures Modernization Act."

This Act began life at a hearing held by the US House Committee on Banking and Financial Services on 17 July 1998. The committee rooms were usually drab places where jowly and bespectacled faces droned into microphones. This day was different. The committee room was packed. It was billed as the battle of the bureaucrats, the regulator-on-regulator bust-up of the decade. It was Brooksley Born, the chairwoman of the Commodities Futures Trading Commission, versus Alan Greenspan, the chairman of the Federal Reserve. The question: should "derivatives" be regulated?

"If somebody says to me, I'm contemplating punching you in the nose," Greenspan said into the microphone, "I don't presume that that is a wholly neutral statement. My inclination is to pack up and move to another neighbourhood."

"I may just add," Born interjected, "I think what we are saying is, in—"

"You don't intend to punch Dr. Greenspan in the nose, do you, Ms. Born?" Congressman LaFalce interrupted.

"It is more correctly stated, do you think you need a punch in the nose? That is the question that is being asked," Born shot back.

"I will yield to your interpretation," Greenspan responded dryly.

"I would say that the implication is that if the answer to that question is yes, then the commission has said it has the full authority to administer that punch," said Treasury Undersecretary Hawke.

At the time, few outside Wall Street had even heard of "derivatives," let alone knew what they were or understood why they made Born feel compelled to punch Greenspan on the nose. Yet they were one of the fastest-growing parts of the American economy. The notional value of these new financial products had tripled from 1994 to 1997 to over $28.7 trillion. Born proposed releasing a white paper to see if these new products required oversight. The pushback was swift. "I have thirteen bankers in my office," Lawrence Summers—then Bill Clinton's Deputy Secretary of the Treasury—warned her over the phone, "and they say if you go forward with this, you will cause the worst financial crisis since World War II." Born released her report. No crisis ensued. Clinton's team feared the report was just an opening shot. Greenspan organised a Congressional hearing to launch the administration's counter-offensive. Greenspan's testimony hinged on what a "derivative" actually was and why they were so deeply connected to commodities. Their invention and regulation, Greenspan testified, "were a response to the perceived problems of manipulation of grain markets that were particularly evident in the latter part of the nineteenth and early part of the twentieth centuries."

When Chicago became the grain capital of North America in the mid-nineteenth century, the market was chaotic. Farmers would arrive in Chicago at the same time with their freshly harvested wheat. Supply soared, prices plummeted, and farmers ended up dumping their worthless grain into Lake Michigan. A contract was invented that would let farmers store their grain at home and then have a guaranteed delivery date at some point in the year. They called them "futures contracts." Farmers could pre-sell their crop in advance to real buyers, such as hotels or bakeries. Since there may not always be enough buyers throughout the year, private investors—later called "speculators"—were invited into the market to make sure that somebody would always be available to buy the farmer's contracts. The speculators guaranteed to pay an agreed-upon price for the wheat in the future, and the farmers could then use this guarantee to get a bank loan to fund the harvest. The speculators were given a small discount to compensate them for the risk they were taking, called the "risk premium." Since the value of these contracts was "derived" from something real—bushels of wheat—they were among the first so-called derivatives.

Like a bacterium multiplying under a microscope, the price of a bushel of wheat had split into two. One price was rooted in the real world, the other in finance. This is the heart of financial alchemy. Derivatives are a magic economy—only existing on bits of paper— but their existence is supposed to make the real economy—physical wheat—far more orderly. This was the promise of finance: a way to reorganise and smooth out the real world and make it more productive. Farmers got security, speculators were rewarded for risk and Lake Michigan was no longer full of perfectly edible grain.

Soon this magic economy became much bigger than the physical economy: there were far more wheat contracts than bushels of wheat. In 1875, the *Chicago Tribune* estimated that the physical market was $200 million, but the paper market was ten times greater at $2 billion. Rather than just taking the risk premium, speculators were making large bets on their future prices. Before these magic pieces of paper, speculating on the price of wheat or pork bellies was prohibitively cumbersome for most. Warehouses would have to be rented, the physical commodity delivered and stored. Now all somebody needed to do was purchase a futures contract. And the wall between these two worlds—physical and magical—didn't last long. Speculators tried to rig the futures prices by trying to corner the physical market by monopolising the supply of wheat or oats or pork. Speculation in the derivative markets was changing the physical market. The tail wagged the dog. Prices swung wildly. Chaos had returned. President Franklin Roosevelt finally regulated the markets and curtailed speculation in 1934. Order had reigned ever since.

Greenspan argued that this historical episode of speculative chaos said little about the brave new world of financial derivatives. For one, he remarked, speculation was largely overstated in Roosevelt's era. The attempts to "corner" the market mostly failed. But there was a deeper issue at work here. Unlike traditional derivatives based on physical commodities like wheat and pork bellies, the new financial derivatives had no corresponding real-world object. Instead, they were magic pieces of paper that bet on the future prices of other pieces of paper, such as interest rates or currencies. This paper could not be "cornered" like wheat. "Because quantities of grain following the harvest are generally known and limited, it is possible, at least in principle, to corner a market," Greenspan said. "Supplies of foreign exchange, Government securities, and certain other financial instruments are being continuously replenished . . . and, as a consequence, are extremely difficult to manipulate." Governments, banks and insurance giants could always just print more of them in a way that farmers couldn't simply grow new crops. They were, after all, just pieces of paper. Magic defied speculation.

When questioned about losses in the derivatives market in the next downturn, Greenspan replied confidently: "All markets will respond." But, he explained, such a downturn would have "nothing to do with derivatives markets. I am talking about the underlying markets." Dogs wag their tails. The magic prices follow the real prices. To Greenspan, the idea that speculators could manipulate the "underlying" physical markets on such a scale as to move prices was fanciful.

Instead, the prices of financial derivatives would stabilise markets and reduce risk. Prices, according to the Efficient Market Hypothesis, are the best possible tools ever invented for synthesising information. So the prices of derivatives are the world's best guesses about what will happen in the future. And institutions can protect themselves from future risks by purchasing derivatives as insurance products. If you're a bank and you're worried about homeowners defaulting on mortgages, you can protect yourself by purchasing a credit default swap that will cover your losses. The proliferation of these derivatives, Greenspan believed, made the financial system fundamentally safer. He told the committee that the Glass-Steagall Act—regulatory legislation passed during the Great Depression to stop speculation-prone investment banks from merging with commercial banks—was an "anachronism" thanks to the incredible "risk dispersion" derivatives allowed for. "[W]e very much would like to have this all reviewed, because there is a new world out there."

Greenspan's gambit won. Born resigned. Glass-Steagall was repealed. Greenspan co-authored a report with Larry Summers that would form the foundation of the Commodities Futures Modernization Act. The legislation was far more ambitious than Greenspan's testimony suggested: commodity-trading would be deregulated alongside financial derivatives. Greenspan had changed the "rules of the game." Now an unlimited number of Friedman's speculative "voters" would be deciding the prices not just of financial products like currencies and insurance on mortgage-backed securities, but also the prices of products in the physical world. It would be a grand experiment in the "spontaneous order" of the market. Prices, not the government, would truly be telling people what to do. Prices would reign.

"I found a flaw," Greenspan admitted to the US House Committee on Oversight and Government Reform on 23 October 2008. His "ideology," he was forced to concede, was wrong. Greenspan's "new world" of derivatives had detonated spectacularly. The global financial system teetered on the brink of collapse. Rather than make the markets safer, derivatives had become, as Warren Buffett had warned in 2002, "weapons of financial mass destruction." The *Washington Post* called Brooksley Born the "Cassandra" of the crisis: the prophet of catastrophe who was exiled for telling the truth. The notorious "credit default swaps" that had fuelled the mortgage meltdown were considered the most destructive of these magical new derivatives. But there were many others. Commodity index funds had also created a global tsunami of suffering through skyrocketing food prices, starvation, riots and revolutions. Greenspan had let these magical prices rule, and their reign had plunged the world into chaos.

In the wake of the crisis, a heterodox economic theory emerged to explain just how the price system had malfunctioned so badly. These "behavioural economists" had run experiments on college students to try to tease out universal psychological biases that could impact prices. Their findings suggested that we are biased towards positive outcomes, to think the status quo will continue, and to ignore information that goes against our pre-existing beliefs. All of these incline us to "vote" the wrong way and pull prices away from their real, fundamental values. This universal psychological explanation gave a scientific basis for the "popular delusions," "irrational exuberance" and "madness of crowds" that had long been used to describe bubble behaviour.

But the more I thought about a universal explanation, the less convinced I became. Why were Masters, Born and Buffett able to see the madness all around them but nobody else could? Greenspan himself coined the phrase "irrational exuberance" in 1996 when he warned of a stock-market bubble. Did he develop a "bias" before his testimony two years later?

It seemed clear to me that any explanation had to take account of this difference: why some were seemingly infected by a false belief and others were not. I remembered one vivid instance where madness, magic and commodities collided—an instance where this fever gripped one group but not another. It happened in 1945 in the Indian Ocean islands of Melanesia, as one European colonist recalled:

This "Madness" is not confined to any one area, but is found among tribes whose dialects and customs differ widely. In all cases the "Madness" takes the same form: A native, infected with the disorder, states that he has been visited by a relative long dead, who stated that a great number of ships loaded with "cargo" had been sent by the ancestor of the native for the benefit of the natives of a particular village or area. But the white man, being very cunning, knows how to intercept these ships and takes the "cargo" for his own use . . . We have seen grave harm to the native population arising from the "Vailala Madness," where livestock has been destroyed, and gardens neglected in the expectation of the magic cargo arriving.

These episodes of "madness" began as soon as the colonisers from Europe arrived in the 1880s. They would periodically bubble up around charismatic prophets claiming that a magic ritual would bring planes and ships filled with cargo—meat, packaged rice, tinned tobacco, steel tools, rifles, clothes—from the heavens. These rituals usually entailed the slaughter of livestock, the abandonment of farms and the construction of makeshift airfields, wharfs and warehouses. In one typical episode, a young girl named Filo claimed to have received a prophecy in a dream. The community had sinned against God. To atone they must stop hunting or gardening, or they would be turned into pigs and weeds. They slaughtered pigs across the islands as an offering. They need not worry about food or money, she said, as God would reward their sacrifice with planes filled with cargo. When the cargo never arrived, the Europeans were blamed. They had intercepted the shipment and kept it for themselves.

How could people believe that abandoning real economic activity for magic would make them richer? It was a puzzle that brought generations of anthropologists to the islands. One was Peter Lawrence. He spent time with one community, the Garia. He discovered that magic was integral to their everyday economy. When they planted seeds in their gardens, sorcerers known as Big Men would utter the secret names of the gods. If the seeds failed to sprout, the Big Man would be blamed for handling the magic incorrectly. They assumed European economies worked the same way. The planes and airports and ships were merely props in elaborate rituals conducted with secret knowledge. After all, they had never seen a European physically make any of the commodities they enjoyed. They just gave magic bits of paper to those unloading crates off planes or ships. When the Europeans told them that the goods had come from Sydney, the Garia assumed that this was the location of heaven, where God manufactured the cargo. Some tried to persuade friendly Europeans such as visiting anthropologists like Lawrence to share their superior magic. Others claimed to have acquired the Europeans' knowledge through divine revelation directly from God. These were the prophets of the cargo cults.

It can be tempting to read accounts like this and see the Garia as a homogenous unit, a walled-off world where beliefs in "spells," "magic" and "secret rituals" are shared universally by all. Beliefs never are, in any society. But even if these beliefs were widely held, there remains a core divide between two groups: prophets and followers. Consider the prophet Kaum:

> Kaum of Kalina claimed to have been killed when in a police jail, that he had gone to paradise and seen angels making cargo. God gave him instructions for how to acquire it on earth together with a sacred symbol, a small gun shell. He held seances in a hut covered with a white cloth. He would place the gun shell in the middle and have his followers cook food and place it, along with tobacco, all around it. They would fold their hands and pray: "O Father Konsel, you are sorry for us. You can help us. We have no nothing—no aircraft, no ships, no jeeps, nothing at all. The Europeans steal from us. You will be sorry for us and send us something." . . . When the seances were over, the workboys would leave Kaum to sleep near the table in company with a trusted lieutenant . . . During this period he claimed frequently that he had dreamt of the souls of the dead, and also that at night they came up to eat the food put out for them on the table.

Kaum's prophecy never came true. The planes packed with cargo never arrived. It's tempting to see them all as victims of a popular delusion. But reading this story, I saw an alternative theory. It hinges on the question: who ate the food Kaum's followers prepared?

If it was Kaum, and not the "souls of the dead," who was eating his followers' food, then his prophecy was not only true, it was self-fulfilling. By performing the prophesied ritual, Kaum would receive cargo. The catch was that his followers wouldn't. The ritual didn't create new cargo for all to enjoy, it simply transferred it from one group to another, from the followers to the prophet's confidants. Often, this transfer was accompanied by the mass destruction of community property, which left everybody—except for the prophet's inner circle—substantially poorer. During the episode of pig slaughter inspired by Filo's prophetic dream, her parents collected money from the community to help "appease" the gods who would deliver the cargo. The so-called madness was not uniform. It was not a "psychological bias" or "collective belief" shared by all.

For prophets, magic was a rational tool, a means of enriching themselves at the expense of others. It worked by manipulating familiar words, imagery and rituals. They adapted common prayers. They constructed buildings that had the outward appearance of an airport or sea wharf. Their followers misread these familiar signals as evidence of plausibility. Their everyday understanding of the world was twisted into a means of extortion. Their culture was used against them. They believed themselves to be acting rationally, but they did not have all the information available to them. It was through manipulating information—and their followers' lack of it—that the magicians were able to sell their rituals to them.

Magic is not a "madness" or a "delusion" but a business model. It is a model based on manipulation: the magician prophesises that goods are destined for their shores, but only if certain costs—or "sacrifices"—are paid to the magician and his or her inner circle. But this transaction is not a straightforward wealth transfer. The wealth of others is destroyed in the process. The rituals the magician performs to acquire these goods are inherently destructive and leave the community far poorer than they were before. When the promised cargo fails to arrive, the problem is not that the magic is fraudulent but that malevolent forces have intercepted it. All are absolved of any responsibility—even the magician who instigated it—and life returns to normal. That is, until the next magician makes a prophecy of future riches.

I wondered if the magic used by Kaum operated with the same economic logic as those magic bits of paper called derivatives. Had the financial alchemists on Wall Street adopted the same business model as the prophets in Melanesia? I went to see another vocal critic of derivatives in the 1990s, one who had, like Born, warned of their destructive powers.

"When I was in the Clinton administration of the 1990s, I was chairman of the Council of Economic Advisers," Joseph Stiglitz tells me in his office at Columbia University. "This was the period when the derivative market began to grow. We became aware that these were potentially dangerous." These new derivatives were different from the futures contracts for wheat and oil sold at the exchanges. Those contracts were regulated, they were simple and standardised, and traded by thousands of people. Farmers and speculators alike understood them, and understood what would happen if a farmer couldn't deliver her quota or the grain delivered wasn't the correct quality. In contrast, this new derivative market was neither regulated, public nor standardised. They were called "over-the-counter" derivatives and sold privately between financial entities. They were bespoke, hundreds of pages long and impenetrable to even seasoned financial professionals. "Their intent was to obscure what was going on," Stiglitz says. "They were an instrument of non-transparency."

Stiglitz was awarded the Nobel Prize in 2002 for his research on precisely this problem: information. His work had challenged the idea that prices were information-processing machines: that from the thousands of transactions between buyers and sellers a magical system emerged that coordinated the economy efficiently. He exposed this story to be a fairy tale. The conditions needed to conjure the magician's wand—the "invisible hand"—were utopian. They require perfect information and perfect competition. "The invisible hand is invisible because it doesn't exist."

Imagine you want to sell someone your used car: you could give it a thorough polish, grease the wheels and pass it off as in better shape than it really is. Your superior knowledge of the car's hidden flaws allows you to get a better price for it. You can charge the buyer the price of a passion fruit and give them a lemon. You can profit from an "information asymmetry" between you and the buyer. Prices don't just *coordinate*, as Friedman and Hayek had argued. They could also *hide* information to *manipulate* others.

But how did derivatives deceive? Before the Financial Crisis Donald MacKenzie, an economic sociologist at Edinburgh University, delved into the world of the "quants"—the financial wizards who priced derivatives. They created the mathematical models that assigned prices to the magic bits of paper—credit derivatives—that bundled and insured thousands of mortgages. The prices of these credit derivatives were crucial for coordinating the business of mortgage-lending. Their price signalled the overall risk in the real-estate market. They told the bank the risk of issuing mortgages and how much risk was on their balance sheet if they held on to them. The higher the price, the riskier the bet.

The problem, MacKenzie discovered, was that there was no established model for pricing these credit derivatives. The quants had twisted a formula originally used by actuaries to predict when a spouse's partner would die into predicting when a mortgage would default. But there was no consensus on how to do it. The results were erratic. The quants admitted to MacKenzie that the formula they used to price the derivatives had the "appearance" of rigour to "give people some comfort" but it was neither rigorous nor reliable. The quants had to manipulate the models to get the prices to look reasonable. Some quants did not consider them real "models" at all. Banks in London had to alter the formulas so that they required less computing power, as their offices didn't have enough air conditioning to keep the computers cool. These diverging prices made buying and selling the derivatives difficult, leading them to settle on compromised prices that both parties knew were wrong.

And yet, despite their importance to the entire mortgage industry, which is valued in the trillions of dollars, they kept producing faulty prices anyway. This is because the prices served another role: they were used to calculate the quants' bonuses. And the more certain the formula's prediction seemed and the longer into the future it forecasted, the bigger the quant's annual bonus became. The accounts departments saw that a complex equation was behind the estimates, so they accepted them. It looked like a rigorous assessment, even if the quants knew that it was not. Some, in fact, did not use the formula at all and, when pressed by auditors, needed to claim that they did in fact use it—if only "for reference," as a quant told MacKenzie—to appease them. This was a classic case of information asymmetry: an asymmetry inside the banks that gave prices the "appearance" of rigour but would soon prove to be explosively wrong.

As Greenspan had lectured Brooksley Born in 1998, derivatives prices were supposed to respond to prices in the "underlying markets." The mortgage-insurance derivatives were supposed to synthesise information about the real-world business of buying and selling physical homes. But soon after the passing of the Commodities Futures Modernization Act in 2000, the relationship reversed. As house prices rose, the quants' formulas calculated that the risk that homeowners would default was declining, and so lowered the price of credit derivatives. This signalled to the banks that it was safe to issue more mortgages. As the formula defined risk through the whole housing market, banks and ratings agencies alike believed— or claimed to believe—that they did not need to know about the specific mortgages inside these supposedly AAA-safe bundles. It was a convenient shortcut and the banks had little incentive to question this "information." Issuing mortgages and bundling them into securities to sell off to pension funds and other banks generated the majority of the banks' profits. And as they lent more money, house prices rose further and the quants' models, once again, showed that the risk that people would default on their mortgages was declining. The quants' models were not just inaccurate, but radically wrong: signalling to the market that mortgages were getting safer as risks were in fact escalating. And as these signals coordinated the housing market, they created a feedback loop that fuelled the bubble. Real-estate construction boomed. The tail wagged the dog. Magic was dominating, reordering the real world, and all thanks to an information asymmetry: a faulty formula that made a deceptive price.

Greenspan had bought into the fairy tale of the invisible hand. He believed that banks had embraced derivatives because they wanted to harness the magical powers of the price system: to understand and manage financial risk. It is true that banks embraced magic, but their business model was quite different from the one Greenspan imagined. It was the kind of magic long practised in human societies, as the anthropologists of Melanesian cargo cults have documented. They embraced magic not as an instrument of knowledge and transparency but as one of deception and manipulation.

This kind of actually existing magic, whether it is on Wall Street or Melanesia, works by promising riches for everybody while covertly transferring it to yourself as collective wealth is destroyed. This deceptive transfer takes place through a ritual that adopts familiar symbols to win the trust of the laity. In derivatives, and the impenetrable formulas used to price them, Wall Street had a perfect ritual "instrument of non-transparency," as Stiglitz puts it. The quants used formulas to project an image of rationality and plausibility onto the products they were selling when, in fact, these formulas were not just faulty but explosive. Rather than reduce risk they amplified it. Their prophecies were no more divine than Kaum's or Filo's. They were, however, many times more destructive. Filo's pig-killing spree was confined to an island, whereas the Financial Crisis was an earthquake that rocked the world. And by blaming everybody—*psychological bias! the madness of crowds!*—the scam is hidden. Those selling faulty formulas or fake rituals thereby cast themselves as victims of the very fraud they created.

Was magic to blame for the commodity boom too? Michael Masters, the turncoat hedge-fund manager, tells me that the answer begins with the bursting of the roaring 1990s tech bubble. Up until then, large institutional investors such as pension funds and university endowments had traditionally invested in stocks and bonds. When the tech bubble burst in 2000, their portfolios imploded. "So having been burnt badly, they were looking for something that was not US stocks," Masters says. They wanted to "diversify" their portfolios. They searched for prices that had no relationship to the stock market, that were, in finance-speak, "uncorrelated" to stock prices and other financial assets. Indeed, there was no reason to believe that the price of Chilean nickel or Brazilian coffee had anything to do with the price of Microsoft stock. Not only would commodities provide a cushion in the face of another crash, but they themselves seemed like a sound investment. "At the same time, you had lower interest rates created by the last recession, a nascent market in China, and emerging markets that were growing . . . So brokers, being the salesmen that they are, said, 'Hey, you know, you don't like stocks, you should look at emerging markets, or commodities, or other stuff that has nothing to do with technology.' And investors were like, 'Yeah, I'd be happy to look at that because I haven't really invested in it, but I haven't really lost any money in it either.'" Institutional investors could diversify their portfolios and get in on the growing emerging markets without the hassle of storing physical commodities or investing in the supply chain directly. All they needed to do was purchase a product "derived" from physical markets: a commodity index fund.

"The crazy thing about commodities was that they were marketed as this sort of great investment that you could buy and hold," Masters says. "And the market was completely different." Commodity index funds were linked to futures contracts that would end with the delivery of physical wheat, pork bellies or barrels of oil. In order to keep the money in the market—and avoid the unwanted deliveries—the contracts needed to be sold right before they expired and new contracts bought. This is called the "roll." This aspect of derivatives, the investors were told, was a feature and not a bug. The banks' salesmen pointed to a paper published by two Yale economists in 2006 which showed that holding and rolling futures contracts over the long term produced a tidy profit. This was because there was a gap in the prices between the old contracts and the new contracts: the new ones were cheaper. This piece of financial alchemy produced a profit, so long as the "roll yield" remained positive. The study had been paid for by AIG, which was selling its own commodity index fund.

With the promise of diversification, rising prices from growing demand in China and emerging markets, and the alchemy of the roll yield, investors piled in. After two decades of sleepy stability, commodity prices began to rise. And as the prices in the future rose, the roll yield turned negative. Expecting to profit from booming commodity prices, investors struggled to understand why their profits had turned to losses. Not only that, the losses were bigger than expected. It was as if traders with insider knowledge were swooping in right before the roll, buying up futures contracts, pushing up the price further, only to turn round and sell back to the bank conducting the roll at inflated prices. It appeared that these rolls—the largest, the Goldman roll, in particular—were being "front-run." It's as if I overhear your lunch order for a tuna sandwich, run to the canteen and buy all the tuna sandwiches, and then offer to sell one to you for a marked-up price. It's a way to profit from an information asymmetry: knowing your order before you have placed it. One study estimated that between 2000 and 2010, front-running cost commodity index fund investors 3.6 per cent a year, or $26 billion. It was over five times the $5 billion Goldman Sachs and other banks were collecting in fees for managing their indexes.

The people best placed to front-run the roll were Goldman's own traders, as they had the inside information. "I don't think that anybody conclusively knew that they were, but I mean, why wouldn't they do it?" Masters says. "It's not illegal to do." These quirks in the changing financial alchemy of commodity derivatives were enough to turn a bet on rising prices into a loss-making enterprise. "In many cases, even though the prices of commodities moved up over time, if enough of these investors that had a buy-and-hold strategy just continued to roll and roll contracts, they actually ended up losing money over that period of time, even though the prices of the commodities actually went up, and in some cases significantly."

By another quirk of how these contracts were written, those who benefited from the roll yield shifting from positive to negative were those who stored the physical commodities. Which, it just so happened, were the banks. During the commodity boom of the 2000s, they aggressively moved into the commodity-storage trade, buying up oil terminals, granaries and metals warehouses. These were not small plays. In many commodities, the banks dominated. Morgan Stanley, for instance, was the world's ninth-largest oil shipper with over 100 tankers, had storage facilities capable of holding 58 million barrels of oil, and was the primary supplier of jet fuel to United Airlines.

Commodities had, in every sense, become "financialised." Not only had they been placed in portfolios as financial assets like stocks and bonds, but the very business of producing, storing and transporting commodities had been taken over by financial institutions too. Neither the pension funds nor the banks had any real interest in the reality of the commodity trade. They were instead exploiting the financial alchemy of derivative contracts. In doing so, they had fundamentally transformed the nature of commodities—those things like food and fuel we all need to survive—into something else altogether.

I struggled at first to understand just what this transformation meant. I found it helped to think about the solar system. Imagine a row of planets, each with a gravitational pull based on the real-world supply and demand of a commodity. Planet Nickel's gravity is the result of the supply of nickel from nickel mines and the world's demand for nickel. Planet Wheat's gravity is determined by the amount of wheat harvested and how many people across the world want to buy it. The price of these commodities is each planet's moon: it moves according to the gravity of each planet, that is to say the real-world supply and demand for it. Then another object appears, one many times the size of each individual planet. Let's imagine it's the sun. The sun's gravity comes from the supply and demand of financial capital, and its size dwarfs every real-world market that it encounters. This sun passes by our commodity planets and tugs on their moons. The price-moons are drawn towards this larger gravitational field. They now orbit the sun. They may be moved by the planets occasionally, but the sun-mass of financial capital overwhelms.

This is what financialisation means. It means that the prices of commodities enter into a constellation of financial prices. They are unmoored from physical reality. Prices become disconnected from very real fluctuations in the real world—the weather, wars, new technologies. This was first noticed in the prices of commodities themselves which, for the first time, began to correlate to one another as financial capital treated them as a singular "asset class." Then, as the housing market collapsed in 2007, capital fled real estate and found refuge in other, apparently unrelated, financial assets. Commodity prices had been growing for years, and since everybody needs to eat food and fuel their home, it seemed like a safe "uncorrelated" asset for financial capital to seek refuge within. And as the capital moved from housing to commodities, the bubble "migrated" from

one financialised asset to another. This is why food prices began
to spike in 2007 even though food production continued to grow.
The "demand" for commodities was not coming from real-world
consumers, but institutional investors searching for a safe haven as
real estate cratered.

**FINANCIALIZED
ASSET PRICES**

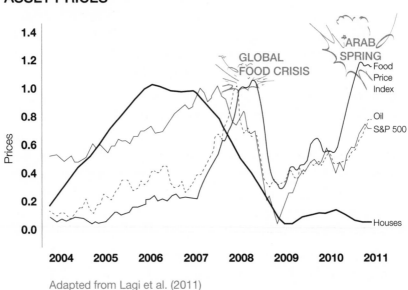

Adapted from Lagi et al. (2011)

But food and fuel are not supposed to be safe havens for pension funds. This strange situation only came about because banks
wanted to sell derivative products to institutional investors. They
presented commodity index funds as a straightforward way to bet on
commodities. But, once again, Wall Street was deploying the cargo-
cult business model. The feverish complexity of the derivatives hid
all kinds of transactions that would transfer wealth from pensioners and universities to themselves. And, just like in Melanesia, the
profits for the prophet were not extravagant. The banks made perhaps tens of billions through these commodity derivatives and the
investments in the physical supply chain. But the destruction that

they wrought—the Global Food Crisis that pushed 100 million into hunger, sparking riots and revolutions—was many times larger.

"The harms to the rest of our society, like the 2008 crisis, was just collateral damage in the struggle to make more money for the financial sector," Stiglitz says. But few on Wall Street were worried about this "collateral damage." "Institutional investors over time got the joke and realised that they were, in many cases, getting ripped off by this kind of activity," Masters recalls. But rather than work to bring commodities back into the real world, they looked instead for new ways to bet on their prices. "They were still enamoured with the potential diversification benefits of commodities in their portfolio, so they switched to other kinds of trading strategies, and one of those trading strategies was Trend-Following CTAs."

"Oh that was a really good crazy period," Jerry Parker tells me in his office in Tampa, Florida. He's the CEO of Chesapeake Capital Management, a Trend-Following CTA. In the summer of 2008, he had bet big that oil's meteoric trend upwards would continue. "I remember where I was. I remember what I was doing. I remember what I was thinking. I think Paul Tudor Jones was quoted in the media saying, 'Energy's gonna crash, 150-dollar price is not gonna hold.' And I was like, hmm, 'I'm not gonna pay attention to that. He's a famous trader, very smart billionaire, but I'm just gonna stick with my trend-following.' And then almost twenty-four hours later I'm already regretting that."

Parker doesn't doubt that he got sucked into a speculative bubble. "The increase of food prices and energy was definitely blamed on speculators. Hard to deny it, seeing as how it pretty much all crashed shortly thereafter." But, as he says, he's a trend follower, he has a system and he sticks to it. There were, I was discovering, lots of different ways to speculate on prices. I had seen how the banks made money by hiding information in complex derivatives and tricking long-term-orientated speculators like pension funds and university endowments into buying their old Hondas with the promise that they were Ferraris. But Parker, like most speculators, is not in the business of inventing and selling new derivatives. He's a small player trading regular futures contracts to bet on prices of everything from soybeans to oil to the Swiss franc.

He has a particular speculative strategy: "Spot trends, follow trends, pay attention to price only." This means that if the price is high compared to where it was last week or last month, that's a signal that an upward trend is forming and it's time to buy. And when prices seem to be going down, it's a signal to bet in the other direction. "Most of the time, 60 per cent of the time, we're wrong," Parker continues, "so we're not good at predicting. It's just a question of those 40 per cent of winning trades; the average trade may be three times as large as the average loss."

Even though Parker lost his bet that the oil price would continue to rise in 2008, trend-following was declared the victorious strategy among the Masters of the Universe. The financial press was filled with stories about how trend followers had earned 14 per cent profit that year as the rest of finance cratered. "Trend-following has produced substantial riches for both the customers and managers," the *Financial Times* wrote in one of many stories hyping the sector. Winton Capital, one of the largest trend-following hedge funds, made a 21 per cent profit. In fact, 2008 was the best year in trend-following history.

In 2009, trend-following was in vogue on Wall Street, but it was by no means new. Parker got his start in 1983, when he enrolled in a training programme inspired by the Eddie Murphy comedy *Trading Places*. Two legendary real-life commodity traders wondered if they could teach novices such as Parker to trade successfully by adhering to strict rules. These rules helped Parker and his fellow classmates to "spot" trends and "get in gear" with the trends. But this strategy is controversial. The Efficient Market Hypothesis says that these rules shouldn't work. "I heard about this idea of Efficient Markets in 1983, and I was like, *whoa*—what the heck is this?" Parker remembers. "What are we doing here? Are these things going to work?"

Imagine a hurricane is heading for Florida's orange groves. A meteorologist puts out a report alerting the world to this fact. Fearing the oranges will be damaged, and overall supply significantly dented, speculators buy orange futures anticipating a price rise. The Efficient Market Hypothesis assumes that this is the end of the story: market information is incorporated immediately into the price. If the price continues to rise the next day, this is assumed to be a "random walk"—essentially just a noise, a random fluctuation before reverting back to the mean. Trend followers take a different view. They believe that market information takes time to get incorporated into prices. That the markets aren't necessarily efficient. That a second-day price rise isn't random noise, but evidence that speculators are slow to absorb new information. They see rising prices as evidence of a trend.

These two different views of prices lead to two different trading strategies. On one side, there are the trend followers: a price goes up and they buy, and if the prices go down they bet against it by "shorting" it. On the other side, there are the trend sceptics, often called "contrarian" traders. They see the price go up and they bet against it; or if prices are declining, they buy. They assume prices revert to the mean. I discovered that there was a simple way of thinking about this fight, how these two opposing forces can shape prices over time. It's a model I encountered when I was looking into the nature of chaos, a model that can predict the "boom-bustiness" of a system.

Robert May's blood boiled as he watched *Jurassic Park*. "The so-called chaotician," May said, referring to Jeff Goldblum's character, "runs around spending most of the movie telling people that modern chaos theory says that the park is going to be unstable . . . You don't need chaos theory to tell you the world is complicated. What chaos theory tells you is that sometimes really, really simple things—not like Jurassic Park—can be unpredictable. I couldn't wait until the dinosaurs ate him."

May was all too familiar with the *Tyrannosaurus rex*–Goldblum relationship. Like blue whales and plankton, foxes and rabbits, it is the relationship of predator and prey. May was born in Australia and trained as a physicist who stumbled into the new field of mathematical ecology. At the same time that Edward Lorenz was exploring the power of feedback in weather—how the tiny gust of wind from a butterfly could be amplified by feedback into a hurricane—May was looking into amplifying feedback in nature. Specifically, he was looking into two very different kinds of feedback and how they might interact with each other over time.

Imagine an island world filled with just Jeff Goldblums and T-Rexes. The Jeff Goldblums are a species that, left to their own devices, will reproduce like rabbits or plankton. Their numbers will grow and grow until there are so many of them that they'll overflow into the sea. Their predators, the T-Rexes, stop this from happening. They gobble them up and prevent their population from getting out of hand.

Now assume that there is a dial on each Jeff Goldblum that can change how quickly they reproduce. This dial, according to May, is the amount of *positive feedback* in the system: if we crank it up, the Jeff Goldblums multiply faster. Let's also assume that the rate T-Rexes hunt the Jeff Goldblums—the opposing *negative feedback*—is constant. T-Rexes don't get to learn new tricks.

When May turns the dial on the Jeff Goldblums to a low number, the populations of both Jeff Goldblums and T-Rexes are stable. The

FEEDBACK & BOOM-BUSTINESS

Positive Feedback Increases

BALANCED   BOOM-BUST   CHAOS

Adapted from Gleick (1987)

negative feedback keeps the positive feedback in check. Their numbers look like a straight line (see illustration). But when May cranks up the dial and increases the rate at which Jeff Goldblums can reproduce, their numbers begin to boom. And because there's more food for the T-Rexes to eat, their numbers boom too. But now that there are more T-Rexes, the Jeff Goldblums are gobbled up more rapidly, and their numbers switch from boom to bust. And because there's less food, the T-Rexes don't have enough to eat, they begin to starve and die off, and their numbers bust as well. Until there are only a few T-Rexes left, and Jeff Goldblums, free from their natural predators, are able to multiply once more, causing the cycle of boom and bust to repeat itself. Indeed, May called the dial the "boom-bustiness" of the system. All May had to do was increase the positive feedback in the system and he could send it from a peaceful order to boom and bust and eventually to true chaos.

We can think of the struggle between trend followers and contrarians as analogous to prey and predator. The trend followers see an uptick in the price, and they pile in and push it up further. As the price rises, this "confirms" the trend, signalling to still more trend followers to join in or double down on their existing bets. The trend grows and grows and grows. This growth is fuelled by positive feedback, a self-perpetuating engine that amplifies a small price move into a big one. Contrarians are the opposing force: they see prices moving in one direction and they bet against it, often taking the "other side" of the trend followers' trades. They stop the trends from growing. They bring negative feedback into the system, bending prices back to the mean.

Friedman and Greenspan, like most economists, believed that negative feedback would triumph in this struggle. That contrarian T-Rexes would always prevail over the trend-following Jeff Goldblums, that the superior power of negative feedback would constrain the chaos-making positive feedback. "People who argue that speculation is generally destabilising seldom realise that this is largely equivalent to saying that speculators lose money," Friedman wrote. In other words, if speculators are chasing trends purely created by other speculators, then it is only a matter of time before prices return to the mean. And since trend followers bet the wrong way, they lose money. The contrarians, who correctly predicted that markets are self-stabilising, that prices tend to revert to the mean, will have bet correctly and be financially rewarded. This is why most economists see speculation as a stabilising force in markets: their bets only pay off if they are correct. The price system rewards the order makers and punishes the troublesome agents of chaos.

When Robert May first formulated his predator–prey model in the 1970s, ecologists shared the same assumption. They believed that nature tended towards balance: that shortly after a shock, such as a hot summer, a flood or a cold snap, animal populations would soon rebalance. But May's model suggested that this wouldn't always be the case. They could settle into all kinds of regular patterns, cycling through boom and bust or even breaking out into self-reproducing chaos. His native Australia had suffered numerous plagues of rabbits since the British introduced them in 1788. The Victorians had unwittingly killed off their only natural predators, a carnivorous marsupial creature called quoll. Without natural predators, their numbers exploded. Introducing new predators—cats, foxes and even mongooses—had no effect, nor did 200,000 miles of supposedly "rabbit-proof" fencing. There was no self-correcting return to a "balanced" or "orderly" ecosystem. Rabbit populations continued to boom and bust for nearly two centuries. It wasn't until the rabbit-killing virus myxomatosis was introduced in the 1950s that order returned.

In the mid-1980s, one freshly tenured Harvard economist investigated a similar instance of protracted disorder in finance. One of the era's most notorious speculators, George Soros, claimed that he made consistent profits not by looking at real-world fundamentals but by guessing where the speculative herd was heading. It was a trend-following positive-feedback strategy, precisely the kind that Friedman—and most economists—believed impossible to sustain over the long term. This young economist and his colleagues found that if there were enough traders jumping on trends like Soros, then they could in fact make consistent profits. There was a tipping point, a point at which enough trend followers could push prices from order into boom and bust and even chaos. Their presence altered the boom-bustiness of the system: the more of them there were, the higher May's dial would be turned up. The troublemaker was Larry Summers. He would go on to be Greenspan's ally in the Clinton administration and co-author of the Commodity Futures Modernization Act of 2000.

Summers, more than anyone else, knew that opening the floodgates to speculation had the potential to transform the market. Which direction it would take depended upon the dominant speculative strategy. The first to dominate was "passive" commodity index investing. From 2004 to 2008, institutional investors parked their capital in commodity index funds, pushing up prices, and then doubled down in 2008 as the housing market collapsed, causing a sharp super-spike. In 2009, this capital flowed into trend-following funds on the news that these speculators were the lucky few to profit from the turmoil of the Financial Crisis. Speculators would, just as Summers's decades-old research predicted, become an engine of chaos inside the market, poised to amplify any real-world disturbances into mega-trends.

It didn't take long. In 2010, speculators feared the Federal Reserve's bond-buying "quantitative easing" programme would cause runaway inflation. They poured their money into commodities to "hedge" against the inflation to come. Then, that summer, wildfires raged across Russian wheat fields. Speculators feared a worldwide shortage, so they piled into agricultural commodities. Both pushed up commodity prices, starting a trend—a trend that the trend-following capital was now poised to amplify, and amplify it did. By December 2010, food prices had surpassed Yaneer Bar-Yam's tipping point of 210. The Arab Spring was triggered.

In retrospect, both of these disturbances had little to do with the real-world fundamentals. The Fed's quantitative easing did not cause inflation. Nor was there a global shortage of wheat. The Americans had a bumper crop that year. Just as in 2008, the world had never produced so much food. The magic of the price system had departed from reality into its own fictional financial world. No one is more aware of this than the traders themselves. "I want the fundamentals to win out and just be a small observer with my position; not determining the prices so much and the speculators not determining prices so much, but I think that's hard to see that happening these days," Parker says. "We're causing a lot of chaotic crashes."

Prices are supposed to coordinate. They're supposed to synthesise information and harmonise vast supply chains. The "magic" of the price system is supposed to bring "peace and harmony" to the world. Instead, prices had plunged the world into chaos. This chaos was the result of a different kind of magic, one that shared the business model of cargo cults where orgies of destruction disguised a manipulative transfer of wealth. This magic was performed through those fast-multiplying pieces of paper called derivatives, whose new role in ordering the global economy would result in three explosions in quick succession. Housing in 2007, food in 2008 and food again in 2010 would each send a shockwave of poverty and hunger throughout the world. For the Middle East, this last detonation would finally push it over the edge of chaos and open a Pandora's Box of horrors. Yet this was only the start of our chaotic decade. There would be many more detonations to come. Many more maze walls would be destroyed, and new monsters unleashed. The chaotic decade, I would discover, was just beginning.

PART II

WARS

3

Perception: Pricing ISIS in Iraq

A concrete staircase descends out of a shapeless grey sky and ends mid-air. I look up and see its precarious connection to what remains of an interior wall of a Catholic church. Beneath where the roof once was, three Iraqi men look onto an acre of cracked concrete boulders sprouting steel wires like flowers. They wear navy-blue flak jackets, khaki trousers and orange gloves. I worry these uniforms won't offer much protection against the horrors hidden within the rubble. A wrong move could trigger grenades, suicide belts, artillery shells and other assorted improvised explosive devices (IEDs). They don't have the metal detectors or robots or spaceman-like protective suits I saw in *The Hurt Locker*. They're not paid-up members of a well-funded army but volunteers for the United Nations Mine Action Service (UNMAS). I channel my anxiety into operating the camera that is digging into my flak jacket.

The men take a slow, deliberate step into the rubble. They crouch, peer down and inspect the debris. Their orange gloves root around the bricks and rocks and plastic fragments. Nothing. They take another step. One raises his hand and calls out. The three men freeze as a fourth joins them. He crouches next to a large boulder and slowly removes the small rocks beneath it one by one. He stops. He stands up and examines the boulder from different angles. He crouches again, reaches underneath it and stands to reveal his find: a foot-long silver shell.

My handler from UNMAS, Simon Woodbridge, gives me a signal that it's time to leave. "Just follow where I'm walking exactly," Simon reminds me, "everywhere else is uncleared rubble." I follow him and two others carrying automatic weapons down a muddy path. Bullet holes rivet the street walls. The plaster is cracked and falling off. Either side I see buildings blown open, exposing what were once private lives. Garbage oozes out of these craters, blue plastic bags, a purple blouse, a turquoise chair, floral bedsheets from happier times.

We step inside the wreckage of a building. "ISIS would have slept here," Simon says, "then we've got the prison cells upstairs." He leads me through a concrete shell and up what remains of the staircase. The room is almost pitch-black. A small window illuminates some scattered plaster on the floor. "We heard stories about people taking turns to sleep because they were so crowded. When this was finally captured, one of the Armenian priests was able to get in here with American special forces, and the church outside was just littered with bodies."

As we walk, a strange feeling comes over me. For a moment I feel my sense of reality slip, as if I've stepped onto a film set about some kind of dystopian future. The prospect of the apocalypse hangs over Western popular culture as a question of *when*. But it should be a question of *where*. It's already here, beneath my feet, in the Iraqi city of Mosul. The apocalypse is not a shapeless menace stalking the horizon but a horror that has already ravaged this city. Monsters are real. ISIS is the worst of them. Over nine months of fighting, ISIS was defeated, but the "liberated" city was reduced to a crater. It is an epicentre of the destructive forces that were uncaged after the Arab Spring.

I've come to Iraq to crack my numbness. I want to witness chaos not as something counted, but something experienced. I want to go beyond the impersonal euphemisms of "battlefield deaths" and "forcibly displaced persons." This kind of horror-accounting can be a banal evil in its own right. Psychologists have found that the larger the death toll becomes, the less we care.

Before I left, I hadn't fully grasped that the person experiencing chaos wasn't always going to be somebody else. It was also going to be me. The report my security contractor had prepared runs through my mind. "There are reports of ISIS members staying behind and merging with the population," it stated. "As a result the threats are now asymmetric, either suicide bombings on crowded areas, security-force checkpoints or shootings towards security forces." The threat was now invisible, which was more dangerous. "The normal nature of daily life in eastern Mosul can give the illusion that everything is fine and lead to a more relaxed attitude, providing perfect cover for sleeper cells to stage incidents," it continued. "Foreigners are seen as prized kidnap targets for political or financial gain." The local police recorded twenty-eight kidnappings in Mosul in the last two months, most blamed on ISIS sleeper cells. The bombings continue: "IED hits school bus south of Mosul. Four Killed. IED kills two near Mosul. Car bomb kills three in Mosul." Mosul may have been "liberated" and ISIS "defeated" but the chaos continues.

Perhaps I should have stayed at home. I am far outside my natural habitat. This world of hunky men with deep voices and flak jackets does not line up with my own boyish, camp demeanour. My mind rushes through various disaster scenarios, assigning a probability to each one. I wonder how long it would take after an ISIS cell kidnapped me before they would notice my pink socks, work out that I am gay and burn me alive on the spot. I already have to pass to the people I'm working with, avoiding the topic of boyfriends, girlfriends and marriage plans that comes up in car rides, at meals and over shisha. I realise it's a bit late for second thoughts. I don't have a different pair of socks in the car.

We arrive at another complex of ruins. An orange digger pulls out a mountain of rubble and dumps it on the ground. Two UNMAS volunteers sweep towards it and go through the bricks one by one. "The Christian Catholic church that we're going into now," Simon says, gesturing to the remnants of a baby-blue wall, "up to 2,000 women were held in there. Some Yazidi women, and quite a few women from Mosul. And they were held in there until they were moved out to Syria to the slave market." The church has been cleared for explosives, so we can step inside. It's a wide-open space punctuated by large pink columns chiaroscuroed by beams of light piercing small windows across the frieze. The light catches the carpet of bricks stretching out across the floor, forming a delicate pattern of gold triangles. There's a lone office chair where the altar was, perhaps a throne to some ISIS bureaucrat who oversaw the atrocities. "The good thing about churches is they're strong defensive positions," Simon tells me. "They make good prisons, and they're good for keeping your equipment and supplies safe. Bomb-making factories, and holding prisoners and women."

We pass UNMAS volunteers laying out their finds on blankets covering the muddy ground: grenades, suicide belts, the odd artillery shell, an improvised drone. Simon tells me that UNMAS estimates that the Old City has one million tons of rubble. It could take ten or twenty years to finish clearing the city. "The level of contamination here is just mind-boggling. We haven't seen anything like this anywhere else."

"In the world?" I ask.

"Certainly not anywhere else I know of. It's just phenomenal."

From this vantage point atop the Old City I can see the Tigris draw a line between order and disorder. Like the River Acheron in Dante's *Inferno*, which marked the boundary of Hell, the Tigris carves out an island of ruins from an otherwise contented landscape. Over the water I see three broken bridges that connect the two worlds. Their mid-sections have imploded; one is just an empty space, another has fallen down, leading the road into the riverbed. Yet this medieval metaphor is deceptive. Mosul is not cut off from the modern world but intimately bound to it. The devastation was created through a butterfly effect that started with magical derivatives traded thousands of miles away. The "financial weapons of mass destruction"— as Warren Buffett called them—had become actual artillery fire, mortars, missiles and grenades. The ruins around me were quite literally, as Joseph Stiglitz told me, the "collateral damage" of the financial sector's pursuit of a few percentage points to add to their balance sheets. And the damage was ongoing. The force of the detonation not only turned the idealism of the Arab Spring into the ISIS nightmare, it also sent new waves of market chaos across the globe. Mosul, like Moria, I would learn, was a node where the dimensions of chaos converged.

Yet life was returning. Peppered through the debris were little shops selling clothes and shoes, food and spices. To me the ruins around them are interchangeable, but to Mosulis each one is an echo of the past. "That was my bank," my translator, Moayad, says, gesturing to one half-collapsed structure. He turns to another one. "That's where ISIS threw people off who were accused of being gay." Yellow cabs and motorcycles swarm around a five-storey structure stripped of its exterior walls and exposed as a bullet-ridden lattice. I look at it. I'm overwhelmed by ambivalence, a disconnect between the horror I should feel and the banality of another bombed-out building. This is where, after all, I would be dragged to the roof, tied to a chair and thrown to my death in front of a cheering crowd. My cracked-open head would be left on the roadside as a warning for a day or two before being cleared away for the next victims. But I find it hard to imagine. The roof is gone. Cars pass by casually below.

For the people that live here, however, imagination isn't necessary. "Walking through this neighbourhood, you would experience a horrible smell, the smell of humans," one Mosul resident, Khaled, tells me. He is a twenty-one-year-old student at Mosul University across the river. We stand next to his family home: a purple house that an NGO helped them rebuild to be a symbol of hope for the city. A few other neighbours have returned too, and their children are running up and down the dirt-covered hillside. In front of us, diggers move backwards and forwards throwing up clouds of debris. Earlier that day they had found a dead body. "I feel fine outside the neighbourhood, but I walk back here and all of a sudden everything is worse, my heart aches, my mind is scattered," Khaled says. "I sit down to study, but my mind keeps thinking about everything: the past, the present and the future. I think about past friends and family that I've lost. The present of living in this zombie neighbourhood of the dead. And the future, what is my future? What more will I see in the future? I can't see anything."

This is what it is like to live in the long shadow of chaos, after the politicians declare "mission accomplished" and The Feed moves on to the next nightmare. Those left must adjust to a new landscape, to a geography beyond the physical ruins and rubble and buried bodies, a psychic geography of lost opportunities, of memories, of a future that moves further and further away. This is life in a chaotic world. The "zombie" existence, as Khaled puts it, of being alive but not living. This ongoing trauma is what is missing from the official statistics, what happens after the "battlefield deaths" are counted and tabulated and plotted into trend lines describing the world as an ever more peaceful place. If one has to count something, then count refugees, the people trying to escape a life reduced to a zombie existence. This is on the mind of everyone I meet here, even those who are being pitched by NGOs as symbols of hope. "If I have the money," Khaled says, "I will leave Iraq."

I ask him about the future of the children here, many of whom are growing up with these ruins as their playground. "Here we have children who come out and play with explosives . . . In the area around the Great Mosque of al-Nuri, there were children going through the rubble and they triggered a mine that killed two of them."

"Did that happen recently?" I ask.

"Around a month ago."

I dart backwards as a donkey chariot hurtles towards me. Standing upright and holding on to the reins is a child no older than twelve. As he passes, another kid seated on the back next to a pile of scrap metal gives me a wave. I turn round, only to see another chariot approach, and then another. It was *Lord of the Flies* meets *Ben-Hur*, an army of medieval children criss-crossing the bomb-filled ruins. The only adults here are dressed in flak jackets, wearing helmets and holding automatic weapons from UNMAS. I walk over to Simon. Behind him I spot another child, this one clambering onto a small mountain of rubble the UNMAS volunteers are cautiously sifting through. He yanks out a large piece of corrugated iron from between two boulders. "How dangerous is it for them to be climbing up there?" I ask Simon.

"Very dangerous," he says. Just this morning, a couple of kids headed into a crater and found suicide belts with explosives still attached. "If we've got children going into that area, and they disturb those suicide belts, then they're gonna have a detonation. We can't tell them to stop. It's their livelihood. We can just try and warn them as much as we can."

I follow one of the chariots down the hill to a clearing by the river. The entrance is guarded by one of the many armed militias here in Mosul. With the Iraqi state barely present, much of the city is divided up between warring militias. The ones backed by Iran have the prized spots in the city, including a beach where they oversee industrial diggers searching for the rumoured $400 million that ISIS left behind. This junior militia has to do with a less lucrative racket, but a racket all the same. Moayad negotiates my access.

Donkeys jostle to park next to a scale so that the day's finds can be weighed. Kids sit in circles close by, chatting as their donkeys drink water. Their faces and hands are covered in white dust from the broken brick and concrete they've been wading through all day. One wears a T-shirt with "FASHION, TURNUP, PLAYER" printed on it in bold white type. I want to interview him, but Moayad tells me this could put the children at risk: ISIS sleeper cells could be watching and later punish the kids for talking to Western media. I retreat and let Moayad approach them. He comes back and tells me that most are from the slums along the city's outskirts and come into the Old City each day. He says that a cart full of scrap metal earns them $1 from the militiamen. These kids are pawns in a spontaneous feudal order, serfs to the militia that rules this tiny fiefdom.

When I set out to look for the human experience of chaos, this is far from what I imagined. It wasn't so much abject suffering or poverty but a peculiar kind of existence: the adult residents living as zombies and the children as feudal serfs. It's a reminder of how limited the human imagination is. How life can slip into arrangements so bizarre that we wouldn't consider them "plausible" if we encountered them in a fictional universe. And yet, it is all becoming quite normal. I'm starting to get into the rhythm of the order in disorder.

I recognised in Mosul something I had seen in Tunisia four years earlier. First, there was an explosion, "the boiling of water" as Yaneer Bar-Yam put it. Then things began to settle. The chaotic movements of individual water molecules slow down. They cool. They bond with each other. They condense into small shapes that are whole but also fluid. Only these molecules are not made of hydrogen and oxygen, but individual people bound by relationships. I was seeing social thermodynamics.

In times of "cold" stability, dictators try to integrate all the social relationships—called "social capital"—into the regime. Rival factions are bought off, given government appointments or special dispensations. But despite their efforts, some social capital always remains outside their control. It often persists among business elites, religious organisations, professional associations, trade unions, sectarian affiliations, organised crime and factions inside the regime itself. When tensions become sufficiently "hot" and society boils over, it is these bonds that lie outside the state that survive. As tensions "cool" once more, it is from them that new political alliances form.

This is why, despite the enormous diversity among the Arab Spring protestors, the political cleavages that followed resembled the old ones. In Tunisia and Egypt, the Muslim Brotherhood was one of these long-oppressed but persistent sources of social capital and was among the first to organise as a political force. Their main opponents were the other major sources of social capital—the lasting fragments of the old regime institutionalised in the police and the military. Syria's diverse religious and ethnic make-up allowed for few nationwide pools of social capital that had not been co-opted by Assad's regime. When militias did form they drew from local pools of social capital, such as defectors from military units, religious communities and members of organised crime. This is why the opposition was splintered into 1,000 independent militias and 3,250 smaller brigades. In Mosul, the dynamic was similar. Militias had formed around sectarian loyalties, bolstered by material support from foreign countries, and were taking advantage of the weak Iraqi state. They mark their fiefdoms with flags. They run protection rackets and road tolls. Some send kids into deadly ruins to extract the metal that remains. Social capital was structuring the disorder, normalising the madness around me.

These same thermodynamics had played out a decade earlier in

Iraq. The US-led coalition destroyed Saddam's regime and liquidated the Sunni-dominated state bureaucracy. No longer integrated into the state, millions of Sunnis who had worked for the army, the police and the government bureaucracy were unemployed, many still with access to Iraq's stores of weapons and munition. It was a tremendous pool of social capital that stretched across the country, but it was also fragmented and disorganised. Right before the invasion, US Secretary of State Colin Powell elevated the profile of one unknown Sunni who would later unite much of it. "Iraq today harbours a deadly terrorist network headed by Abu Musab Zarqawi," Powell announced to the world at the UN General Assembly in 2003. This low-level Al-Qaeda operative residing in Kurdistan was the best connection the Bush administration could come up with to tie 9/11 to Iraq and justify the war.

But he was a nobody. "He wasn't that smart," his mother said in disbelief when asked about her son, the alleged terrorist mastermind. Later the Americans themselves would publicise his idiocy, spreading the out-takes from one of his propaganda videos showing him struggling to fire a machine gun. Yet Zarqawi did understand the order in disorder. How smaller molecules could be manipulated to form larger structures. And thanks to Powell's UN speech, he was elevated from bumbling soldier to a potential leader who could fashion an army out of the disaffected. Zarqawi broke with Osama bin Laden, the leader of Al-Qaeda, when he decided to fight a war not against the secular West but inside the Muslim world itself. His own organisation would be called the Islamic State of Iraq and Syria. He mobilised many of the disenfranchised Sunni minority against Iraq's Shia majority and launched an insurgency against the Americans.

By 2011, Zarqawi was dead and ISIS diminished. But its new leader, Abu Bakr al-Baghdadi, saw an opportunity across the border in Syria. The Arab Spring protests had escalated to civil war. The opposition was weak and fragmented, just as it had been in Iraq seven years before. He branded ISIS as the most extreme of the Sunni Islamist militias, managing to unify the disparate brigades under his banner and turn his small army into a proto-state. In 2014 he set his sights on Mosul. The city's Sunni majority offered a strategic opportunity. Many resented their mistreatment by the Shia-dominated government in Baghdad, which had violently repressed their protests two years earlier. Before ISIS's army arrived, Al-Baghdadi's lieutenants managed to recruit sleeper cells among the disaffected. When his army of 1,500 did approach it was dwarfed by the 25,000-strong Iraqi force. Then ISIS sleeper cells let off bombs across the city and, amid the carnage, managed to slip through a suicide truck that detonated in front of the Iraqi army HQ. The Iraqi forces fled. Al-Baghdadi had used social capital to take the city, but he would need another source of capital to keep it.

Moayad hadn't even heard of ISIS when they took Mosul. He was a schoolteacher who enjoyed racing his car and going to the gym. He'd learnt to avoid the news. "If you turn on the news," Moayad tells me, "you hear the word 'died' like twenty times—'got killed,' 'someone died,' 'someone got kidnapped.' I hate those things." Now he was the news, a prisoner in Al-Baghdadi's caliphate. To stay sane, he undertook small rebellions against the ever-expanding rules. He played dominoes at a friend's house, shaved his moustache, bought contraband cigarettes and smoked shisha. He played music at home, even after one of his brother's friends was beheaded by the ISIS morality police, the *hisba*, when they found music on his phone. Music was important to him. He'd learnt to speak English by listening to George Michael's "Jesus to a Child" and Madonna's "Like a Prayer" as a teenager. Like most Mosulis, he retreated to his home with his brothers and parents, a bubble where they lived out some semblance of their life before the so-called caliphate.

One day this bubble popped. A visitor knocked on the door. Moayad's sister-in-law opened the door with her naked fingers wrapped around the frame. A *hisba* officer saw the offending fingers from the street. This was a serious offence: women's hands were to be covered outside the family home. Someone needed to be punished. If his brother went, "He would 100 per cent curse and he will be beheaded for sure," Moayad says. "So I went. I told them she was my sister." The ISIS officers told him he had to learn to be a "good Muslim," to take care of his family, and twenty lashings would help do that. As the first blows hit his back, Moayad began to laugh. He couldn't take it seriously. The officer was so put off he gave up after six strokes. They let him go.

Such abject cruelty shouldn't happen in civil wars like this because militias are dependent upon locals for support, housing, food and soldiers. This dependency creates an incentive for cooperation. But Al-Baghdadi wasn't dependent on his subjects. His forces had captured Assad's oil fields in the Euphrates valley, bringing in between $1 million and $2 million a day. With this money Al-Baghdadi could offer hefty salaries to foreign soldiers and fund his growing state bureaucracy. The commodities markets had first created the opportunity for him in Syria—by raising food prices and sparking the protests that would escalate into civil war—and now they were funding his expansion. High oil prices on the global markets meant that even the revenue he lost from selling oil to the black market still brought substantial revenues. Without either of these market interventions, Al-Baghdadi would have never left hiding in Iraq. But these sudden changes in the market maze in 2011 uncaged him and fuelled his growth into a monster among the monsters.

As horrific as ISIS was, it was far from the only disordered episode that Moayad had lived through. Born in 1987, his life could be counted in wars: Iran–Iraq, the Gulf War, Operation Desert Fox, Bush's invasion, then years of warring insurgencies. "I would hear the sirens and four or five missiles hit," Moayad says about growing up in Saddam's Iraq. "But to us it was normal. People went to their jobs. I used to go to school each and every day. It was a simple life. We didn't have car bombs, suicide bombers or explosions, or you'd be stuck all of a sudden in a fire fight."

This isn't normal. But it is, statistically speaking, normal for people like Moayad who are blessed with being born in a country with abundant oil reserves. What can read as a personal curse or a string of unfortunate events is, in fact, the "resource curse." Oil is a source of both wealth and mischief. Political scientists and economists have filled libraries with studies demonstrating this "paradox of plenty." When compared to their oil-importing neighbours, oil-exporting countries are more likely to be ruled by dictators with oversized militaries, be riven with inequality and corruption, start invasions and be invaded, and be ravaged by unusually long civil wars.

The resource curse is another amplifying engine of chaos. Just as speculators can turn small events into major price shocks, and the news media and populists can turn a few thousand refugees into an "invasion," the resource curse can turn a local crisis into a global catastrophe. The engine amplifies through the combination of the commodity markets and state power, through the corrupting influence of an easy supply of money, and those willing to enable or excuse their worst behaviour to get a slice of it. Oil fields can strengthen regimes as the revenues are traded for arms. But those fields can also be captured by militants who can use the black gold to starve the state and fund their own campaign. It is why oil-exporting countries are twice as likely to have outbreaks of civil war and why those wars last longer. What is often forgotten in these comparisons is that the resource curse is lived by people like Moayad and millions of others.

This curse is not a passive process, but a visceral and violent struggle. "From one side, we were facing bullets, getting injured and shedding blood, and from the other side, our people were getting attacked," Ajwan, a young Peshmerga fighter, tells me at a military base on the outskirts of Erbil. As ISIS entered Iraq she dropped out of college to join the army and quickly found herself in a battle near Kurdistan's prized oil refinery at Kalak. "Here we were trapped," she says, pointing to her smartphone screen. She made this video while the battle unfolded all around her. I see her in her truck, crammed into the back seat along with three other uniformed women. Out of the window, desert sand is being kicked up as other trucks swerve in and out of view. "Suicide bombers have not appeared yet. Snipers were firing. The Ford we were riding in had a shooter who was injured. There was a car ahead of us and a sniper shooting. Because it was open land, it was easy for them to shoot us. Here wireless phones were used to warn us of upcoming suicide attacks. They were so close and I could easily see them." It wasn't long before one showed up. "We tried to run. We had no shield and we had to save our lives. In order to keep fighting our enemies later. Here, they were giving signs to go right or left. But there were ISIS fighters on both sides. They were in all directions and we were surrounded by them. But we had to take a long path to be rescued."

They escaped, and the Peshmerga eventually beat back ISIS's advance. Kurdistan kept its oil refinery. "That was a gloomy day," she says, "but its fruits were sweet."

"Iraq violence lights fuse to oil-price spike," announced the *Financial Times* on 20 June 2014. "A loss of Iraqi exports could add $40–$50 to crude price." Oil prices surged 5 per cent on the news that ISIS had captured Mosul, to a nine-month high of $115 a barrel. The violent chaos that Ajwan and Moayad were trapped in was new "information" being fed into the oil price. Mosul was the nexus of these different dimensions of chaos: the zombie existence, a bloody war for oil, refugees forced to flee and now the financial markets. What had started as a food-price spike had become a civil war, and now this civil war was causing the oil price to spike. It was an incredible feedback loop between reality and the markets, where chaos in the markets had caused chaos in the real world which was now being fed back into the markets. Out of the other chaos amplifiers—the media, the algorithms, the resource curse—prices are the most powerful because they incorporate them all. Whether the disturbance is a hurricane, a war or images of outside "invaders," they are all, ultimately, "information" to be "priced into" the markets. And because these prices are global, the chaos in this small region of the world surged at the speed of light to every corner of it.

On the surface, there was nothing unusual about this oil-price spike. Prices had risen to triple digits as the Arab Spring brought down Gaddafi and temporarily halted Libya's oil production. Indeed, the greatest price shocks to the commodity markets took place in the 1970s as the Organization of the Petroleum Exporting Countries (OPEC) embargo and later the Iranian Revolution disrupted the global oil supply. If supply goes down prices are supposed to go up, whether the market is dominated by speculators or those trading physical barrels of oil. What was unusual is how far back in history you have to go to see a similar shock. Even Bush's 2003 full-scale invasion of Iraq barely shifted the oil price.

Indeed, one person was particularly irate about the failure of Bush's Iraq invasion to send the oil price to the heights of the 1970s. "Its price today should be $100 at the very least," Osama bin Laden complained in 2004. He had long blamed America for decades of low oil prices, believing it was "the pressures exercised by the US on the Saudi regime to increase production and flooding the market that caused a sharp decrease in oil prices." He had calculated that if oil had stayed at its peak in 1980, then the Arab oil producers would have made an additional $405 million a day which, over the subsequent twenty-five years, amounted to a loss of $36 trillion—$30,000 for each of the world's 1.2 billion Muslims. "You steal our wealth and oil at paltry prices because of your international influence and military threats," bin Laden said. "This theft is indeed the biggest theft ever witnessed by mankind in the history of the world." He had successfully lured Bush into a Middle Eastern war with the 9/11 attacks but failed to achieve one of his core objectives of raising the oil price. As ISIS battled in Iraq in the summer of 2014, the oil price was more than double—nearly three times, even—the price in 2004, yet the disruption to Iraq was just a fraction of what had occurred a decade earlier.

I asked commodity speculators what they thought of the price spike. They too said that there was something strange about the market's strong reaction. For one thing, ISIS hadn't captured any of Iraq's major facilities. Nor were there many to capture in that part of the country. Unlike in the 1970s, the oil supply hadn't been disrupted. "As news of ISIS spread throughout the media, speculators pushed into the market," Emad Mostaque, the former Chief Investment Officer of Capricorn Capital Management, tells me. "What speculators didn't understand was that ISIS was a Sunni army. This is why Mosul fell quickly and it seemed like they were going to take over the whole of Iraq. However, as they pushed into the Shia areas of East Iraq and the Kurdish areas of North Iraq, where the majority of oil-producing facilities were, they met far stiffer resistance and the oil kept on flowing." The speculators miscalculated. They didn't understand the order in disorder: how pre-existing social capital—in the form of sectarian bonds—was structuring the conflict. How it was working to keep Iraq's oil out of Al-Baghdadi's grip. ISIS's early success and growth was built around recruiting disaffected Sunnis to fight a sectarian war. It shouldn't have been a surprise that the areas in Iraq dominated by the sects they had fought for over a decade would put up greater resistance than Sunni-majority cities such as Mosul. Why had the speculators got it so wrong?

"Anytime you see stock prices or oil prices or land prices going up rapidly there's a story," Robert Shiller tells me in his Yale office one snowy January morning. "People see a price movement that is big and that justifies their attention to a story that might explain it. Big price movements also suggest that a lot of money is being won or lost right now, new millionaires are being made, former millionaires are going to be committing suicide . . . You have lots of people even among the so-called professionals who are not that professional, who hear stories and they just jump at it." Shiller is famous for his Nobel Prize–winning work on economic bubbles. Stories, however, do not need a bubbly episode to move prices. Stories, he believes, are an intrinsic feature of how all markets work all the time.

"People who believe that financial markets are perfect and efficient will readily say that price is determined by stories about the future," Shiller continues, "but the difference is that they think of these stories as rational and optimal forecasts of the future. The Efficient Market Hypothesis says that the stock market or other speculative markets represent a vote of all the smartest people in the world about what the future will be. The other view of speculative markets that I've been pushing is a narrative view. Yes, the markets do respond to stories, but it's not the optimal forecast. It's the popular story, the one that is tellable and contagious that gets invited into market prices . . . The strength of these narratives does not correspond to scientific reality. It represents feedback and contagion of stories."

In other words, all the "information" that is factored into prices comes to speculators in the form of a story. There is no pure information that exists outside their interpretation of it. And their interpretation is emotional and subjective. When a certain story becomes particularly popular among traders, it goes from merely influencing prices to becoming a self-reinforcing price-escalation machine. "The feedback loop for speculative bubbles is," Shiller explains, "investor A bids up the prices of stock, then investor B sees that investor A made some money and feels envious and finds out that there is a theory that it went up for some—God knows what—reason and the theory is an optimistic one. So, investor B buys into the bubble, pushing the price up again." The optimistic story about rising prices is the very thing that pushes the price up, and the higher price "confirms" the story, even if the story is, in reality, wrong. The story becomes a self-fulfilling prophecy.

I ask Shiller about another amplifying feedback loop I had come across: trend-following. These speculators say that they ignore stories and only focus on the price. If the price goes up, that's a good enough reason to buy. But, Shiller tells me, "trend-following" is itself a story, one that started in the 1950s. "Trend-following may be a fashion for a while among a group of investors, but it will eventually be forgotten or pushed away by some other theory," he says. Indeed, the rise of trend-following in 2009 came from stories in the financial press about the strategy's astonishing success in profiting from the 2008 collapse.

Trend-following amplifies any price move, and that includes the price moves of other stories embraced by speculators. In 2010, I had seen how stories about Russian wildfires and the prospect of Fed-induced inflation had bid up food prices. And how trend followers—many of whom had adopted the strategy upon hearing the story of its success in 2009—further amplified these trends. These narratives were all combining and feeding off each other, fuelling a bubble that would send a shockwave throughout the world. Looking back further, I saw how the rise of commodity-index investing was also driven by narratives, from the benefits of "portfolio diversification" to China's "industrial revolution" and "peak oil." I was beginning to see how the markets were not just reacting to stories but being built by stories. How one story about trading strategies amplified another story about wheat or inflation. Stories amplify and amplify and amplify.

Not all these tales originated in the market or the financial press; they could spill over from anywhere. In 2014, one of the most powerful stories was being told by Al-Baghdadi. "ISIS played a paradoxical game," Shiller says. "They showed videos on the internet that would by many accounts inspire anger at them. Beheading Christians, for example, is not a popular thing to show, but it had a paradoxical effect of making their story contagious among a small element of the population who were very enthusiastic about it. That's testament to the power of narratives, and the same narrative can spill over to oil prices, surely, because it had such vivid attention driven to it."

From Shiller and Stiglitz I had learnt two truths about prices. On the one hand, prices narrate. They tell a story, a story that can excite and spread and become a self-fulfilling prophecy. In this view, prices are driven not by scientific rationality but emotional contagion. On the other hand, prices deceive. They can hide information, they can manipulate the unwitting and extract their wealth. In this view, prices are a carefully deployed rational weapon. Were these two perspectives compatible? I went back to my original model of financial markets: the cult. I found one in the US that combined prophecy and deception, and suggested how prices could manipulate and narrate at the same time.

One summer's day in 1973, Marshall Applewhite and Bonnie Nettles were on a beach in the Pacific Northwest when they were struck by a "vibration like thunder." The divine had intervened. They believed they were the two witnesses prophesied in Revelation 11. They would be assassinated, rise from the dead and board a cloud to heaven, but "the cloud" would be a spaceship.

Applewhite and Nettles refashioned themselves as Bo and Peep: space-age shepherds who would guide lost souls through the UFO age. They prophesied a final "Harvest" of mankind. Only those who had achieved the "Level Above Human" would be permitted to board the single spacecraft to escape to the "Next Level." A few dozen believed that their revelation was a prophecy, and as they became a cult Bo and Peep's prophecies were codified into daily routines. Strict rules would help them escape their humanity: no sex, no relationships, no friends, no drugs, no alcohol, no personal possessions or identities. Members had to change their names, shave their heads and wear the cult's uniform. TV was permitted, to study human behaviour, but *Little House on the Prairie* was banned because it "vibrated on the human level." The cult would later become known as Heaven's Gate.

In 1975, Bo and Peep left the cult for a month to embark on a spiritual journey. On their return they discovered that one member, Aaron, had claimed a revelation of his own. The space aliens had told him that he could drink, smoke marijuana and have sex with his girlfriend. The cult split. Half of them abandoned asceticism for hedonism. Bo and Peep were horrified. They banished the heretics and reinstated the old rules. But they also announced a new revelation directly from outer space: the aliens were no longer in communication with everyone, but only The Two.

The problem facing Bo and Peep, I discovered, was not unique to Heaven's Gate. I went back to the sociologist Max Weber's classic study of religion. There he found that Catholic priests and Jewish rabbis confronted the same nuisance of ordinary people claiming a connection to the divine. Their solution was to simply declare that the era of prophecy was over, and that God had stopped talking to people until His return. "The closing of the canon," Weber writes, designated that "a certain epoch in the past history of the religion had been blessed with prophetic charisma. According to the theory of the rabbis this was the period from Moses to Alexander, while for the Roman Catholic point of view the period was the Apostolic Age." What had taken hundreds of years in these religions had taken Heaven's Gate just two. But the message was the same: God has stopped talking to you, it's only us now. This convergence in spiritual doctrine, Weber believed, was because all religions have the same business model. The priests and prophets pass on sacred knowledge to the laity, and in return the laity provide the material possessions—money, food, land—that support the religious bureaucracy and pay their salaries. If the laity are able to produce their own divine knowledge, then the priests would lose their spiritual monopoly and, with that, their material income. Their power comes from controlling information.

To a non-believer, the narrative here is just a tool of deception, a tactic for extracting material wealth out of the laity to support an economically unproductive class of so-called priests. The laity are suffering a "popular delusion." But suppose that a layperson challenges religious doctrine about the workings of the here and now. Take one famous example, that of Galileo, who, contrary to the Church's teaching, claimed that the earth went around the sun. He was denounced as a heretic, subjected to a show trial, forced to retract his "false" statements and then imprisoned by the Church authorities. Galileo was, of course, correct. But his fate was determined by a set of rules, a kind of social game defined by the authorities that reigned over him. This game rewarded conformity to the Church's official narrative and punished any challenge to it. Knowing the objective truth about the state of the world had no value in this game and could, in fact, incur great personal costs, as Galileo discovered. Conforming to the orthodox narrative, on the other hand, could lead to social advancement, status and wealth.

In other words, it can be rational to be wrong. One does not need to be "deluded" to espouse a false belief. Communities based around false narratives—about the arrival of cargo, of spaceships, the sun orbiting the earth—used these narratives to amass wealth at the top of their hierarchies. In the long term, knowing how manufactured goods are really made or that the alien apocalypse is not nigh or that the earth moves around the sun is economically productive information. But in the short term, it often isn't. Wealth can be acquired simply by transferring it from one group to another, rather than actually engaging in the physical process of making things like food, fuel, housing or clothing, or providing services like education, health care or entertainment. One can be a member of the group that receives wealth by playing a social game of figuring out the dominant orthodoxy and conforming to it before anyone else—and more zealously, too.

It is precisely this model of a social game that John Maynard
Keynes saw as the basis of all speculative activity. He likened it to
a popular game played in a newspaper in the 1930s. Readers were
presented with the faces of young women. They had to write into
the paper and guess which women the other readers—presumably
men—considered the most attractive. The goal was therefore not to
know who the most attractive woman was, but who they thought
everyone else thought the most attractive woman was. It was about
anticipating the narrative of beauty and not who was, objectively
speaking, the most beautiful. Putting aside the strange misogyny of
his chosen example, Keynes's point was a profound one. Speculative
markets are social games that are won by anticipating the moves of
other speculators. In the long term, the truth will win out. But, as
he famously put it, in the long run we're all dead.

Winning the speculative game follows the same logic as the game
of religious advancement. They are both games that reward conformity to the dominant orthodoxy. They are games where wealth
is acquired not by creating something new—tangible goods and
services—but by anticipating the emergent "truth" that the other
game-players will embrace. Wealth is transferred, not grown. Stiglitz
and Shiller are not describing two different games, but two aspects
of the same one. A game where rational players publicly embrace
ideas they know to be irrational.

Anne Hathaway is a famous Hollywood actress. Warren Buffett is a
famous investor whose company, Berkshire Hathaway, trades on the
stock market. When Anne Hathaway hosted the Oscars, Berkshire
Hathaway stock rose by 2.94 per cent. When her film *Bride Wars*
opened, Buffett's stock rose 2.61 per cent, as it did at the openings
of *Passengers* (1.43 per cent), *Rachel Getting Married* (0.44 per cent),
Valentine's Day (1.01 per cent), *Alice in Wonderland* (0.74 per cent)
and *Love & Other Drugs* (1.62 per cent). But when Anne got into a
car "crash" in 2011, the stock dropped by 0.84 per cent. Something
was treating the two Hathaways as one: connecting them together
and executing a trade.

"These programs are looking for key words, looking for key data, looking for key movements in other markets," Doug King, the Chief Investment Officer of the commodity hedge fund RCMA Asset Management, tells me. The headlines in The Feed were not just a representation of our chaotic world, but of the data that feeds trading algorithms. "You can see it instantaneously, you can see it as I do every day looking at trading volumes going through, and the swiftness of the whole situation responding to certain headlines that are in the marketplace." These algorithms read the news to anticipate the new orthodoxy, the new market narrative that will be factored into prices. The new orthodoxy may be wrong, but that doesn't matter. What matters is being the first to move, to stay one step ahead of rival traders. The incorporation of narratives into prices is not the result of our psychological failings as human beings selecting stories based on their emotional virality. It is simply rationally following the incentives of a social game, a game that can be played by emotionless computers all the same. As long as other computers are also confusing Berkshire Hathaway with Anne Hathaway, then the false prediction becomes a self-fulfilling prophecy and, as far as the prices go, becomes true.

The same algorithms that confused the two Hathaways were also reading the news that Ajwan and Moayad were engulfed in war in Iraq. Before the printed words "Iraq" and "war" had landed on a human retina, algorithms had already made the connection, anticipated a rise in the oil price and bought oil futures. They were wrong, but they were right. Wrong about the oil disruption, but right that the other traders—the other algorithms—would make the same call and buy oil. "The systems that then were looking at these headlines were highly sensitive to them," King says. *Sensitivity*, remember, is the main feature of a chaotic system, the butterfly effect that makes something small into something big.

The computers are scanning headlines from all over the world, searching for chaos, looking for a small disturbance that could send prices higher and—before anyone has even read the headline, let alone verified it—trade automatically. The sheer volume of the algorithmic trades magnifies the mere suggestion of chaos—such as an army approaching a refinery—into an all-too-real price shock. "The fluctuations in price today are enormous, larger than I've ever seen, and not down to a Gulf War, not down to a financial crisis," King continues. The cause "can be nothing to do with commodities at all."

Yet I found a further twist to this story of war and oil. These algorithms were trading on the conventional wisdom that conflict will lead to a surge in the price as the oil supply is reduced. "No regime will come in and say, 'We're not going to produce,'" Mahmoud El-Gamal, an oil economist at Rice University, tells me. "The only thing that really reduces supply is the destruction of physical infrastructure and trade routes." There was no reason why any new government or militia who seized the oil fields would want to destroy them, no matter their ideology. "ISIS were trying to build a state, and they were relying on oil revenues. So they're going to take over the fields, and still keep the oil pumping. It was an incoherent story of why ISIS would shut production. That's the goose that lays the golden egg." Indeed, Al-Baghdadi was fighting for control of Iraq's oil infrastructure in order to smuggle the oil to Turkey and sell it on the international markets. Even if Ajwan and her fellow Peshmerga fighters had failed to beat back ISIS and lost the Kalak refinery, it would have made little difference to the global oil supply. It would just be that the petrodollars would flow to ISIS rather than Iraqi Kurdistan.

It turned out that, rather than being the beginning of a new super-shock adding $40–$50 to a barrel of oil, the ISIS-in-Mosul spike would be the end of a three-year trend, not the start of a new one. Oil prices had been in the triple digits from the start of the Arab Spring in 2011, so this $5 jump was just adding to already historically high prices. "During the Arab Spring," El-Gamal explains, "the story was that there could be regime change in the North African republics that would eventually lead to regime changes in the major oil exporters, and then lead to disruptions in oil exports, and that's the story that maintained the bubble, even though clearly there was a glut in the global oil market." Libyan oil production was disrupted once Gaddafi fell, but only temporarily. Otherwise, oil continued to flow throughout this period. "And yet with these soaring inventories in the US and around the world, prices were still held high because people were afraid that there would be major disruption and therefore gobbling up whatever they can find at these inflated prices."

It was the narrative that the Arab Spring would bring chaos to oil production that had inflated the oil price over these years. Not only was that untrue, but it was highly unlikely that regime change by itself would impact production, as regimes want the power that petrodollars bring. Chaos in the markets had triggered chaos in the real world, and the *perception* of this chaos brought chaos into the markets once again. Whether it was a persistent story that began with the Arab Spring or a sudden newsflash sparked by ISIS invading Iraq, perception was always being priced in: predicting a future disruption that didn't happen, wouldn't happen and had little chance of ever happening. El-Gamal predicted in 2013 that the Arab Spring oil bubble would burst, and shortly after the ISIS spike it finally did.

The closer I got to understanding prices, the weirder they became. They were supposed to be synthesising information, coordinating global supply chains, moving people and goods and services to the most productive parts of the economy. Instead, prices were caught up in a social game that revolved not around reality but around collective perception of a reality, an orthodoxy. Just as in a cult or a religion, it is through the quick and public embrace of the emerging orthodoxy that material benefits are accumulated, be they wealth or status. In the long term, orthodoxies often crumble. But in the short term they can appear invincible, as unquestionable arbiters of truth and fortune.

An orthodoxy is, by definition, a monopoly. And monopolies have their own way of extracting wealth—called "rents" by economists. A field of oil wells is a textbook example: a militia or army takes over the land, declares the wells under their sole ownership, and can reliably enjoy the revenues from the oil produced. It is this ready supply of easy "rents" that fuels the resource curse, making oil fields and oil-producing countries the targets of corrupt politicians, warring militias and foreign armies. Religious rents operate in the same way. A church claims a monopoly over religious orthodoxy in a given territory. Competing churches are banned. They are the sole providers of salvation, and so congregations—at the pain of both physical and spiritual punishment—must transfer a portion of their wealth to them as a "rent." Economists from Keynes to Stiglitz have likewise shown how finance is able to acquire all kinds of ill-gotten "rents." Through a combination of collusion and political patronage, financial institutions are able reliably to extract wealth from the people they are supposed to serve.

At first, there doesn't appear to be anything "monopolistic" about speculative markets. They are, by definition, competitive. But this competition is far from fair. As the Anne Hathaway price bump suggests, investment banks and major hedge funds have an array of state-of-the-art weapons at their disposal to consistently outgun their rivals. They do not monopolise the emerging market narratives, but they also don't need to. They just need to anticipate them before their rivals, to maintain a superior position in the information hierarchy. To always hear the new orthodoxy first.

This competitive yet durably hierarchical social structure reminded me of the militias I had encountered in Mosul. I had seen a competitive, spontaneous order of vying fiefdoms where the strongest took the prized neighbourhoods and the weaker ones settled for lording over children digging for scrap metal among the explosives. Like Central American cartels or medieval barons, this loose feudal tapestry has the same extractive logic of rentier monopolies. They fight to acquire each other's territory, but the boundaries between them remain more or less stable nevertheless. The financial markets are a kind of financial feudalism where information, rather than territory, is the prize.

This "information," however, is less about the reality of Iraq's oil infrastructure and which factions control them than about the perception of them held by traders in New York and London. Their collective perception, their orthodoxy, was what drove prices, prices they profited from predicting. It didn't matter that the orthodoxy was wrong: that the Arab Spring revolutions were never a serious threat to oil supplies, that no matter who seized power the oil would continue to flow. For three years, the orthodoxy reigned nevertheless.

The resulting high oil prices orchestrated an incredible transfer of wealth, and not just to winners of the speculative game in finance. Yaneer Bar-Yam and his colleagues estimated that over a ten-year period, deregulated, financialised commodity prices had bestowed an incredible windfall on oil-producing nations. From 2002 to 2012, speculative finance delivered *excess* windfalls of up to $820 billion for Saudi Arabia, $580 billion for Russia, $230 billion for Venezuela, $290 billion for Iran and $190 billion for Kuwait. These were transfers directly to some of the world's most corrupt and unscrupulous governments. They would power another flap of the butterfly's wings, another tsunami of chaos that would sweep across the world.

4

Contagion: Typhoons, Trump, Brexit, Brazil, Belt and Road

"Last week I was in Tripoli and Benghazi," Britain's new prime minister, David Cameron, said in his first address to the UN General Assembly on 22 September 2011. "I saw the hunger of a people eager to get on with reclaiming their country, writing themselves a new chapter of freedom and democracy. This has been the most dramatic episode of what has been called the Arab Spring." Cameron urged his fellow leaders to break with their self-interested *realpolitik* and join him in supporting this idealistic movement to build a better world. "Just as after 1989 we helped those who tore down the Berlin Wall to build robust democracies and market economies," he continued, "so now in 2011, as people in North Africa and the Middle East stand up and give voice to their hopes for more open and democratic societies, we have an opportunity and I would say a responsibility to help them."

A year later he was in Dubai. The lofty rhetoric was gone. At the top of his agenda was sealing a deal with Saudi Arabia for seventy-four Typhoon fighter jets and flogging another hundred to the Gulf states at £70m apiece. Why was he now trying to strengthen the very regimes he had asked the international community to help the protestors overthrow? "We have one of the strictest regimes anywhere in the world for the sale of self-defence equipment," Cameron said in a statement, "but we do believe that countries have the right to self-defence." The words rang hollow. Just a year ago Saudi Arabia had rolled their troops into neighbouring Bahrain with British-made vehicles to "quell" the demonstrators. This was not "self-defence" but crushing pro-democracy protests in a foreign country.

Those uprisings were long over. Some were now civil wars that financial speculators were "pricing in" to the commodity markets. They were pushing the oil price sky-high and drowning Saudi Arabia, Kuwait, Iran, Russia and Venezuela in an awesome wave of black gold. Cameron was in a long line of foreign dignitaries, real-estate developers, tech entrepreneurs, movie producers, defence companies, investment banks and money managers who had come to feast on the windfall. Boris Johnson, then the Mayor of London, was one of them. "They eat camel. They milk camel. They race camels. They even have camel beauty contests," Johnson wrote in the *Daily Telegraph* on his return from Qatar. He acknowledged his conservative readers' hesitation at these exotic foreigners dressed in "flowing white robes with knife-edge creases," while reminding them of their incredible wealth and how they could get a piece of it. "The opportunities for Britain are enormous," he wrote, "there is so much we can offer."

But what does a politician with petrodollars want? How about siphoning off the windfall for himself and storing it safely abroad? No safety deposit box is safer than London real estate, and there's no better way to get it there than Britain's network of tax-haven islands. Want to shower one-off gifts on your most trusted supporters right before an election? British and American banks will happily lend you the money against future oil revenues—for a hefty fee, of course—as they did when Venezuela's Hugo Chávez ran for re-election in 2012, throwing houses, washing machines and TVs at voters like an episode of *Oprah's* "*Favorite Things*." How about new weapon systems to crush dissent at home and invade your neighbours? Britain's prime minister will come to negotiate the deal personally.

I discovered that these three desires—steal money, reward allies, embolden the military—are how all oil exporters spend their bonanzas, whether it's "socialist" Venezuela, "nationalist" Russia or "theocratic" Saudi Arabia. And while many countries help them do this, particularly the US, none are as singularly focused as Britain, whose economy is dominated by finance, real estate and defence. It is as if the plundering of foreign riches and fomenting chaos abroad from the Empire's heyday had never ended—instead it simply took on a new form.

As I traced these petrodollars through international finance across the world, I discovered that the windfall and its subsequent plunder were not two different transactions but a single circular one—a boomerang. I had first seen how capital from the financial markets—pension funds, university endowments, banks, hedge funds—had flowed into oil futures, pushing up prices and swelling the bank accounts of oil exporters. But these dollars soon found their way back to bank accounts at nearby addresses: in arms companies, investment banks, or via the stock market and real estate. The money had boomeranged from New York and London to Riyadh, Moscow and Caracas, back into New York and London. In fact, to make the round trip, the money may well simply have been shuffled around different accounts within the same Western bank. During this digital dance, guns were delivered, opponents bought off and riches plundered.

This circuit, I realised, didn't enable the resource curse, it *was* the resource curse. It is how petro-politicians retain their grip on power as ordinary people suffer. It is the reason why those living in oil-exporting nations earn less, have fewer freedoms and receive a poorer education and worse health care than those living in their oil-importing neighbours. Their national wealth doesn't stay in the nation, it is sent abroad. The beneficiaries of this capital export are not the people but the politicians who are strengthened. It is thanks to the architecture of the global maze that these petrocrats—despite their contrasting professed ideologies—govern similarly. The market not only provides the resources to unlock their cages, it also offers the opportunities and incentives to be more authoritarian, more corrupt and more belligerent—to behave like monsters.

Soon after Cameron finalised his arms sales with Saudi Arabia, the Saudis led a military intervention in Yemen. It was not even a week after the bombing began before human rights groups reported multiple instances of civilian-targeting, including of children, nowhere near military activity. Yet Cameron continued to pick profits over people; he too responded to financial incentives over his publicly professed belief in democracy and human rights. Days after an Oxfam warehouse containing humanitarian aid was bombed, the UK government approved another £1.75 billion arms deal to Saudi Arabia. In 2016, a UN committee would find "119 coalition sorties relating to violations of international law . . . [including] three alleged cases of civilians fleeing residential bombings being chased and shot at by helicopters."

Fragments of British-made missiles were pulled out of civilian buildings once occupied by the very people Cameron had told the UN it was his "responsibility to help." Instead, he helped create one of the world's greatest humanitarian catastrophes. In July 2015, the UN reported that 9.4 million struggled to access water, 13 million lacked adequate food and 21.1 million needed international aid. But the war in Yemen would just be one ripple in this beat of the butterfly's wings. The glut of oil money that the financial speculators bestowed on petro-states sent ripples everywhere, including the West itself.

"Let me be clear: leaving Europe would threaten our economic and our national security," Cameron said as he announced that Britain's membership in the EU would soon be up for a vote. "Economic security" would be the Remain campaign's central message, and Cameron had good reason to be confident the strategy would pay off. Those cap-in-hand trips he and Johnson had made to the Gulf states after the Arab Spring had worked. The oil windfall flowed through tax havens into UK real estate, pushing up house prices by 19 per cent across the country and even more in London, where 70 per cent of all high-end properties were sold to foreign buyers. Seeing prices rise, ordinary Brits jumped into real estate, pushing up prices even higher. Bubbles are contagious: the oil bubble had become a property bubble. Cameron's finance minister, George Osborne, went on TV to warn the British public that leaving the EU would threaten their new wealth: "There would be a hit to the value of people's homes by at least 10 per cent and up to 18 per cent."

"What the fuck was that?" Ryan Coetzee shouted at the TV. He was director of strategy for a Remain campaign group, Britain in Europe, and feared Osborne's message would backfire. True, the middle-class Conservative Party base had seen their wealth rise thanks to the housing boom, but what about everybody else? The boom had benefited homeowners in major cities and the South-East, but many parts of the country had been left out. The traditional Labour heartlands in the de-industrialised part of the country had seen prices decline or stagnate. They had suffered from Cameron's austerity budgets, which cut the safety net and social housing. Large swathes of the electorate didn't feel wealthy. As the vote neared, the economic message was falling flat. And now the news was filled with images of the global refugee crisis: boats packed, borders crossed, tent cities erected. All of these anxieties were colliding with Brexit. "My disabled mother missed out on SIX bungalows because immigrants jump the council house queue," one Brexit voter told the *Daily Mail*.

The Leave victory was an earthquake. The seismic tension—austerity, economic stagnation, housing insecurity, the refugee crisis—reached a critical point. The political landscape fractured. This new fault line didn't follow the traditional divides of left/right, Labour/Conservative, north/south. It followed another cleavage, one that Ben Ansell, Professor of Comparative Democratic Institutions at Nuffield College, Oxford, discovered through a granular geographic breakdown of the island nation. He found a single number that predicted who voted In and who voted Out. It was what Ryan Coetzee had feared. It was house prices.

"House prices are a health check for people," Ansell tells me, even for renters. "You might not like expensive house prices, but you do like the booming economy." People living in neighbourhoods with rising prices perceived it as a sign that the economy was doing well, whereas those who lived in places with falling prices believed that the status quo was failing. Brexit represented a vote for change. What is striking about Ansell's data is how localised the effects were. Even within different towns, like poor Wakefield and rich Cambridge, he found both Leave and Remain neighbourhoods, all conforming to

BREXIT & HOUSE PRICES

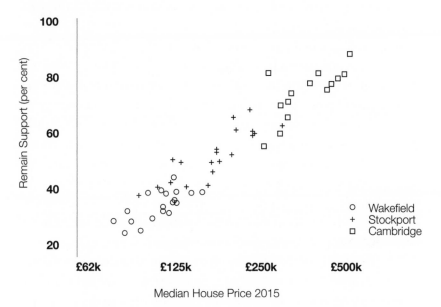

Adapted from Ansell and Adler (2019)

the same principle: the higher the price, the more they supported the EU.

Ansell explains that house prices figure so large in our minds because they are the cornerstone of the social contract in advanced economies. I had already seen in the Middle East the outsized role that bread plays: it's the most important source of sustenance for people as well as a symbol of the relationship between ruler and ruled. In wealthier countries, from America to Japan to Europe, home ownership is a similar source of security. People see it as their ultimate insurance, pension and nest egg should something in their lives go wrong. Ansell found that as people's property values increase, their support for the welfare state diminishes, as they no longer believe they need it. In 2016, both pressures bore down on voters. Austerity was gutting the welfare state, rolling back the safety net the propertyless relied upon. And rising house prices meant that the only alternative—the insurance of home ownership—was moving further and further out of their reach. For them, the social contract was broken. It was time for a revolution.

In the US, Ansell and his colleague David Adler found the same dynamic. In the years running up to the 2016 presidential election, a chasm had opened up between the coastal cities that saw house prices boom and the "left-behind" interior of the country. Much of the rise in prices came from oil money, as American real estate has been a prime place for stashing petrodollars ever since the 1970s. Some of these dollars were courted openly, such as Donald Trump flogging his apartments to wealthy Russians. Other money streams found indirect routes to real estate. Saudi Arabia ploughed $60 billion into the venture capital Vision Fund which flooded Silicon Valley with fresh investment dollars, re-inflating a tech bubble that was on the verge of bursting and, in doing so, sending Bay Area house prices past Manhattan's.

But the wave of black gold had flown over flyover country. Detroit's empty streets and boarded homes looked like sets from *The Walking Dead*; house prices had sunk so low that many properties couldn't be given away. In 2016, the anxiety of economic decline collided with the global refugee crisis, just as it had in Britain. "Hillary Clinton would rather provide a job to a refugee from overseas than give that job to unemployed African-American youth in cities like Detroit," Donald Trump told a crowd in Diamond, Michigan. Trump railed against the state's physical decay, from crumbling infrastructure to closing factories, blaming the incumbent Democrats. Helpfully, the Clinton campaign supported his message by touting the alleged booming economy, just as David Cameron had done.

When the votes were counted, Ansell and Adler found that yet again house prices predicted the swing to Trump. The left-behind neighbourhoods turned from voting for Obama in 2012 to Trump, whereas those with rising prices switched from Romney in 2012 to Clinton. The inequality in house prices, and the Democrats' failure to see their significance, is how Trump turned their Midwestern blue wall Republican red. It's an incredible demonstration of the power of prices and how deeply they've become ingrained in our collective psyche. Those numbers are integral not just to our economic well-being, but to our morality: our sense of fairness, justice and order.

The Trump–Brexit episode shows how prices can be a hidden causal force. Their power can be all too easily deflected onto apparitions of chaos—the foreign "invaders" who populate The Feed. But prices may also create chaos more openly, as they do the very thing that Friedman and Hayek believed they were built for: coordinating the economy.

A turboprop plane flew over Brazil's rolling hills. Looking out of the window at the deep valleys and dirt roads was Jane Mendillo, the Chief Investment Officer of Harvard University's $32 billion endowment. It was the summer of 2012 and commodity prices were high. "What I want is properties that produce something that the world is going to want more of, and the increase in the supply is difficult," Mendillo said. She reasoned that as the world's population grows and land remains finite, the land below could well be "green gold," as Wall Street analysts were calling it. She had already plunged 10 per cent of Harvard's fund into farmland in the US, Russia, Ukraine, New Zealand, Romania and South Africa, but Brazil would become her biggest bet. These investments, she said, would be "environmentally driven" since "increasing the health of the forest" meant they could "sell at a better price" in the future.

The high commodity prices after the Arab Spring were feeding the "green gold" story: invest in commodities now because supply is limited and demand is sure to grow. Remember, this is, according to Friedman, the function of prices: to coordinate the economy. Rising prices are supposed to mean that supply isn't meeting demand and investments should be channelled to boost production. Banks, hedge funds, university endowments, pension funds and sovereign wealth funds all poured money into the commodity supply chain. Financial entities were leading a global "land grab" as well as buying up water sources, mines and storage facilities. They funded the global fracking boom. High prices made oil trapped in shale rock—traditionally costly to extract—suddenly affordable. Fracking rigs sprang up across the US, from Oklahoma to Pennsylvania to North Dakota, to blast out this new supply of oil. This was all perfectly rational provided that prices reflected reality. But if prices were artificially inflated and this story of "green gold" or "peak oil 2.0" was just, as Robert Shiller puts it, not the "scientific story" but the "tellable story," then the commodity investment boom would prove disastrous. It would ramp up supply without the anticipated demand to absorb it, causing prices to crash and investments to implode.

It wasn't just finance buying up the supply chain: nation states joined the commodity frenzy too. "I can almost hear the camel bells echoing in the mountains and see the wisp of smoke rising from the desert," China's premier, Xi Jinping, said in Kazakhstan on 7 September 2013, as he launched the $1 trillion New Silk Road (or Belt and Road, as it is also known). Rather than camels carrying the commodities across the deserts of Central Asia, as they did long ago, it would be pipelines. China was planning an incredible investment in commodities and infrastructure across the globe and it was starting with a new gas pipeline in Kazakhstan. Xi Jinping would go on a tour of the other Central Asian states, announcing investments in oil, natural gas, uranium, gold, rare-earth metals and agriculture. Soon China's capital flooded not just Asia but Africa as well, investing in copper mines in Zambia and the Democratic Republic of Congo, and oil wells in Sudan, Nigeria and Angola.

China's investments were in one sense unremarkable. Prices were, as Hayek put it, "telling people what to do," and that was to pour capital into commodities. But unlike financial investors such as Harvard, China has an army and geopolitical strategic interests beyond profit-making. There were local fears that these investments were a colonial power grab. "We respect the development paths and domestic and foreign policies chosen independently by the people of every country," Xi Jinping reassured his audience that day in Kazakhstan. He pledged that China would not "establish any sphere of influence" but would instead "strive to build a region of harmony."

Investing in commodities, it turned out, was far from harmonious. The global shale boom alone was met with a fierce anti-fracking movement that staged large demonstrations, from the US and Mexico to the UK and France, Bulgaria and Romania. Harvard University created chaos everywhere it went. The university's subsidiaries bulldozed indigenous burial sites in Australia; in South Africa they tried to evict workers off land that had been granted to them in the post-apartheid settlements. Even in the US, Californian farmers launched legal actions against Harvard, accusing it of stealing their water. The most serious claims, however, came from Brazil. The World Bank warned investors in 2011 that illegal land-grabbing was rife in Brazil, where indigenous people were removed through violence and fraudulent land documents were being sold to investors. Harvard went ahead anyway, using shell corporations to hide their involvement. Now they face multiple investigations from Brazil's state authorities, one of which alleges that their companies engaged in a "festival of irregular and illegal procedures which resulted in usurpation of public lands," while another directly accuses their subsidiary of violent and forced evictions. Harvard was not the only player: land grabs were endemic as financial capital sought to acquire this "green gold." Brazil is now the world's leader in land-grab murders.

China's efforts were no more "harmonious." Protests break out periodically in Central Asia. In Pakistan, Baloch rebels routinely kill and kidnap Chinese engineers working on the oil pipeline. Many of China's "investments" in fact turned out to be loans that countries had to take out to pay Chinese companies, creating a form of colonial debt-bondage. The most extreme case was Sri Lanka. When the government could no longer service the debt to pay for a new port, China annexed it with a ninety-nine-year lease, just as the British had done to China with Hong Kong in 1898. The commodity boom even sparked chaos inside China's borders. The western province of Xinjiang connects Central Asia to the rest of China and is home to 30 per cent of the country's oil reserves and 40 per cent of its coal. Xi Jinping's brutal crackdown on the region's Muslim minority—the ethnic Uighurs—coincided with the launch of Belt and Road. Everywhere I looked, high commodity prices had coordinated chaos across the globe.

—

I call Yaneer Bar-Yam. I tell him how the chaos in the oil markets that followed the Arab Spring created its own wave of real-world chaos. I tell him how the ungodly riches that finance rained upon the world's petro-politicians only made them stronger. How David Cameron sold weapons to Saudi Arabia which were then dropped on the very people he had promised to help in Yemen. How the money had flowed through tax havens into real estate and sparked a property bubble in the UK and pushed the country, together with the global refugee crisis, towards Brexit. I tell him about how this happened in America, too, and how the high commodity prices had coordinated the shale revolution, the global land grab, Belt and Road, and how each of these produced their own eruptions of chaos.

Bar-Yam pauses. "Why aren't you looking into Ukraine?" he asks.

Boom: Putin's Chestiness Engulfs Ukraine

A TV built into the train carriage plays animal videos on a loop. A cat has a birthday party. A squirrel is confused. A show horse jumps over a fence. It's a six-hour train journey from Kiev to the war in Eastern Ukraine and I'm bored. I stare out of the window. The landscape cycles through miles of flat, snow-covered fields and grey, brutalist towns. The oldest Slavic languages have no words for beach or coast or sycamore or larch because it's in this marshland that they emerged 3,500 years ago. It's also the mythological home-land of a united Slavic people under the empire of Kievan Rus' and its Orthodox Christian king, Vladimir the Great. Ever since the end of his reign in 1015, the boundaries of Ukraine, Belarus and Russia have been caught in an endless loop of wars for independence and empire. Everything feels monotonous. History, landscape, TV—it all has the rhythm of a metronome.

In the winter of 2013, the pendulum swung again. The Ukrainian president, Viktor Yanukovych, had just dropped his plans for an economic arrangement with the EU. Protests erupted in Kiev. Camped in the capital's Maidan Square, the protestors feared Yanukovych was turning from Brussels to Moscow and would make them Russian subjects once more. When snipers fired at protestors on 20 February 2014, everything changed. Yanukovych fled. Amid the chaos, militias sprang up in Crimea and Eastern Ukraine to defend "Russian-speakers" who they claimed were under attack from neo-Nazi vigilantes and the Ukrainian army. By the summer, Putin had formally annexed Crimea and Eastern Ukraine had broken off into two rebel statelets: Donetsk People's Republic (DPR) and Luhansk People's Republic (LPR). Now in its fifth year, this European war has claimed 10,000 lives and turned 1.5 million people into refugees.

I find that idea—*European war*—strange. Sure, Europe has been, historically speaking, a horribly violent place. And I remember when I was ten years old hearing about ethnic cleansing in Kosovo on the evening news. But that, I was told, was just a blip: the last gasp of History. I had come to find out why History had returned to the very place it had been declared dead two decades ago.

The train arrives. The animals on TV are still going strong: cat birthday, confused squirrel, jumping horse. I lug bags of equipment onto the platform. A man runs towards me. He's shouting in Russian and throwing his arms towards a beaten-up old car. This must be my taxi driver. He speaks no English, but I detect panic. My translator sends me a text: we're running late, the checkpoints close soon.

We race down empty roads. The first checkpoint is to leave Ukraine. We drive past long lines of old people in coats with fur collars snaking around retro cars and tiny buses. After an hour of waiting, we're free to leave.

The car weaves around makeshift barriers made of tyres and corrugated iron that are tied together into the kind of improvised barricades you'd see at a student demonstration. We are in no-man's-land and heading towards a black box: the self-proclaimed Donetsk People's Republic. I had heard that this new country was a police state, a mini–North Korea. But I don't see towering monuments or heroic murals. I see a petrol station.

The separatists had converted it into their border control. There are no clerks or bureaucrats here, only men with walkie-talkies in military uniforms and black boots. They don't speak any English. I get my translator on the phone. I'm nervous. I'm not at risk of kidnap like in Iraq, but I was entering, for the first time in my life, a rogue state. It isn't recognised by any other country. They have signed no trade agreements, no international treaties, no conventions upholding human rights. Should I ask the wrong question or be overheard saying the wrong thing, anything could happen.

There are no embassies to hide in. So I just try to keep it simple. I assure them that I'm not a spy or a hostile journalist. They pretend to check some paperwork. I'm free to go.

We drive into the darkness. Ten minutes in: sirens. The taxi pulls over to the curb. My heart sinks. They must have changed their minds. They found something out about me. Something on my Twitter account had been flagged. A uniformed man approaches the window. The problem seems to be with the driver, not with me. Relief. He'd run a red light. He pays a fine—or a bribe—and is free to go. The driver turns to me and starts throwing his arms up and making explosion sounds with his lips. He turns back, starts the car and we set off into the darkness. It's only a minute before I hear the thud of artillery fire.

The hotel seems like a little bubble of normality, except for the "Entry with Guns Is Strictly Prohibited" sign on the door depicting a machine gun pointed at a woman and two children. "Mr. Russell," the hotel receptionist says as I enter the lobby. Business must be slow. I'm the only person checking in tonight.

My translator—let's call her Nadia—comes to the hotel bar for dinner. The other tables are filled with portly men in garish shirts puffing on shisha pipes. Loud Russian techno drowns out every-thing, but she insists that we speak quietly anyway. There are spies here. My room is probably bugged. I feel like I'm in a straight-to-video Cold War thriller. The knock-off, Ukrainian version. I play along. Whispering, I tell Nadia I'm here to find what has brought this 1,000-year-old conflict back from the dead. Is it just the inevi-table return of a cyclical battle between East and West? Or was this a new kind of war: a war that had its roots not in geopolitical division but in integrated global markets? Was the war, as Yaneer Bar-Yam suggested, really a price war?

I'm sitting in a nondescript office buried deep inside a square box of a government building. Two women chit-chat as they prepare my press pass. They work for the Ministry of Information, the DPR's propaganda operation. But the chair I'm sitting on isn't just a chair. It's a link to Moscow. It's an itemised expense found in a trove of hacked emails belonging to Putin's star propagandist and "political technologist" Vladislav Surkov. The chair revealed not just that the Kremlin was paying the bills, but that it was micro-managing this newly "independent" state. And this press pass is my ticket into the world that Surkov built.

Surkov isn't your run-of-the-mill propagandist. He's a mythologiser with his own mythology—the "puppet master," "the grey cardinal," "the Wizard of Oz," "the Lord of Darkness." With two framed photos on his desk, one of Putin, the other of Tupac, he was no ordinary Kremlin apparatchik. He tore up the Soviet playbook of enforcing a singular party line from the centre. Drawing on gangster rap, surrealist painters and postmodern French philosophy, he formulated a radical new strategy. Truth is fragmented. Grand narratives are dead. Everything is theatre. The conflicts in Russia's new democracy would be scripted. He invents opposition parties and casts protest groups and writes their speeches only to then expose them as frauds under Kremlin control. Contradictory conspiracy theories are spread. Nobody knows what is real and what isn't, and that's the point. He doesn't try to convince you of the truth, but rather that nothing is. He creates a thick cloud of cynicism and paranoia to choke anything that might become genuine opposition to Putin's rule.

In November 2013, just such an idealistic opposition movement was flowering in Kiev. The Kremlin needed to keep its ally, President Yanukovych, in power, and Surkov made regular trips to Ukraine's capital to support him. It wasn't long before Surkov's theatrics began. "Homosexuality is a threat to national security!" chanted a new protest group at the long-standing opposition protestors camped in Maidan Square. Their support for Europe, the counter-protestors told them, "will lead to the inevitable homosexualising of Ukraine." Then, right on cue, a group of pro-gay, pro-EU protestors appeared in clownish make-up waving rainbow flags. Social media lit up with evidence that they were frauds. Screenshots showed they had been recruited on Facebook and paid $150 to dress up and pretend to be a villainous queer army of EU-lovers. Both sides of the "homosexuality debate" were fake. It was an attempt to rewrite the protest script, split the Maidan movement and poison the atmosphere with paranoia. But Surkov's gambit failed. The Maidan protests grew.

Surkov made another visit on 13 February 2014. The Kremlin had changed its position: Yanukovych had to go. Seven days later, Surkov orchestrated—according to an investigation by the Ukrainian army—a sniper attack on the protestors and the police. Chaos reigned. As Yanukovych escaped, Ukraine appeared to collapse into anarchy. Social media was awash with reports that neo-Nazi thugs and the Ukrainian army were attacking Russian speakers. On 24 February unmarked soldiers appeared in Crimea. Despite having 22,000 soldiers stationed at a naval base on the peninsula—with four new divisions deployed there over the winter—Putin denied they were Russian. "There are many uniforms that are similar," Putin proposed, "you can go to a store and buy any kind of uniform." Locals jokingly called them "little green men" because they had seemingly come from outer space. But later, the Kremlin ministers justified the invasion. Maps appeared on TV of a "New Russia" that cut Ukraine in half. Putin was chosen by God to unify the Slavic people. Some even suggested that Vladimir Putin was the literal reincarnation of King Vladimir the Great.

Surkov's fairy tales were contradictory and fantastical. The monsters were gay European activists but also neo-Nazi thugs. The prince was Putin, who both never intervened and intervened by divine right. The stories were clichéd, even ISIS had used them: Al-Baghdadi as the great avenger of the homosexual menace and also a direct descendant of the Prophet. Nevertheless, the fairy tales worked. Everyone accepted that the chaos was real. Some blamed European elites for pushing EU and NATO expansion eastwards and poking the Russian bear. Others saw Putin as an imperialist who had used the chaos as an opportunity to expand his reach. But in reality Surkov had invented the opportunity; the chaos was his creation.

I leave the ministry with my press pass. My next meeting is with the head of communication for the army. I'm still thinking about Surkov's hacked emails. There was one that included a script for a TV movie about the war to be aired in Russia. I begin to worry that

I am walking into a trap; that I am an unwitting actor with pre-written lines in a drama that Surkov has scripted. Surkov's information warfare campaigns are famous for their irony and misdirection. How could I spot it?

"You are part of our information warfare campaign," the commander assures me. We're meeting in a restaurant basement. He is dressed in military camouflage and sits on a cow-skin chair. A purple chandelier hangs over his head. Behind him, a TV plays a runway show called *Life in Fashion* on CBS. He takes a puff from a tiny white e-cigarette. The commander explains that it is very important that I stay alive. The Ukrainians are going to target me just so they can blame the DPR for my death. "They will say, we killed you because you saw a Russian tank!"

He reminisces about the early days of the war. He fought in a battle where just a few hundred separatists defeated thousands of Ukrainian soldiers. They called themselves the "300" after the famous Spartan battle and more famous Hollywood movie. I make a note to look it up later.

A scantily dressed waitress wearing a tiara and bunny ears takes my order.

"How do you think the war will end?" I ask.

He looks down for a second. "I don't know," he says, lifting his head. "Maybe Ukrainian army will enter Donetsk and we will have one final battle," he chuckles, "like Stalingrad."

My taxi is hurtling towards the front line. I'm nervous. Not of the snipers or unexploded bombs or artillery fire. It's my driver. He's clearly stoned. He reminds me of a 1990s emo-kid: baggy jeans, greasy long hair and that blank, pseudo-philosophical stare. He hasn't said a word to anyone all morning. "He gets high because he finds the passengers so boring," Nadia had warned me. "He doesn't want to hear their conversations." But there's only a few taxis that go to the front. So here I was, with my baked driver winding through icy roads and frosted fields only pausing to wave at the separatist soldiers manning checkpoints. I sit uncomfortably in my flak jacket and helmet labelled "PRESS."

Dima, my military handler, is sitting in the front passenger seat fiddling with his phone. He turns round to show me something. "Here, you can see the Ukrainian army," he says, zooming into a photograph of masked militia men covered in swastikas in a Facebook post. "The Ukrainians are Nazis!"

Nadia rolls her eyes. She's clearly heard this all before. This must be Chapter 1 of the propaganda playbook: show the journalists pictures of the "Azov Battalion" and claim that this ultra-nationalist militia represent the Ukrainian army and government at large.

"So, what did the Ukrainian government do that was so bad it made you want to fight?" I ask, playing along.

"They banned Russian in the passports. So if you had a Russian name it would become Ukrainian," Dima says.

"But is that worth fighting a war over?"

"We have to fight for our names."

I'm disappointed by his answer. I was hoping for something a bit more imaginative, such as the story that the Ukrainian army had crucified a ten-year-old girl which was proven not just to be fake, but not even defended by the Russian minister responsible. He boasted that his Russian audience enjoyed such fabulist stories, which were great for ratings. I think Dima can tell I'm unpersuaded that he joined a revolution over his passport. He changes the subject.

He shows us photos of his newborn son. A Rabbi is in one of the pictures. He says he's happy to be a Jew fighting Nazis.

"I wish I was a Jew," Nadia says.

"Why do you wish you were Jewish?" I ask.

"Because then I could go live in Israel and not live in a fucked-up country like Ukraine."

They chat in Russian. They are familiar but not friendly. They know each other from high school. This must be what happens when a tiny province breaks away: the organs of the state, business and journalism are suddenly filled from a tiny pool of locals. I try to imagine what would happen if an American state like Maine or a British county like Kent just broke off and declared its allegiance to its foreign neighbour. Bank managers would run the Treasury, police officers would command the army, and local journalists who once covered village fetes would file articles for the *New York Times*. Politics is often compared to the psychodrama of high school: the cliques, petty jealousies and resentments. Here, it literally is.

The taxi pulls up alongside a thicket of trees. The other side, I'm told, is no-man's-land. Across a field, the Ukrainian army are guarding their position with guns pointed our way. A small wall of car tyres protects us from their view. Beneath them a staircase descends into the ground. Dima takes me down the steps and into the trenches.

My head bobs well below the firing line. The walls must be eight feet high. I try not to slip on the snow-covered floorboards. I'm disoriented; it's not what I expected. As a kid, I'd visited elaborate re-creations of the First World War trenches at the Imperial War Museum. They'd made a show of re-creating the smell of disinfectant and the sounds of artillery fire. Only now I'm in the real thing and I can't hear or smell anything. It's dry, empty, silent. My only view is of the walls made of tree branches to either side and the grey sky above. It doesn't feel real.

Dima pauses by a strange-looking rifle several feet longer than himself. "We got this from the museum. It is for fighting tanks. It is from the Second World War," he says. The subtext is clear: Russia isn't arming us, we're the underdogs.

We duck and dive through more tunnels until we find the soldier Dima has prepared for me to talk to. He's standing in his white camouflage uniform holding an automatic weapon. He tells me that before he came here, he was just an ordinary Ukrainian living in Kiev working for an internet provider. Then, in 2014, his cousin was killed at a checkpoint. He wanted to join the fight but couldn't until he moved his aunt to Donetsk. When he did in 2016, he joined the army. He's had friends killed and injured. "That's what revenge will be for if we receive the orders," he says.

But for now, he waits. "Trench wars are considered to be the most intense ones because we are constantly on the front line," he says. He doesn't go to a nearby military base when his shift ends, he eats and sleeps here too. "The most exhausting thing is anticipating. Anticipating when the Ukrainian army will come at night, when shooting will start in the morning." Staring onto an empty field all day long sounds like the path to madness. And, sure enough, the void gets to some. "A [Ukrainian] sniper was dressed up as a sort of witch. We first thought the binoculars were distorting our vision. We didn't understand. He just sat there for ages. He thought he wouldn't be noticed. We all got out and looked at him. I don't know if he saw us or not, or if he was on drugs."

He leads me out of the trenches, back up the stairs, to a small building and yard obscured by the tyre wall. This is where he and a dozen other men live. He shows me a large pot of soup sitting on a fire. He points out their pet cat and some artillery shells. He takes me to his dugout. It's a small subterranean room with a single bed and a DVD-player. He says three of them sleep here. Finally, we go into the canteen. It's another cramped underground room. Five soldiers are eating soup. They ask me to sign the wall. It's covered with the names of all the other journalists who have visited them.

I begin to wonder what exactly this place is. Is anything here real? Is this just Surkov's idea of a Disneyland ride for war correspondents? I hadn't seen no-man's-land or the Ukrainian positions, just a trench and a wall and these camouflaged soldiers. I could be anywhere. A military base, perhaps. A converted construction site.

One of the superior officers calls out something in Russian to our soldier. Nadia translates: "Hey, Muscovite, come over here!" I guess his story about travelling from Kiev to avenge his cousin's death may not, in fact, be true.

"I want to see the Ukrainian positions," I command Dima with all the authority I can muster.

He talks with his superior officer for a minute. He comes back and tells me they've agreed.

He takes me past the towers of car tyres to the thicket of trees. "You can see the Nazi Ukrainian army through here," he says, pointing to a small gap in the thicket.

I peer through my telephoto lens. Blurry branches criss-cross blobs of white snow. "I can't see anything. I can't see past the branches," I say.

"Try over here," he says, pointing to another opening.

I frame up. "That doesn't work either."

"You can see them through here!" He points to yet another gap.

"More branches."

I'm exhausted. The weight of the body armour and the camera together is taking everything out of me.

"Try here."

"You try!" I throw the twenty-pound camera rig towards him. He nearly topples over but manages to catch himself.

He places the rig on his shoulder and peers down the viewfinder. He tries to find a space between the branches but can't. I take the camera back. He leads me back into the trenches, sulking.

After ten minutes of walking through the maze of mud walls we arrive at a hole dug deep into the earth.

"You cannot have the camera here for long," he says. "The Ukrainians are very sneaky. They will see the light reflect on the lens and they will shoot at you."

Another lie? Was there really a Ukrainian sniper staring at this position, waiting for a journalist? I didn't know, but there could be, so I say, "OK."

I step into the dugout. It's barely big enough for the one soldier here. He's leaning against a mound of earth with his rifle pointing out of a tiny opening, several inches high and about two feet wide. It's a window to a white-frosted field and a row of trees about 800 feet away. Imagining a sniper peering through his binoculars back at me, my mild anxiety seeps into panic. My heart rate rises. I grab the telephoto lens and aim it through the opening. I can make out some grey shapes that could be something military. I hold the shot for thirty seconds and duck out. I let out a deep breath. Dima leads me back through the trenches.

PHHHHHHT! I hear echo around me.

"It is good if you hear the bullet," Dima says. "If you don't, you are dead."

While Surkov was spinning tales of murderous homosexual neo-Nazis, the Americans had long been telling a monster story of their own. They rebooted the Cold War story, the story of East versus

West, of a free Europe against an expansionist Russia fuelled by Soviet nostalgia. "[Putin] gave us notice of his strategy seven or eight years ago," Trump's national security advisor, John Bolton, told Fox News, "when he said, 'The break-up of the Soviet Union was the greatest geopolitical tragedy of the twentieth century.'" America's national security establishment worked hard to up the stakes of this sequel: it wasn't just a reboot of the Cold War, it was an escalation. "When the history books are written, it will be said that a couple of weeks on the Maidan [square protests] is where this went from being a Cold War–style competition to a much bigger deal," Obama's top diplomat, Ben Rhodes, told *The New Yorker*. "Putin's unwillingness to abide by any norms began at that point. It went from provocative to disrespectful of any international boundary." From the neoconservative right to the liberal left, the story was the same: Putin was an expansionist, a warmonger, a treaty breaker and a norm ignorer. When others, including Putin himself, point out the hypocrisy of this story—that America routinely ignores norms, breaks treaties and invades countries—they are dismissed as pushing a dangerous *whataboutism*. America's record doesn't change the story's central truth: Putin is a monster.

Indeed, these Putin-as-monster stories have plenty of biographical colour to draw from. Putin started his career as a KGB operative in East Germany. After a stint as the deeply corrupt mayor of St. Petersburg, he became Boris Yeltsin's prime minister by chance. Yeltsin's team was having difficulty deciding on a successor, so they polled the public, asking them who their favourite fictional heroes were. It just so happened that Putin bore the closest resemblance to the winner: Max Stierlitz, a fictional spy, the James Bond of the USSR. When Putin was installed as prime minister his approval rating was a dire 2 per cent. Then bombs destroyed apartment buildings in Moscow, Buynaksk and Volgodonsk, killing 300. Putin blamed Chechen terrorists and invaded Chechnya. His approval ratings soared and he won the presidential election. Many Kremlinologists believe he staged the attacks so he could brand himself as the nation's saviour. It set the stage for a monstrous presidency filled with foreign invasions, domestic assassinations and human rights violations.

Yet the rise of this monster, like the rise of the Soviet monsters before him, was not powered by a villainous personality or a bold ideology. Yegor Gaidar, one of Russia's foremost economists and one-time acting prime minister, argues in *Collapse of an Empire: Lessons for Modern Russia* that his country's power comes from a familiar maze. Whether under communist or capitalist rule, Russia's fortunes have been dictated by its vast Siberian deposits of natural gas and oil.

The Eastern bloc that Stalin had conquered in the Second World War was bound to the Soviet empire through a network of economic dependency. During the 1960s Stalin's successor, Nikita Khrushchev, constructed a web of pipelines that delivered subsidised natural gas and oil directly from the mother country to Poland, Ukraine, Belarus, East Germany and the other states of the Warsaw Pact. Moscow's control of both the supply and the price could be used either as carrot or stick. When the Solidarity Movement threatened the Polish regime, the Kremlin slashed their gas prices to bribe their disgruntled subjects into compliance. Those who strayed from Moscow's orbit, such as Nicolae Ceaușescu's Romania, were forced to pay the full international price for natural gas. And when oil and gas prices rose dramatically in the 1970s, the Kremlin's grip over its energy-hungry satellites strengthened as its carrot rose in value. In 1979, the oil price surged again and the USSR felt emboldened to expand its empire. Soviet tanks rolled into Afghanistan.

Yet this power was fragile. The oil revenues had long been used to cover up a crumbling agricultural sector, one that had been destroyed through decades of failed "collectivisation" programmes. Before the First World War, Tsarist Russia was the world's largest wheat exporter, but by the 1960s it had become the world's biggest importer. And the bill for these imports was paid for in dollars earned from its oil exports. So when the oil price crashed in the mid-1980s, the Soviet energy empire unravelled. Without an abundance of dollars from oil exports, the Kremlin was forced to borrow dollars from Western banks and governments to pay for foreign food to feed its people. And, now desperate for every dollar it could squeeze from exporting oil and gas, Moscow could no longer afford to subsidise energy for its Eastern satellites.

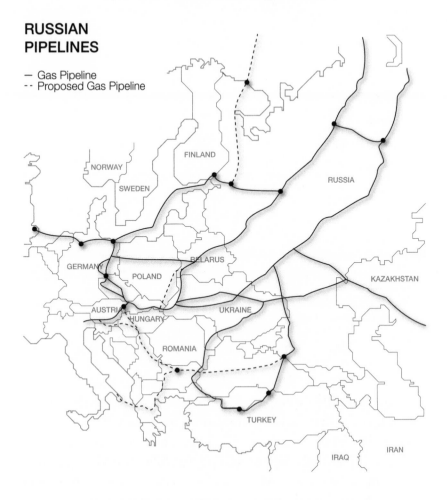

**RUSSIAN
PIPELINES**

— Gas Pipeline
-- Proposed Gas Pipeline

In 1988 the harvest was weak, and all Russia's oil revenues were spent servicing its existing foreign debt. To stop his people from starving, the Soviet premier Mikhail Gorbachev needed a new round of loans. The Western governments exploited his desperation. They demanded that, should the loans be granted, the Soviet Union could not use force to oppress its own people. Gorbachev agreed. With neither the economic carrot nor the military stick, Moscow lost control of Eastern Europe. And despite the loans, the crisis escalated. The Kremlin was forced to raise food prices, with bread going up by 300 per cent. Unable to feed its own people, the regime collapsed.

When Putin came to power in 1999 he set about rebuilding Rus-

RUSSIA & OIL PRICES

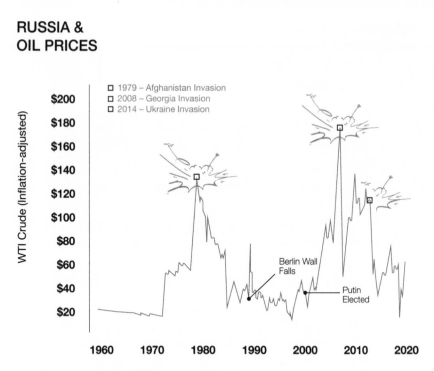

□ 1979 – Afghanistan Invasion
□ 2008 – Georgia Invasion
□ 2014 – Ukraine Invasion

WTI Crude (Inflation-adjusted)

$200
$180
$160
$140
$120
$100
$80
$60
$40
$20

Berlin Wall Falls

Putin Elected

1960   1970   1980   1990   2000   2010   2020

sia's economic energy empire. He took back control of the oil and gas companies that had been privatised by Yeltsin. Thanks to the Commodity Futures Modernization Act, the price of oil and natural gas surged as financial institutions poured billions into commodity index funds. Not only was this a direct wealth transfer from Wall Street to Russia and the other oil-exporting nations, it also gave the Kremlin back its "gas weapon."

Putin was now able to bind the former Soviet satellites to Moscow once again through generous gas subsidies. The chief beneficiary was the "last dictator of Europe," Alexander Lukashenko of Belarus, who has enjoyed essentially free gas from Putin in exchange for his fealty. Georgia and Ukraine initially received generous subsidies too. However, as the 2000s went on Putin tussled with both regimes, raising prices and even shutting off supply to enforce compliance to the Kremlin. Georgia was cut off after the 2008 conflict, and the two Russian-backed states that broke away from Georgia—South Ossetia and Abkhazia—received a new pipeline all of their own. Ukraine had its gas prices raised and shut off periodically in 2005, 2006 and 2009 as Kiev flirted with Western allegiance.

The EU became increasingly alarmed at Putin's brazen deployment of the gas weapon. In 2012, Russia supplied 39 per cent of the EU's natural gas. Of the three major pipelines, two of them ran through Ukraine. "The question of Ukraine is a question of EU's future, EU's safety," Poland's prime minister, Donald Tusk, said. "We will not be able to sufficiently fend off potential aggressive steps by Russia in the future if so many European countries are dependent on Russian gas deliveries."

Neither the EU nor Ukraine planned on being trapped by Putin's pipelines for much longer. In 2012, enormous gas reserves—2.3 trillion cubic metres—were discovered under Ukraine's share of the Black Sea. Russia tried to negotiate access to the deposits, but the talks fell through. Then, in January 2013, Ukraine struck a deal with Royal Dutch Shell to start drilling in Eastern Ukraine, where another major deposit of natural gas had been discovered. In April 2013, the Ukrainian energy and coal industry minister declared that the projects in Eastern Ukraine and the Black Sea around Crimea would soon start producing so much natural gas that the country would no longer need to import it from Russia or anywhere else. In fact, Ukraine would become a net exporter to Europe—competing with Russia—by 2020.

If these plans came to fruition, Putin's leverage over Europe would evaporate. He had no intention of overseeing the same unravelling of energy dominance that the USSR had suffered in the 1980s. But Putin still had time. Ukraine's plans for energy independence had yet to become reality.

"We call this the Road of Death," Dima says from the front seat of the taxi. "You can only take this road because I am with you." I can't see much out of the window. The forest is thick along the road. My anxiety seeps in again. Our emo taxi driver has yet to speak. The car turns a corner. Two figures are walking along the road. I tense up. But it is just two pensioners. They smile and wave as we pass.

The forest clears. Perfectly formed mountains, as if from a kid's colouring book, pop out of the fog. These pyramids are man-made piles of debris, tombs to the once-thriving coal-mining industry that made Donetsk the richest city in Ukraine. Their peaks are decapitated by low-hanging clouds. Everything appears in monochrome. Occasionally I see a flash of yellow as old buses appear and disappear through the white mist.

Dima directs our taxi driver to an intersection. I'm not quite sure why he's brought us to this street. The shops are boarded up. Buildings are bombed out. Through a gaping hole two storeys high I see the skeleton of a staircase barely hanging from the ceiling. A single shop is still open—a kiosk selling newspapers and cigarettes.

The war is very much alive here, but the city is economically dead. The young, working-age population has fled. Nothing is made here. Everything is imported from Russia. People keep asking us if we have Ukrainian cigarettes. The Russian ones are full of woodchips, they say. I wonder how people are surviving without jobs or how this proto-state can survive without taxes.

I head to the suburbs near the airport. The neighbourhood looks like a snowy Mosul, only rather than kids clambering over rubble it is drunk pensioners. Most of the homes are just shells; a few surviving walls suggest what might have stood there. I see a made-up bed covered in dust. A TV antenna in a bathtub. A kitchen stove dangles from the second floor. A man on a bicycle appears at the top of the street. A dog runs out to greet him, wagging his tail and circling the bike as he rides past. The dog doesn't know he's living in a post-apocalyptic wasteland. I envy the dog.

One resident gives me a tour. He points to where his daughter's house once was. "It got burnt down completely," he says. Like in Mosul, this graveyard is one of bodies and ruins but also memories that never really go away. "Many people were killed. That house burnt down. They got killed there. My relative got killed. Not many would come back here." But here he is. One of the leftovers.

His house was destroyed too. "As the projectile hit the ground so hard, I lost all my teeth." He then smiles and points to a gap where they once were. There were fourteen bombs dropped on his little plot of land. But he managed to rebuild much of it. He has walls and windows but inside it's a mess. There was a flood, so he spread chestnuts out on the floor to soak up the moisture. He keeps a rifle under the mattress he sleeps on. There's a white bust of Lenin sitting next to a little painting of the Virgin Mary. But the most important thing he has is in the backyard.

He lets out about thirty pigeons from a hutch. "My pigeons. They all are my favourite. I survived the war with them, I hid them in the cellar. I won't get rid of them. I might starve myself but I won't let the same happen to my pigeons . . . I have been keeping them since I was six. I wasn't even going to school yet . . . I will starve, but I will feed my pigeons."

But why isn't he starving and how is he feeding his pigeons? He lives in a barely functioning state with no economy. "We survived," he says. "It was hard, yes. We had no gas, no light. But then Russians connected gas and electricity here. They helped us to survive. I, myself, am a Ukrainian but there is nobody in the world like Putin." His Ukrainian pension was cut off from Kiev, but the Russians replaced it with something called "material benefits." "It's the same as the Ukrainian pension used to be, we get the same amount." For all the conspiracy and propaganda, there remains an undeniable truth that cannot be erased: money.

In February 2014, Cullen Hendrix, a political science professor at the University of Denver, was thinking about chaos. Putin's Ukrainian invasion was his first major military action since he invaded and "liberated" South Ossetia and Abkhazia from Georgia in 2008. That year had seen military disputes flare up all over the world. The Venezuelan president, Hugo Chávez, sent ten tank battalions to Colombia's border. Both Chávez and Bolivia's President Evo Morales ratcheted up their beef with the US and expelled US diplomats. In the Middle East, Hamas launched rockets into Israel with Iran's money and support. There's nothing particularly surprising about these conflicts. Disputes between the US and South America, Israel and Palestine, Russia and Georgia, are relatively routine. But what if these conflicts had a rhythm beyond retribution and retaliation?

Russia, Venezuela, Bolivia and Iran had something in common:

they were all exporters of oil and natural gas. And in the summer of 2008, when Putin's tanks rolled across the Georgian border, oil was trading at an eye-watering $143 a barrel. It was the highest since 1980, another year that saw the Kremlin send tanks across a border, in that case Afghanistan's. And now, in 2014, Putin's army was marching once again as oil traded at historic highs. Looking at 1980, 2008 and 2014, Cullen wondered if the beat of the rhythm was prices—the price of oil.

"I got data on international conflict and I merged that with information on oil price," he tells me. The conflicts here aren't outright wars. Those rarely happen any more. They are "militarised interstate disputes" or "MIDs." A MID would be recorded when Pakistan fires artillery over the border in Kashmir or when China shoots down a US drone. He found that the higher the oil price, the more likely an oil-exporting regime like Russia, Venezuela or Iran was to start a militarised dispute. Prices didn't need to be at record highs to significantly increase the chance of a conflict. In fact, a jump in the oil price of just $20, from $40 to $60, could make military action 40 per cent more likely.

Hendrix had measured how prices operate as the levers and pulleys of the monster's maze. Whether it's Putin, Nicolás Maduro or Mohammed bin Salman, petro-politicians face highly structured obstacles and opportunities. The opportunities for mischief, for confrontation and invasion, rise with the oil price. Spikes in the prices of 2008 saw a spike in conflict, just as the last previous record high price, in 1980, saw Saddam's invasion of Iran and the Soviet invasion of Afghanistan. These spikes were moments when monsters were uncaged.

I wanted to know if the high oil and gas prices in 2013 and 2014 had uncaged Putin, and how much more likely the bubbly oil prices—then around $100 a barrel—made an armed confrontation. "When the price of oil was at $100, they were 65 per cent more likely to start a dispute than if at $45, or 80 per cent more likely than if it was $23," Hendrix tells me. He takes me through the four locks that high prices open: the mechanisms that turn a single digital number into violent conflict.

CONFLICT
& OIL PRICES

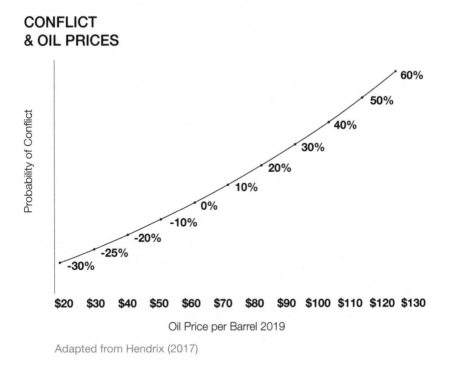

Adapted from Hendrix (2017)

The first and most immediate lock that high prices open is the *gas weapon*. "When prices are low and Russia needs all of those dollars, it's not nearly as credible a threat," Hendrix explains. "To say we're barely scraping by, we're running massive budget deficits, and we're going to cut off our nose to spite our face, and to stop exporting the energy to you—it's just not as powerful a lever when the prices are much lower." Putin's use of the gas weapon against Georgia and Ukraine in the 2000s was dependent upon the first commodity bubble inflating prices. It's the high prices that gave the considerable subsidies their value and provided the Kremlin coffers a cushion, should supplies be temporarily cut off. Its effectiveness is compounded by the nature of gas: it's very difficult to transport. Unlike oil, which can be moved around in barrels with ease, gas needs special facilities on the boats and at the ports. This makes it hard to get hold of substitute supplies. However, when prices are low, such as in the 1990s, the dynamic is reversed. Not only was Yeltsin desperate for every dollar his energy exports could bring into Russia's depleted coffers, but this desperation gave Ukraine and Belarus leverage. They siphoned off gas from the pipelines knowing that Yeltsin could not afford to retaliate.

In the winter of 2013, just months after Ukraine announced its timeline for energy independence and while oil and natural gas remained at historic highs, Putin deployed the gas weapon against Ukraine's President Yanukovych. He offered to cut Ukraine's gas bill by 33 per cent if Yanukovych cancelled trade talks with the EU. Yanukovych accepted the offer, but the pivot to Moscow sparked the pro-EU Maidan protests. Then, when Yanukovych lost control of Ukraine and fled, Putin's posture changed. He hiked the gas price by 80 per cent in April 2014, and then in June cut off the country's supply. At each turn, Putin pulled Kiev towards his will without firing a single shot.

The second lock is longer-term: the oil *windfall*. During the years of inflated oil and gas prices, Putin was able to rebuild Russia's economy and military. Oil revenues make up half of Russia's federal budget. In 2002, when oil was hovering around $35 a barrel, Russia earned $53 billion a year from oil exports. In 2014, the high oil prices had seen annual revenues rise nearly sixfold to $330 billion. Much of this windfall had come directly from Wall Street and the City of London. Yaneer Bar-Yam estimates that from 2002 to 2012 Russia received up to an additional $560 billion from financial speculators alone. And Russia, like other oil-exporting regimes, spends a far higher percentage of GDP on defence than oil-importing countries. It is another way in which the resource curse manifests, amplifying the chaotic effects of high commodity prices.

Yet, as I had seen among the pigeons in Donetsk, the costs of war extend far beyond arms and soldiers. A former member of Donetsk's puppet government told Reuters that Russia was funding the "budget sector and the pensions" as well as the army. "Without outside help, it's impossible to sustain the territory even if you have the most effective tax-raising system," the former official said. "The level of help from Russia exceeds the amounts that we collect within the territory." Wall Street has been, in effect, not just funding Putin's growing military, but funding a rogue state on the outskirts of Europe too.

The third lock is the *shield*. Not only do high prices provide a weapon and a windfall, they provide protection too. Commodity exporters are harder for the international community to punish. "Imagine Norway and Sweden have become rogue states," Hendrix explains. Maybe they've invaded Denmark. Or they're sponsoring terrorist bombings in Finland. The international community unites: they ban their exports. "It's much easier to punish Sweden than Norway, it's much easier to say no one can buy a Volvo than Norwegian crude oil." Sweden would have a hard time getting around an embargo. Even if its products ended up in Germany or France, they'd be hard to sell on the black market. Volvos, like IKEA furniture and H&M clothing, are easy to spot. They're branded products. But smuggled oil is very easy to sell. This is true for most commodities, whether it's gold and diamonds or cocaine and heroin. They are commodities precisely because they can be so easily standardised as near-identical products. Once they enter the international markets, they become impossible to trace.

That is, of course, in addition to the bigger problem: Europe needs Russia's natural gas exports. Indeed, the timing of the war, and Russia's willingness to risk exclusion from the international community, was driven by Putin's desire to maintain his leverage not just over Ukraine but over the EU as well. Their dependency on Russia's natural gas acted as a shield for all kinds of nefarious behaviour he might have planned. And it's not a coincidence that the two territorial claims he made—over Crimea and Donbas—were the two regions that had recently discovered deposits large enough to threaten Russia's energy dominance. Putin's annexation of Crimea brought with it two-thirds of Ukraine's claim to the Black Sea and the natural gas buried deep within it. Not only that, but it also offered a route for a new Black Sea "South Stream" pipeline from Russia to Europe that could bypass Ukraine altogether.

The EU's dependency on Russia's natural gas protected Putin from an outright embargo on his oil and gas exports. Instead, the rounds of sanctions targeted Putin's elite, their foreign holdings, and Russia's future oil exploration and production. Those amounted, to be sure, to a cost. However, Russia's oil production continued to grow and in 2016 reached an eleven-year high.

The fourth and final lock is psychological: *chestiness*. "They're more likely to initiate disputes because they're feeling more chesty, their economy is on steroids and they're feeling very confident about their prospects," Hendrix says. The rising prices bring increases in revenues, the power to wield the gas weapon, and the strength of the shield from international retaliation. As these grow, so too does confidence, and rising confidence breeds a bubble all of its own: hubris. It's a form of contagion: the bubbles jump from the market to the government to the mind. This psychological inflation is what turns opportunity into action.

Putin's price war in Ukraine was a different kind of price war than I'd seen in the Middle East. There, high food prices triggered unrest, riots and revolutions, and from that an entire Pandora's box of monsters was born. These monsters thrived in the disorder of failed states. But the price war in Ukraine is its mirror image. The monster here wasn't unleashed by the chaos of a collapsing state, but rather the enrichment of one. Price wars are found at the extremes: when states are too weak to fend for themselves or so strong they can take on their neighbours. Financial speculation had enabled both wars. In Russia, it had unlocked the monster Putin from his cage.

"We are going to meet some Russian volunteers," Dima announces. Bizarre. He had spent all of yesterday telling me over and over again that there were no Russian soldiers, no Russian equipment, no Russian tanks, no Russian money. But there were, it turns out, "battalions" of Russian volunteers working with the DPR army. He claims they aren't fighting, though, only handing out humanitarian aid to villages on the front line. And they weren't the only foreign volunteers here. They had volunteers from Brazil and Colombia as well.

"Why did they come?" I ask.

"Because they want to join the struggle against the Nazis," Dima says.

"Isn't it because they are hitmen? They have got into trouble and now they are on the run?"

"Well, yes, that as well."

I was curious why Dima is taking me to meet a Russian battalion when the DPR's entire "information warfare" campaign was based around denying Russian involvement. Incompetence? Or one of Surkov's games? I can't tell if this is just a piece of a far grander manipulation strategy designed to confuse and bewilder and distract. I hate to admit it, but it's working. A wave of paranoia crashes over me.

My taxi arrives at a forward operating base and we transfer into a small, beaten-up military jeep. We're now driving through the "grey zone." The boundary between the Ukrainians and the separatists isn't carved into the ground with trenches but with invisible lines that cut through fields and forests. A wrong turn, and we would be driving straight towards enemy snipers or even fortified military positions.

The jeep pulls up by a row of houses. Half are standing, half are bombed out. Amid the crossfire, people still live here. There's a meeting under way: ten pensioners are talking to a military commander. They fire off their demands. "We need a fridge and one light bulb," one states. "In winter we can survive without a fridge but not in summer." Their homes have been raided, possessions stolen and destroyed. They accuse the separatist army of being involved.

"I talked with my team, they say that never happened," the commander says. "Things get stolen, but not by us. If I at least catch one of them I will punish them to show everyone. Do not panic, everything will be fine."

"People are just scared. Some people were burnt alive," one pensioner replies.

The commander tries to reassure them. "The raid is not cool with me. I will be firing them if I find out that is true, or put them in prison. I am very tough in such situations. I have been here for five years. I came as a volunteer and I can honestly say that I haven't stolen anything from anyone in all these years."

I'm not supposed to be hearing this. This can't have been on

Surkov's script. The so-called separatist army sounded more like bandits than liberators. I get a tap on the shoulder. Alexey Smirnov, the head of the volunteer battalion "The Angels," is ready for his interview.

He claims he can speak English but tells Nadia that he "doesn't want to speak in the language of the enemy." He hands me a book about his group. I open it up and it's filled with pictures of himself in humanitarian poses: chopping wood, kneeling next to schoolchildren, that sort of thing. He's a good-looking guy. Nadia tells me that Donetsk is full of Russian men who come here to look macho and get girls. She shows me his Russian IMDB page; he's an actor with a few credits in short films. He doesn't mention any of this. He says he came from Russia to help people. His battalion of volunteers work side jobs and receive donations to buy supplies for those still living on the front lines.

I am impressed he's sticking to the volunteer script. In April 2014, proud Russian soldiers got fed up with their official cover story. They began telling the locals that they weren't volunteers. "We are special forces from the GRU" (an elite Russian military unit), they said. And, like them, I think Alexey wants to tell his own story. "People were almost ripping us apart," he says of one of their aid drops in 2015. "The kids were almost black from starvation. They had no water to drink. That's when animal instincts awaken, when people are ready to rip each other apart. They scrambled over our volunteers to get their hands on food and ate it all immediately."

I realise the irony here. This was a price war enabled by wealth—a glut of commodity money transferred from Wall Street to the Kremlin. It is a war of excess, of Putin's indulgences. But the reality on the ground was one of want, of absence. This point isn't lost on Alexey either.

"Meanwhile some people lead an upper-class life, some people starve and get shot at in war," he says. He laments how the artillery shells that destroyed houses cost thousands of dollars but today they only had $500 worth of aid for the people who continue to live in them. "It's strange how there is always not enough money for peace, but they always find money for the war."

A line is forming behind us. Alexey, and the other Angels, begin handing out plastic bags from a car boot. The residents put their aid packages on sledges, which they drag through the snow like a scene from a period drama set in Tsarist Russia. Dima holds a small video camera. "We're filming this for our Instagram," he tells me. He asks if he can interview me about the "humanitarian work" they are doing today. I realise that this is the Surkovian move I've been waiting for: I'm not here to bring their message to the West, but rather to be an actor for their message to the East. The war is never-ending, the Russian public needs to be kept invested. The Western audience lost interest long ago. I politely decline.

The taxi pulls up by the side of the road. It's the middle of nowhere and it's dusk. Through the dark-blue light I can make out the silhouette of a small hut and the edges of a few large trees. As I approach the hut, I duck under a wire holding up two frozen socks. I open the door. There's a light bulb hanging at the bottom of a stairway. A blond Labrador is taking a nap. There must be three flights of stairs.

At the bottom, there's a bank-vault door, several inches thick with a spoked, circular handle. It's been left ajar, but it's heavy. I struggle to cleave it open further.

It's a bunker and it's cold. Half a dozen beds fill the room. They are neatly made up with woollen blankets on top. Four bodies shuffle around. They look like upright beetles. They're hidden in a blob of layers: dark-brown shirts and sweaters and overcoats with frayed seams and missing buttons, topped with bobble hats. No one is talking. Two sit watching a news report on TV. Another slurps her soup.

The walls are covered with Soviet propaganda. There's a two-foot-high mural running right across the top of the room that depicts scenes of military greatness: submarines, missile launchers, bombs. An astronaut looks deep into outer space. A naval officer surveys the sea. It must be from the 1960s. On the few blank spaces left on the walls there are flashes of gold and red. The current inhabitants have put up little framed pictures of Orthodox icons and the Virgin Mary. There's a calendar filled with photographs of puppies wearing bow ties sitting under rainbows.

I ask one of the residents about a mural showing little grey men in gas masks carrying the injured on a battlefield. "It is instructions on how to use gas masks," she tells me. She looks like she's in her fifties. Her name is Olga.

When the war started, she was living with her mother in their flat in Donetsk. Her mother was seventy-five years old. "When we were in our flat and the shooting had started, she was very scared. She was coming out from the flat to the building entrance, she wanted to go somewhere. But where could you go then? The bullets were getting into doors . . . And then we decided to get into the bunker . . . But this is like a cellar . . . Two hundred people lived here. People slept on the floor, on mattresses, on benches. Now only twelve people live here. Everyone is used to the cold, we have an electric oven, so can have hot tea sometimes . . . Once a day we make something to eat. The atmosphere is hard in the bunker."

I remind myself why I am here. I have followed the butterfly's path from a bubble in the wheat markets to the chaos of the Arab Spring to a bubble in the oil markets and the chaos of Eastern Ukraine. Amid this chaos I am, once again, in a bubble. But this one is physical.

These concrete walls are the leftovers of the atomic age. They were defences for the atomic war that never came. The battle between communism and capitalism ended without a nuclear exchange. But the end of the Cold War ushered in a new kind of war, one fuelled by the chaotic engine of finance capitalism. These wars are invisible to most of us. They aren't fought with physical weapons, but ones and zeros. Travelling at the speed of light through thousands of miles of fibre-optic cables, they form the invisible labyrinth all around us. Explosions in the real world—a failed Russian harvest, the fight for Iraq's oil—become explosions in this digital realm. The electronic fallout once again took on the physical form of soldiers and tanks and munitions.

The resulting price war is far from the blinding flash of a nuclear bomb. It is the drip-drip of disorder. Olga's mother developed heart problems in the bunker. She was constantly in and out of hospitals. "She was eighty years old and said she wouldn't go anywhere else.

She died on Saturday. The funeral was today." They had left her dead body in the bunker for five days waiting for authorities to collect it. With her mother gone, maybe Olga can escape this place. "I really want to move back to the flat and live there."

For Olga and these bunker dwellers, there is no freedom in chaos. The victory of capitalism nearly three decades ago had made little difference to them. The free market's road from poverty to prosperity never came here. Instead they are trapped, staring up at communist propaganda once again. Meanwhile, the financial bubble that had entombed them in this one had burst. Just months into the war, the oil price collapsed. Another seismic wave shook the world. In another country, thousands of miles away, millions of people would soon live in a different kind of apocalyptic landscape. One not made from missiles or tanks or artillery shells, but from prices themselves.

Bust: Venezuela's Fractal Apocalypse

I walk off the plane and into Simón Bolívar International Airport feeling ridiculous. I have $10,000 in cash stuffed in my underpants. My embarrassment is a helpful distraction from why it is stashed there in the first place: fear. My fixer—let's call him Carlos—had warned me that carrying so much cash would be dangerous. People kill for a $100 bill in Venezuela, and I was carrying 100 of them. If the immigration officers discovered them, they'd tip off *malandros* waiting in the parking lot ready to ambush a clueless *gringo* like me. But there's no other way to get the cash into the country. I will get ten times more bolívars for these green bills on the black market than I'd get from a Venezuelan ATM machine.

I arrive at immigration. Two men in blue uniforms sit behind a desk. I hand one the customs form with "nothing to declare" ticked. He examines it. He reaches for a stamp. Clank. He gestures towards the metal detector. I step through. I tense up, expecting the inevitable beep. Nothing. I'm waved towards the exit.

Carlos finds me. He takes me out to the car and we set off on the highway. I let out a sigh of relief. I had survived the airport. Next is Caracas, a city that holds the dual distinction of being the world's capital for both kidnap and murder. And I'm not sure that this beaten-up former taxicab offers much protection from either. "Um, do you really think that this, erm, car is safe enough?" I ask Carlos from the back seat.

"Sometimes American news crews or businessmen from Mexico insist on armoured vehicles with armed guards," Carlos says. "That is just a giant bullseye. Last month, a gang pulled over an armoured truck. They waved grenades outside the window. They said they'd blow the car up unless this businessman from Mexico inside got out. So he opened the door. It was a bloodbath. His guards were killed on the spot." We can't fight the gangs, we can only hide from them. This old banger is the best disguise available. And my driver is a former policeman. His nickname is *Bachaco*, after the Leafcutter ant, because he's small and violent. He can spot the *malandros* coming a mile away.

"And besides, the best-case scenario is that we get caught by the kidnappers," he says. My relief evaporates. *Best case?* "We pay them and we can go free." What is worse, he explains, is when the kidnappers are not the gangsters but the police. When the police kidnap you, there's no one to call. But they too can be bought off, just for a higher price. Worse still is being caught by the National Guard reporting a story critical of the government. Just three months ago, a BBC crew had been deported for trying to interview an opposition leader. If I was found doing anything other than reporting on the government's triumphs, I would be put on a plane home and Carlos could face imprisonment and torture. And if I was caught by the intelligence services—the *Servicio Bolivariano de Inteligencia Nacional* (SEBIN)—who patrol the city in armoured cars, wearing black masks and brandishing machine guns, then the consequences would be worse. We'd all be tortured. But this wasn't the worst-case scenario either.

"Who is next?" I ask.

"The *colectivos*," Carlos says. "They are the unofficial private army of the government. They are the ones who drive motorcycles into protests. They beat up activists. They have killed opposition members and Venezuelan journalists. They act with impunity."

I stare out of the window, looking for a distraction from what I've just been told. I see a cityscape of concrete buildings with soaring green mountains behind them. On wall after wall, I spot the same mural again and again. It's of two large eyes. The colour and size vary, but the design is identical. "Whose eyes are they?" I ask Carlos.

"Chávez's eyes," he says. Hugo Chávez was Venezuela's larger-than-life president from 1999 until his death in 2013. "Chávez is looking down at us from heaven, looking after the Fatherland." His chosen successor, Nicolás Maduro, used the design for his election campaign and it has been a staple of state propaganda ever since. To me they look like a Big Brother pastiche, as if George Orwell's *1984* was not a warning but a how-to. I realise that the danger I face here is less from the gangs of a Central American–style narco-state and more those of a Stalinist cult-of-personality police state. The eyes are a warning to me and all others who might question the unquestionable eternal Leader and those that rule in His name.

We arrive at the restaurant near my hotel. I struggle to assess each of these threats and how I should proceed. I decide to let it go for now. I'm jet-lagged and hungry and just glad to have a proper meal and a beer. I can think about my impending kidnap and torture tomorrow.

The food arrives. Grilled chicken and vegetables, fried plantains and a sliced pineapple-sized avocado. I take a sip of my beer. I look around. Diners are eating. The waiters are chit-chatting. I'm struck by just how normal it seems. Venezuela has filled The Feed for years with images of months-long riots, bloodied protestors, police shooting bullets into clouds of tear gas and processions of coffins carrying dead dissenters. Venezuela seemed like a logical step on the butterfly's path. I had come to see if this crisis-stricken petro-state was a victim of the resource curse and the commodity markets. Now that I'm here, I wonder if the answer was no. Perhaps the protests were just a natural response to a repressive regime. This calm little restaurant seems a world away from the horrors of The Feed.

Then the bill arrives. I take a look at the piece of paper. It doesn't make sense. The numbers run into seven and eight digits. Some are broken up with dashes like a secret code. I hand it to Carlos. "What does this mean?" I ask.

"This number," he says, pointing to one row of digits, "is the international bank account for the restaurant, and this one," pointing to another, "is the international bank account of the waiter for the tip. And this number here is how much the meal cost."

I take the paper back from him. I squint to make sense of it. The meal cost 45 million bolívars.

I see a street vendor selling lemonade from a white wooden cart. He takes out a piece of paper and writes a price on it. The number is six digits long. He cuts it out and walks over to the front of his cart. There I see a wooden board, thick like papier-mâché, where one price has been stuck on top of another and then another. He places this new price over the old price. He says that he does this throughout the day. This is what hyperinflation looks like.

I see such strange scenes everywhere. On the next street over, a teenage boy is playing with what looks like a skipping rope. I get closer. It's actually a belt made out of old bolívars woven into a geometrical pattern through symmetrical folds. A few years ago, these bills could have bought a car. In history books at school, I remembered seeing cartoons of Weimar Germans burning bank notes because they were cheaper than firewood. Now I was witnessing this historical curiosity in front of me.

The consequences of inflation soaring at 1,000,000 per cent a year are everywhere. On street after street I see the Spanish word for hunger—*hambre*—graffitied in large capitals. Scattered down the sidewalks, piles of open garbage rot in the midday sun. Passers-by bend down and rummage through the remains. I see one man take out a chicken bone and pick off the scraps as he walks away. Storefront windows display empty spaces. Long lines stretching far down the street point to the few that are open and trading. Above one line I spot a relic from the country's prosperous past. There's a billboard featuring John Travolta sitting on a film director's chair next to a fighter jet. He's wearing a luxury Breitling watch. "Welcome to My World," he says.

"I have seen my friends' kids go to bed without eating anything. Just because they do not find food," Maria, a twenty-two-year-old mother of two, tells me. She sits on a single bed in her two-room home in the *barrios*, one of the many slums scattered across the city's mountain tops. She says everyone here is struggling to feed themselves and their children. "The [monthly] minimum wage is not even enough to buy a kilo of cheese." Inflation has reduced the value of the minimum wage to the equivalent of one or two US dollars for *a month's work*. "I cannot get a job with the minimum wage because it's not enough to feed my children or to pay a kindergarten while I am working," she says. "I have relatives in Cumaná who send me goods, such as citrus, coconuts, things that I can resell here. That is how I support myself."

Her life wasn't always like this. "Four or five years ago, you could buy your food, you could go out with your kids, you could buy a present for them, you could take them to the park," she says. That was 2014. The year that the oil bubble inflated by the Arab Spring burst. Ever since then, life here has been almost indistinguishable from a war zone. "My neighbour got pregnant a year ago. She did not have good nutrition, but she stayed pregnant for nine months. Her child died before the birth," she says. "At this moment, if you tell me that I am pregnant I really would not know what to do because the situation is hard . . . I mean, if the minimum wage is not enough to buy food, it's useless for buying contraceptives. All of that has disappeared. The most effective is the IUD but it is really expensive, and also difficult to find . . . That is the reason why I have decided to get sterilised."

She says this as if sterilisation is an ordinary thing. And as we talk, I discover that for her it is. The government refuses to release the numbers, but among Maria and her peers it's becoming the new normal.

Maria takes me to visit her friend Alicia. She's already had the operation. "Well, I decided to do it because of the bad economic situation with diapers, clothes and that stuff," she says. "I already have three children and the current situation is really hard, we cannot find the basic products. It is always a mess: the queues, the searching for products. I said to myself, 'I have to get sterilised because it is really hard.'" Does she regret her decision? "I don't have that trauma I had before: 'Oh my God, am I going to get pregnant again?' I can't handle it!"

Maria chimes in. "Of course! We are always concerned about it. So it is better to sterilise."

"Are you nervous?" Alicia asks her.

"Well, I'm quite nervous because I don't know how it will be. I was unconscious when I got the caesarean section, so I don't know anything about it. But . . . does it hurt?"

"Yes, it hurts a little bit."

"That's my fear."

"It was great. 2014 was a great year. That was a great trade," Jerry Parker recalls. Parker's mathematical model had detected repeated dips in the oil price over the summer of 2014. A downward trend was coming. When ISIS launched their ill-fated attack on Kurdistan, reports swirled that oil could be going up by $50 a barrel if ISIS was to take Iraq. But when that didn't happen, sentiment turned in the opposite direction. Stories of scarcity were replaced with stories of abundance.

American shale oil was flooding the market. The Saudis were increasing production to push down the oil price to fight back against both American shale—which needed a high price to maintain profitability—and the Russians, who were supporting their arch-nemesis Assad. Libya's civil war had cooled, and ISIS was on the defensive in Syria and Iraq. There were also stories that China's building boom was ending, and worldwide demand was slumping. Speculators began shorting oil, betting against the price by taking the "short" side of the futures contract and pushing it down in the process. Parker was one of them. He shorted oil, but the price bounced back. He shorted again and again and again, only to see the oil price shoot back up each time. "And then on the fifth time it finally goes," he says, "so then we just have to hold on."

The oil price plunged. It dropped from a high of $112 a barrel in June to $47 a barrel in December. Just as the price earlier in the year had been artificially high—pricing in oil disruptions to Middle Eastern production that never came, and most likely would never come—now it was artificially low. Whatever the "fundamental" drivers—shale, China, Saudi—the reaction was violent. Speculators had turned a modest decline into an extreme one by aggressively shorting the market, creating a "negative financial bubble," as one economist put it.

The major oil producers such as Venezuela took a massive hit immediately. Oil is the lifeblood of their entire economy. Smaller oil producers were impacted too. African nations—Zambia, Angola, Nigeria—had borrowed against their oil reserves to pay China to build infrastructure; when the prices fell so too did their currencies, leaving them not just out of pocket but spending extortionate amounts of money servicing debt. The investments the artificially high prices had encouraged were now worthless. Fracking companies went bankrupt. Harvard's commodity investment lost the endowment $1 billion. It was not just high prices that could cause chaos—as I had seen with Ukraine, Brexit, Trump, Yemen, Brazil, and Belt and Road—low prices could trigger their own waves of destruction too. Of course, some benefited. "I don't really remember how much I made on that trade," Parker says. "I do remember that we made 20 per cent that year. My guess is maybe a lot of that was the crude—half to a third."

Through the tinted windows of my taxicab, I stare up at the concrete jungle that is downtown Caracas. After a short while, I notice something. Many of the buildings haven't been finished. Their concrete skeletons remain exposed. There are some cranes nearby, but they don't seem to be doing anything. I recognise one of the unfinished structures as the notorious forty-five-storey Tower of David, a lawless city unto itself filled with drug dealers and ruled by gangs. I had heard that it was first built when the oil price rose after Saddam invaded Kuwait in 1990, only to cease construction when the war ended and the oil price collapsed. I realise that the abstract digits of the oil price are realised here in steel and concrete.

In fact, the cityscape is a bar chart of oil prices, each tower a price spike and its decay a price decline. The prices are etched in concrete: you can read the last fifty years of oil prices just by looking at these buildings. The zombie constructions stand as cautionary monuments to the speculative boom and bust that followed the Arab Spring. But while that bust had hurt oil exporters everywhere, for some reason it appeared that Venezuela was hit harder than the others. Over my time here, I would discover that the oil labyrinth that Venezuela is built on is—and has always been—unique among petro-states. I would trace the maze's architecture from the bottom, through the lives of the ordinary people who inhabit it.

"When I tell people that I work playing video games they say, 'Oh wow, that's so cool, that's everyone's golden dream,'" Octavio says, sitting on his bed as red and blue reflections of *World of Warcraft* glimmer in his glasses. The sound effects blend with the gunshots I hear coming from outside his bedroom window. Before the oil-price collapse in 2014, he had wondered what life would be like if he could play his favourite video games all day. He now finds himself in that strange reality. "Be careful what you dream of because it might come true," he says.

When the economy first collapsed and inflation reduced his wages to nothing, he didn't know what to do. A month's salary wasn't even enough to pay one day's bus fare to work. He could only think of ways to slow down his starvation. "If I don't stand up, I won't need so much food," Octavio reasoned. "I ate once a week, it was just like a hunger strike. I would stay on my bed all day long drinking water and only got up to go to the toilet and once a week I got up to prepare the food."

He gets up and reaches inside his closet. He holds up two T-shirts that resemble blankets more than clothing. "If I put them on it looks like I'm wearing a parachute or a coat," he says. He shows me a photograph of his former self. The enormous figure looks like a different person. The man in front of me is slender with a narrow face. Although he's forty years old, he says he now wears clothes he bought as a teenager. "Now I have like a rubber skin around me," he says. "I miss the time when I was fat, when I looked ugly from the fat and not from malnutrition."

At first, Octavio's route out of the chaos was to sell parts of his computer. He then realised that the machine was a gateway out of Venezuela, and, most importantly, to US dollars. He didn't have many skills that he could sell online, but he had been a long-time player of *World of Warcraft* and he knew he could become a "farmer." He could take over other people's accounts and do the boring parts of the game for them, like earning their avatar points to buy new weapons and power. At the time, it was Chinese teenagers who offered these "farming" services to other gamers. Now it's Venezuelans. "I consider myself privileged because I have access to a salary that only lawyers, engineers, doctors and professionals with long careers have," he says. "I earn from $30 to $50 per month . . . I keep alive because of it. Thanks to that money, I've been able to buy food."

Even with his "professional salary," his existence has morphed into a mirror image of the video game he is playing. The moment he converts his precious US dollars into Venezuelan bolívars it's a race against time. "I need to go out urgently to spend that cash, because every minute I have these bolívars in my hands, the less they're worth." He runs straight to the supermarket to buy rice, canned tuna and spam—he has no refrigerator—but often they're out of stock. By the time he finds a supermarket that has them, he may not be able to afford them. The prices can double in a single afternoon. Octavio is trapped in a maze of prices. He's forced to navigate an Escher-like labyrinth that moves at the speed of hyperinflation. He climbs a staircase only for it to flip upside down. He dashes for an exit, only to see a new wall slide in front of him. The price of the bolívar, the dollar, of spam, tuna, rice and the wages of Chinese "farmers" thousands of miles away are the levers and pulleys. Trapped inside, he must navigate a series of Kafkaesque challenges that escalate at each turn with higher levels of surrealism and debasement.

I begin to see this life-bending labyrinth all around Caracas. I spot a hundred people lining up to buy cartons of eggs. They hold enormous wads of cash several inches thick, then hand them to a lady who quickly flips through the notes at lightning speed. After a few minutes she's counted them, and her co-worker hands over a few dozen eggs in cartons held together with red string. But this is, I find out, not what it seems. They are not in the business of selling eggs but acquiring the paper cash. Hyperinflation has pushed everyone to use electronic banking, usually in dollars or Colombian pesos, but paper cash is still needed for a few services like bus fares and road tolls. So when people with cash at home want to get rid of it, they need something to trade for it. In this case they'll accept eggs, and the people taking the cash are going to sell it on for a higher price than its printed value.

I go into a supermarket. I understand why people aren't buying their eggs here. There aren't any. Instead I see rows of empty shelves. Occasionally there is a full aisle, but it is filled with just one product. I find one aisle just filled with hundreds of bottles of mayonnaise. Another aisle is row after row of ketchup. The next is one brand of bottled water. It's like an Andy Warhol lithograph, the sublime pattern of consumer products repeated in all directions.

I pull out my smartphone to capture this strange sight in front of me. Carlos says it's not allowed. It's not just against the supermarket rules, it's against the law. The government said that the empty shelves were a conspiracy of the supermarket owners against the *chavista* government. So they ordered the supermarkets to fill the shelves. The supermarkets responded by filling the aisles with the non-perishable goods that they had in storage. When this looked ridiculous, the government simply banned any photography of it. But there was no way I was going to leave without a shot of this. I subtly place my smartphone in the palm of my hand and point it at the shelves. I manage to film the three aisles before a woman approaches me. Busted.

Neither street vendors nor the supermarkets seem to be where people actually buy the things they need. They're just dead ends in the market maze, zombie monuments to a functional past. I ask Carlos where he gets his food. He takes me back up the winding roads into the mountains and into the *barrios* to a house made of concrete breeze blocks on the side of the hill. There's a small shrine inside with the Virgin Mary and a line running across the ceiling with clothes hanging from it. The house belongs to Ellenor, a thirty-four-year-old mother of two.

"I worked at family houses, cleaning," Ellenor says, "but I realised that reselling would give me more money. Of course I keep my other job, but I also help myself with this one." The chaos in the markets has proved to be an opportunity for her. "Customers come to my house to buy the food, because they do not want to queue or face a massacre in the supermarket." She explains that the supermarkets have a limited amount of government-subsidised food sold at a fixed "fair price." Most people do not want to queue up or have to hop from supermarket to supermarket looking for goods. So she gets in line at 2 a.m. for the government-subsidised food. Then she doubles the price for her clients, who come to her house for the convenience.

"I have decided not to sell anything before elections because we have heard so many rumours: a strike against the government, the prices will get higher, there will be no food. The few goods I have got, I want either to save for me or to sell at a more expensive price later. People are saying that prices will rise soon because of national strikes. We are just holding on to see what will happen." This is a classic speculative strategy: there's a story of higher prices, so people withhold goods and restrict supply, causing the prices to rise, fuelling a self-fulfilling prophecy. She has no formal education but she had instinctively adopted the strategy of highly trained financial speculators. It shows that the market logic is readily available to all and that, with the exclusionary jargon stripped away, speculation is very simple. "Yes, scarcity gets harder, then one starts to gather, to monopolise food, goods," Ellenor says. "And then people start purchasing excessively or by impulse."

I wondered if, in the right circumstances, we would all become speculators: gouging prices from others given the opportunity. That is certainly the libertarian view, the view of *Homo economicus* that dominates economics. Are we all just secret hedge-fund managers waiting for the opportunity to strike it rich by pushing up the price for others? Would she scale up her operation if she could? "If I had more money," she says, her voice shaking a little, "from the bottom of my heart—I would not do it. It is really sad to resell food to your family, a friend, something which is a basic need. But I do it because it gives me more money and I think of my family first. I do not know. Maybe, I would think about another business in which I did not need to resell food to anyone. I would not mess with food or medicine. I mean, I would figure out a way to do something different."

The chaos in Caracas was different than the chaos I had seen in Iraq and Ukraine. Those conflicts had been triggered and enabled by prices, but the chaos that rained down on those caught in the crossfire was of armed struggle: suicide bombers, snipers, artillery shells. In Venezuela, chaos hadn't just been triggered by prices: it brought chaos to people's lives through prices themselves.

It reminded me of a paper I had come across when I originally looked into the mathematical models of chaos, a paper that said the coastline of Britain was perhaps infinite in length. This is because coasts are *fractal*. A snowflake, the green buds on cactus or broccoli, or the branches of a lightning bolt are fractal. You see something with jagged edges, zoom in and see more jagged edges, zoom in further, and you just see more jagged edges, and no matter how far you zoom in, the lines never smooth, there is always a broken surface. Each of these "zoom-ins" is just a different scale, and at each scale the jagged pattern of the coastline repeats itself like a leaf. It is never resolved; it never reaches a smooth plane. It is "self-similar." There is always more coastal edge to measure. The length becomes infinite.

The chaos in Venezuela appeared to me just as fractal. The logic of prices and speculation repeated itself at every scale: from the financial speculators moving hundreds of billions around the international oil markets, to the black-market resellers, video gamers and lemonade vendors speculating on currencies, crises and commodities to eke out a few dollars. These descents into the fractal void reveal the madness of the principle: the irrationality we recognise at the smallest scales is the very same irrationality operating at larger ones. The irony is that it is Venezuela, an allegedly socialist state, that has its people living as pure market beings.

It is precisely Venezuela's two-decade socialist experiment that most pundits point to as the cause of the nation's outsized woes. Sure, low oil prices do not help, they argue, but some kind of reckoning was inevitable in a state governed by outdated central planning, tinpot authoritarianism and naked corruption. But is Venezuela really more corrupt, authoritarian and centrally planned than the other cursed petro-states such as Russia or Saudi Arabia? It's certainly possible. Even if Venezuela is the worst among its peers, however, it would not be by much. Certainly not enough to explain the gap between the SUV-driving Saudis and the self-sterilising Venezuelans.

I came across a study that showed how the resource curse could inflict economic pain independently of the political drivers of corruption, authoritarianism and militarism. There was a lethal economic logic to it that could operate within even the most benign of governments. All it would take was a boom in commodity prices. "A basic idea of the resource curse is that the boom period makes the currency so strong that any other internationally traded sector of the economy—including foodstuffs, fertiliser or other manufactured goods—cannot profitably be produced in the domestic market," Jeffrey Sachs, a Professor at Columbia University and one of the study's authors, tells me. "The currency is so strong that the ability to import whatever you need, whether it's fertiliser or other inputs for industry, becomes the dominant form of international trade. Export oil, import just about everything else that's tradable, and use your wealth for the domestic economy alone. Maybe there's a construction boom, a housing boom, a boom in the service sector. But when it comes to manufactured goods, food production and food processing, that can all be imported. When the boom ends you don't have a tradable goods sector in agriculture, food-processing or fertiliser because it wasn't profitable to keep those sectors alive, much less upgrade them and keep them up with modern investment and modern technology. And so you lose twice."

This phenomenon of a highly valued currency destroying local industries had originally been observed in Holland in the 1960s shortly after it became a major exporter of natural gas. It's where the phenomenon gets its name: Dutch disease. This disease, Sachs tells me, lay at the core of Venezuela's crisis. Oil revenues had kept the bolívar high and imports flowing into the country. Agriculture had atrophied and manufacturing declined: they couldn't compete with cheap imports from abroad. When the oil price collapsed in 2014, the value of the bolívar fell too, and the price of imports rose, causing inflation. The farms were in disrepair and they couldn't afford to import the machinery and fertilisers to get them running again. They "lost twice." The price of food spiked and riots broke out.

I press Sachs on Chávez and Maduro. Aren't they to blame as well? To my surprise, Sachs seems reluctant to see anything unique about Venezuela's current regime. "Venezuela has gone through lots of booms and busts. It has been basically an oil economy for half a century and through many different kinds of governments. It went through excess spending in the good times and financial collapse in the bad times."

Sachs is not known to be a natural defender of leftist populists. In fact, he's long been cast as one of their most effective adversaries who, as the IMF's star economist, transitioned Russia and Poland from communism to capitalism in the 1990s. Nobody could accuse Jeffrey Sachs of being a *chavista* or a Maduro apologist. Rather, he sees them as little different from the governments that came before them. For fifty years in Venezuela, each government mismanaged the cycle of commodity boom and bust. "Right now, we're seeing the worst of these cycles," he says, "the most extreme, but not the only one."

The last cycle started with the 1973 Arab–Israeli War. After the US sent support to Israel, the Arab-led OPEC states doubled—and then quadrupled—the oil price. As petrodollars flooded Venezuela, the bolívar soared. Famous chefs from around the world flocked to Caracas to set up restaurants, Concorde began flying direct to Paris, and Venezuela became one of the largest importers of champagne. As cheap imported goods flooded the economy, domestic agriculture and manufacturing couldn't compete. Farms and factories closed, wages fell. The government filled the gap by expanding the public-sector workforce with boondoggle jobs. When the oil price cratered in the early 1980s, the government responded to the lost revenues by taking out bigger and bigger loans from banks on Wall Street and in the City of London, just as the Soviet Union did. By 1989, interest payments equalled the country's oil revenue. The music stopped. Three years of crisis ensued: inflation, shortages, rioting, IMF interventions and austerity. The military was called in to crush the protestors rocking the capital: 350 were killed and 2,000 injured. It was the same old story of boom and bust, inflation and chaos.

One man who witnessed it all was a young paratrooper named Hugo Chávez. During the attack on the protestors he had been in bed with chickenpox. But he, and many others in the military ranks, deeply resented being asked to unleash violence against starving people, many of whom were their neighbours, brothers and sisters. The military attempted two coups in 1992, with Chávez leading one of them. They both failed and Chávez was imprisoned for five years. Shortly after his release he ran for president. It was 1998. He railed against decades of corruption and mismanagement that sent the country lurching from one crisis to another, leaving the overwhelming majority of Venezuelans impoverished while a tiny elite feasted on the oil wealth. The voters agreed.

"I met him very early in his presidency," Sachs recalls, "and made a couple of points: 'Please, Mr. President, don't let your currency get wildly overvalued because that would stop the development of other sectors.' . . . I think it's fair to say he did almost exactly the opposite of what I had suggested twenty years ago." The exact same cycle of boom and bust, inflation and chaos of the 1970s and 1980s repeated itself in the 2000s and 2010s.

The strange thing is that Chávez didn't need Sachs to give him this warning. He had come of age in the chaos. It was what he had pledged to end in his campaign. In his inaugural address he promised a future for Venezuela without oil. He warned of the dangers of black gold, of how it bred the "terrible cancer" of corruption and mismanagement, of how it had sparked a series of "disturbances" that had snowballed over the 1980s into a national "catastrophe" that they were still suffering from. He promised to take the country on a different path, "to get out of this horrible labyrinth in which we all find ourselves." Even if oil rose above the $8 it was trading for in 1999, he would resist temptation. "If the oil arrives again—hopefully not!—at $40 a barrel, we don't want it, we don't want it to reach $40 a barrel, but even if it did come and even if it rained petrodollars and a lot of money, it would be a momentary relief, but we would sink a little further into an ethical and moral swamp." So what went wrong? Why did Chávez court the very catastrophe he himself had warned against?

"He set a good tone for a very ambitious agenda," Clinton's Energy Secretary, Bill Richardson, said of Chávez's inaugural address. "It's a good start in the American–Venezuelan relationship." In particular, Clintonworld was impressed by his pledge to pay the country's foreign debts, cut domestic spending and raise taxes in order to balance the budget. Like Clinton, Chávez was advocating a Third Way in politics. "We are looking for a middle position," he said, "between the invisible hand of the market and the visible hand of the state." Chávez visited the US, met with Bill Clinton and rang the bell at the New York Stock Exchange. He wore sharp grey suits with dark-blue ties. He cosied up to Venezuela's business leaders, appointed conservatives to his Cabinet, and published plans to privatise the state telecommunications company. The Venezuelan left felt betrayed. "You haven't touched a single hair on the ass of anyone in the economic sector!" Chávez's political mentor, Luis Miquilena, told him, deriding his "fake revolutionary" agenda. "You have created the most neoliberal economy Venezuela has ever known."

Chávez's cosy relationship with the White House didn't last long. In 2001, George Bush installed Cold War veterans in Washington's foreign-policy apparatus. Many had cut their teeth organising the overthrow of leftist governments in South America by funding rogue military generals and death squads. The same officials who were drawing up plans to bring "freedom" and "democracy" to another petro-state, Iraq, began openly discussing overthrowing the democratically elected leader of their top oil supplier. "Washington might green-light a coup against Chávez," Jon Anderson reported in *The New Yorker* in 2001, betraying how casually his sources in Washington weighed Chávez's overthrow. "But that sort of rhetoric has died down . . . Despite all his inflammatory language, Chávez has not actually done much to alter Venezuela's economy."

But the "moral cancer" that Chávez was elected to stamp out lay at the heart of the country's economy: the state oil company,

Petróleos de Venezuela, S.A. (PDVSA). He derided it as a law unto itself, run by a foreign-educated elite who held the purse strings, deciding how much money the Venezuelan people would get from the oil extracted from their own lands. Chávez wanted it to be accountable to Venezuela's elected government. "You, sir, are dismissed!" he said on live TV after reading out the name of a PDVSA board member, and then blew a whistle like a football referee. He read out another name and another, blowing the whistle each time he announced their dismissal. Neither Venezuela's business elite nor their friends in Washington would tolerate any interference with the country's golden goose. Discussion had long been taking place between them on how to remove this "monkey in the palace." Messing with PDVSA crossed the line. A week later a *coup d'état* was launched. Chávez was ousted. But two days later he was back in office: he cut a deal whereby the old PDVSA directors would return. The Venezuelan opposition behind the coup remained dissatisfied. They started strikes, shutting down banks, schools, restaurants and the oil industry, plunging the economy into chaos, sparking shortages, hoarding and inflation. Chávez scrambled to restore order. He fixed the exchange rate and food prices. The strikes ended, but the opposition struck back with a referendum campaign to remove him from office. The vote was scheduled for 15 August 2004. He was behind in the polls. Failure seemed inevitable.

Chávez was handed an incredible stroke of luck. Thanks to the financial capital flowing into commodity index funds, oil prices were steadily rising for the first time in two decades. Chávez finally had some petrodollars to spend and, facing a fight for his presidency, dismissed the warnings he gave in his inaugural address about the cascading crisis that oil wealth inevitably brings. He instead did exactly what his predecessors had done: he used the windfall to lavish gifts on voters. He struck a deal with Fidel Castro: Cuba got 95,000 barrels of Venezuelan oil in exchange for 20,000 doctors and nurses. They would provide free health care in what would be known as *misiones*: social programmes to provide food, education and housing.

The gambit worked: he won the election. He ditched the suit and ties for a revolutionary pastiche costume of a red beret and combat jacket. He finally took decisive control of PDVSA and seized businesses and farms in a tsunami of "expropriations." By gifting Chávez the political crisis and the financial windfall, together the Bush administration and Wall Street fuelled his transformation from the business-friendly, US-supporting, Third Way liberal he was at the start of his presidency to the very leftist populist they feared him to be. Chávez now called himself a "socialist" for the first time.

Chávez's charisma, his theatrics, his televised pageants conjured the image of a "socialist revolutionary" embraced by his supporters and critics alike. But studies into his social programmes—the *misiones*—tell a different story. The aid didn't go to the poorest Venezuelans, but to loyalists and swing voters in middle-class neighbourhoods. Chávez was not deploying his country's vast oil wealth to further an ideology. He was, instead, using the money to cement his grip on power. It's a strategy known as "clientelism" and it's practised by most petro-states, from "nationalist" Russia to "theocratic" Saudi Arabia and Iran. Peel back the showy ideological rhetoric, and each of these regimes governs in much the same way. The state and civil society are integrated into the oil economy through a bloated public sector that hands out useless jobs as patronage. These jobs do not just reward loyalty but enforce it: workers are surveilled by the managers, who look out for any signs of dissent. Should entrepreneurs succeed in building a business independently, they will suddenly find it "nationalised" for any number of spurious reasons. In Russia, Putin and his cronies raid (*reiderstvo*) companies and effectively steal them by "discovering" violations of business regulations or fraudulent activities. In the Gulf countries, these reallocations are often done in the name of corruption crackdowns, such as when Mohammed bin Salman got the Saudi elite to hand over $100 billion by imprisoning them in the Ritz-Carlton hotel. Such re-appropriations are no more socialist than Chávez's televised outbursts of marching up to buildings and commanding: "Expropriate it!" The justification differs, but the logic is the same: keep the economy under their personal control.

Clientelism is expensive. When Chávez was first elected, oil was trading at $8 a barrel: it was easy to reject a strategy that he couldn't deploy. But once the commodity markets were deregulated, and money flowed from American pension funds into commodity index derivatives, clientelism was viable. The Wall Street windfall released Chávez from his cage and, with ample prodding from the Bush administration, grew him into an authoritarian monster: he co-opted the military, expanded the security apparatus and launched paramilitaries, imprisoned opposition leaders, replaced judges with loyalists, clamped down on free expression and sanctioned those who voted against him. This was the Big Brother Chávez whose eyes adorn the cityscape. Chávez was not, however, just a passive recipient of financial capital circulating in the commodities markets. When he ran for re-election in 2012, he borrowed heavily from Western banks against future oil revenues in order to lavish key constituencies with giveaways. Chávez had used the very "neoliberal" forces that he railed against to secure his grip on power. But this source of strength was fragile: it was built on an ocean of debt. And these debts were not denominated in the Venezuelan bolívar but in American dollars.

When the oil price collapsed in 2014, the economic crisis was no different from those that had come before it: a severe recession, soaring food prices, riots and unrest. The oil revenues had evaporated, and Venezuela struggled to service the debt. Chávez's successor, Nicolás Maduro, tried to renegotiate with the banks, but was blocked by the domestic opposition which controlled the legislature. Then, in 2017, Trump escalated the US's long-standing conflict with the *chavista* government by imposing sanctions blocking Venezuela's access to US dollars. This is what Jeffrey Sachs and his colleague Mark Weisbrot believe turned Venezuela's recession into an apocalyptic catastrophe. Confidence in the bolívar collapsed completely. Inflation rose from 1,000 per cent to 1,000,000 per cent. Foreign imports became impossibly expensive. Not only was food now unaffordable, but so too were the machines and spare parts needed to keep the oil flowing. Oil production cratered, causing revenues to plummet further. Hunger became endemic: in 2017 the average Venezuelan lost twenty-four pounds. Sachs and Weisbrot estimate that the sanctions inflicted 40,000 deaths that year. The Venezuelan

VENEZUELAN & COLOMBIAN OIL PRODUCTION

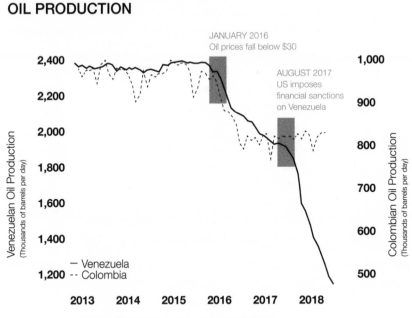

Adapted from Weisbrot and Sachs (2019)

apocalypse was made in the markets: the *chavista* regime was built on a wave of black gold and then suffocated by a shortage of dollars.

It's pouring rain and I'm huddled under somebody's porch. I crouch on the ground with four kids. They're between eight and sixteen years old. None of them have shoes. They swap rude jokes, laugh and take turns rolling a cigarette. Every once in a while one stands up, takes off his T-shirt, runs over to the gutter and washes it in the gushing rainwater.

One of them, a thirteen-year-old named José Angel, starts chatting with me. He's short for his age, but his confidence and cheeky grin lend him a certain charisma in the gang. He tells me about the last time he saw his mother. She dropped him and his brother off at some kind of group home. She told him she'd return later with some food. Only she never did. He says he was beaten at the group home, that the adults barely fed the children, and that one of the other kids stabbed his brother in the stomach. They both escaped. He joined a gang of two dozen young boys like him who hang out during the day by the Chacao subway station and spend their nights sleeping on cardboard boxes under the highway. Their patch is right next to the Guaire River that runs through the city. "When the river floods," he says, "some drown because they sleep on their stomachs." This isn't what they fear, though. Just three days ago, a rival gang of street kids came into their territory brandishing knives and other improvised weapons. He saw them coming and ran away, but one of his friends was caught. When Angel returned the following day, he found him next to the highway. "They had taken apart his head, he was burnt, eyeless, his nose cut, his arms were scattered everywhere in the grass."

What is worth murder, decapitation, immolation? "They want our garbage," Angel says. "If we allow them to take our garbage we don't eat." Every evening they sift through the trash that is thrown out by restaurants, looking for edible scraps. Without access to the dumpsters outside these restaurants they starve. Gangs guard and fight over these dumpsters like other gangs would fight over territory to sell drugs.

The rain subsides. The kids run out from the porch into a small public square between two roads. Led by the eldest, Ignacio, they begin their "training." Using flip-flops as stand-ins for knives, they pair off and mock-fight each other. They dance around, dodging and weaving, trying to strike a blow on the other. The eldest of them acts as a kind of coach, giving them words of encouragement as well as fear. "Respect the iron!" he commands. The training is fun. Angel is enjoying himself. He manages to land a blow on his opponent. "You're such a little backstabber, Angel," Ignacio says.

We meet up again that evening. They've invited me to go "recycling" with them. They take me to a shopping mall. I walk down the ramp to the underground car park, past the cars and through a corridor behind a fast-food restaurant to the mall's back lot outside.

Two teenagers in clean clothes are already there. They live at home, but their kitchens are empty. They have an agreement with the street kids: they get the first round of garbage delivered each evening. They are just finishing up. I sit with the kids as they wait for the next delivery. They play the same game as always, taking turns throwing a bottle into the air and trying to get it to land on its narrow top.

After fifteen minutes, an elderly worker arrives pushing a cart of garbage filled with black bursting bags. They greet each other like they know each other. As soon as the worker goes, they pull the bags apart. The smell is rancid. I retch a little. The kids start ploughing through the leftover food, sorting it out. They discard the cardboard, plastic wrappings and scraps of lettuce soaked in mayonnaise. There seems to be a hierarchy at work. The young kid hands bones with slivers of meat to the older kid, who finishes them off. The young one doesn't seem to eat much. He just takes a small pot of a leftover condiment and rubs his finger around the inside.

After half an hour, Carlos tells me time is up and we need to go. I am relieved. I am nauseated. Not from the smell any more, I have got used to that, but from the realisation that this is not just how these kids eat but what they fight for. To get access to this—the garbage of a fast-food restaurant—is why their friend was decapitated, his eyes removed, body burnt and limbs severed and scattered in the grass by the highway. And that none of this is an accident, a freak act of cruelty.

It is the order in disorder. It's a microcosm of the commodity markets, of how violence and wealth, poverty and survival combine to make the resource curse. Garbage is the commodity and these restaurant dumpsters are the source; like oil wells, they are physically fixed in the ground, delivering a steady supply over time. As a result it's a source of wealth and power, a resource to compete over, to be fought for, to be monopolised. None of these kids, many of whom are eight and nine years old, have any interest in monopolising anything. They are just trying to survive, to get enough scraps of food to stave off hunger. And yet they are pulled into this violent game, a set of rules they're forced to abide by. They are trapped in a maze from which they cannot escape.

These rules scale. They are fractal: "self-similar" at every level. Here is the bottom: the commodity that to most but the starving has no value, the refuse of restaurants, the literal scraps from the city's table. Zoom out a level higher and it is the familiar world of gang territories: competition for street corners to sell drugs, run brothels or protection rackets, as well as zones for kidnapping and extortion. Zoom out further and it's the biggest racket of all, the nation's oil, the monopoly of which continues to be fought over: between the *chavistas* and the old business elite, Venezuela's government and the US. Here, too, the players are trapped by the market incentives that structure the maze, the "labyrinth" that Chávez promised Venezuelans they would escape from. And yet he did not keep the promise. Finding himself trapped in competition inside his own country and with the Americans, he deployed the same tactics as other petro-politicians in Saudi Arabia, Iran and Russia: use the black gold to strengthen and co-opt the military with one hand and shower gifts on supporters with the other.

Perhaps this slide was inevitable, the temptation too great to resist without outside help. Yet the problem is that we never get to find out: in almost all these cases foreign nations intervene, seek to exploit internal political turmoil, back rival factions, seek favourable treatment or even launch military campaigns, as Bush did in Iraq. This geopolitical game is one played out in the markets with prices creating the incentives. Playing a moral blame game misses the point. They have all become monsters in the maze, in a competition where the worst of them is rewarded. A war against this kind of corruption is as pointless as the war on drugs: remove Maduro or Saddam and you simply replace them with another petro-politician who will be facing the same incentives, the same temptations, the same threats from foreign powers. The curse makes chaos, and this chaos is built out of numbers, out of weapons and out of lives.

"I was sterilised last Thursday," Maria tells me, lying down on her bed. She's tired. Her voice is quiet. "I don't know what happened when I entered the surgery room. Perhaps I was nervous. The anaesthetic didn't work. I was supposed to have an anaesthetic for half of my body but I spent twenty minutes waiting for it to work. But nothing happened. When the doctor started the surgery, I could feel everything he did." Eventually they put her under a general anaesthetic. Her body, however, still aches today with the pain from the operation. "I'm struggling with the painkillers because they are difficult to find and also expensive." Nevertheless, she has no regrets about going ahead with it. "I feel relieved, it's better like this. I'm fine with my decision because I know I'll no longer have the fear of becoming pregnant."

I talk to her about her kids. "They play as if they were queuing for flour, or they cannot find food, or their credit card is declined, or the electronic payment does not work. Our children focus on what they live, and that is what they play: the queues, the reselling. That is normal for them, that is their lives now." To her, this is a life not worth living. It is, as I saw in Mosul and again in Donetsk, a zombie existence. The chaos here looks so different from those bombed-out cities of ruins, but over time they converge. The damage becomes psychological. The trauma of a thousand fissures with normality.

I say goodbye. I get back into the car and descend from the *barrios* to downtown Caracas. It's my last day in Venezuela. I need to post the footage that I've shot here back to London before I go to the airport tomorrow. My bags will be thoroughly searched and there's a chance the drives will be confiscated.

A police siren. My driver slows down and pulls up next to some graffiti of Chávez in a heroic pose etched in bright yellow. We get out. There are four uniformed officers. One peers into the back seat where he sees me—a *gringo*—sitting next to a large camera. Bingo. His officers search the car. They open the boot. They see the rest of the equipment, the other lenses and sound recorders. They also see the two hard drives that I was on my way to post. If they were to load them up, they'd see that I was hardly reporting on the government's glorious achievements.

"What are you doing here?" the senior policeman asks Carlos.

"I have no idea," Carlos says, "I'm just a translator."

"If I report you to the intelligence services what do you think will happen?" This is the part where he's asking for a bribe.

"I don't know. He has a visa. I just met him today."

"If I call, and I report all this equipment, what do you think will happen?"

"If you feel you should call, just call. I don't know anything about the equipment. I'm just a translator."

The bluff worked. The policeman got bored. I'm free to go.

I had survived my lone encounter with Big Brother. The monstrous security apparatus had taken a sniff and decided that I wasn't worth the trouble.

In my three weeks in Venezuela, I had seen how the price movements in the oil market had transformed from Arabic numerals on computer screens into the physical world: the cycle of boom and bust, erecting new skyscrapers, new governments, new hopes and dreams, only to turn against them and destroy them. I had seen how Chávez rode these waves: first in opposition during the bust, then benefiting from the boom to build his own fiefdom, a clientelistic regime built with black gold. He would not have been able to do this without the onslaught of financial capital that pushed up oil prices. It was these high prices that fuelled the Chávez monster, that enabled him to become the very thing that he swore he would never be. At first I thought that this was an impersonal process, an unintended effect of speculation, but then I saw how active finance had been: offering Chávez fresh capital to siphon off to corrupt elites and to buy elections directly. This, in turn, became the regime's Achilles heel: when Trump embargoed Maduro's access to the capital markets, the house of cards fell. The country spiralled downwards into a strange apocalyptic world.

As these global market forces set the stage for the monsters, down on the ground ordinary people were free to choose among impossible options presented by the spontaneous order of a hyperinflating economy. House cleaners became speculators, buying up government-subsidised products, hoarding them, making bets on their future prices. Children formed their own micro-corporations and looked to monopolise the one commodity they needed to survive: garbage. As jobs ceased to pay a subsistence wage, people

turned to all kinds of ways to make money from money, from reselling paper bolívars to playing video games for precious US dollars.

I had followed the butterfly effect from the food-price spike to
the Arab Spring to ISIS in Iraq, from the surging oil prices to Brexit,
Brazil, Belt and Road, to the war in Ukraine and now the collapse of
Venezuela. I had traced how chaos in the financial markets created
chaos in the real world, and how this chaos has been fed back into
the markets, only to spark more real-world chaos once again. I had
discovered how this feedback loop had been powered by a speculative machine, amplifying the chaos in every instance. I had also seen
how this chaos had been amplified by other engines too: by populist
politicians exploiting human crises, by The Feed boosting images
of invaders crossing borders, by the resource curse turning changes
in commodity prices into full-scale wars, clientelistic regimes and
economic collapse.

But Venezuela stands out to me as a unique episode. In Mosul and
Donetsk I had seen the physical destruction of warfare: destroyed
buildings, unexploded bombs buried in the ground, missing neighbours presumed to be buried among the pile of bricks that was once
their home. But here the chaos was expressed through the market
itself: a topsy-turvy world of ever-changing prices, of shortages and
queues, of supermarkets ordered to display food and turning them
into curious attractions filled with ketchup and mayonnaise. The
chaos here is blamed on the failure of a "socialist" experiment. But
what I had discovered was that most people's economic activity took
place in an anarchic market of speculation, hoarding and violence. It
was a fractal of finance capitalism. A mirror image—at every social
scale—of the very free-market forces that had powered the chaotic
decade.

I have enough time to make one last stop. I go to the bus depot.
People are lining up with suitcases and saying their goodbyes. Ever
since I started my journey in the Moria refugee camp in Greece,
I've seen how chaos creates migration. Five million have already fled
Venezuela, and here a queue is forming to join them. The bus is
boarding now. It's heading for Colombia. "My youngest daughter

is leaving," Elaiza, a forty-two-year-old mother of three, says, wiping a tear from her face. "She is twenty-three years old. She leaves the country without even finishing her schooling, she is about to graduate . . . She is the third of my children to leave . . . My oldest son is in Spain. He stayed two years in Ecuador, but he is in Spain now. My second son is in Peru. He works as a manager in a store. He left the country just in the middle of his schooling in computer science . . . I have not been able to see my second son, who left last October . . . I feel frustrated. I mean, the law of life says that your children are borrowed and that at some point they will get married. But it does not say that they will be out of your country, you will not be able to hug them, you will not enjoy Mother's Day with them, and they will not be next to you but via the internet on your birthday. They are my three children and I am a single mother, but it is what I've got to live for. Now I stay here all alone."

PART III

CLIMATE

Multiply: Climate Chaos in Kenya from *Mad Max* to *War Games*

"Last night we heard gunshots," Newton tells me as he fiddles with his rusty AK-47. His red necklace and turquoise collar pop against his camouflage shirt and midnight-blue skin. The sun hasn't risen and I can just about make out his homestead against the indigo sky behind him where he sleeps with his wife and two children. Newton is a twenty-two-year-old goat herder, which I'm discovering is a dangerous job in rural Kenya. "The Pokot were spotted in another area close by," he says. "We don't know if the cattle were stolen." This is Turkana and the Pokot are a rival tribe. "That's why we want to patrol this area," he says, gesturing to two friends. "Just to check and see if we find any footprints. Or perhaps we will run into them and a fight will ensue."

We set off. They lead me down a narrow path that runs through a light forest. The three of them each wear a green shirt, a woven skirt and feathered hat, and carry a vintage AK-47 on their shoulders. Whatever danger there may be, I find myself forgetting it, mesmerised by the emerging bronze sunlight flickering between the trees. It's serene. A flock of black-speckled goats cross our path with two herders behind them. Three young girls follow, carrying yellow buckets of fresh water on their heads.

The trees clear. "Can you see any grass? There's none," Newton says, pointing to the ground. "That's why the sheep are getting thinner. Because there's no rain. The grass isn't green, it's white."

We arrive at the river. On the other side is the green land. That's where Newton's goats are. The sun has just peeked above the horizon and is beating down on me. I had come here because I wanted to see how the climate was changing, and now I could feel it. The heat pierces my skin and it's still several hours until the midday peak. I take off my shoes. I step into the water. It's already lukewarm. But there isn't much of it, it barely clears my ankles. Looking down the river, I can see the little oval sand dunes that carve up the water which not long ago would have been submerged. East Africa is supposed to be getting wetter, but over the last two decades it's become drier instead. The climate is changing. Chaos began as an idea about the weather, and now the weather itself is becoming truly chaotic.

The shoreline is thick with trees whose roots thread the loose soil. Newton's goats are not far from here. They are near a watering hole along the fuzzy boundary between Turkana and Pokot. "It's getting hard," Newton says. "If I have cattle now, I have to protect them. Regardless, they are still stolen." Cattle are a prize possession. They're frequently stolen on raids. And as the rain dwindles, the attacks increase. "The goats are stolen, and you have to go back home. You go home to think about what you're going to feed your children. Your kids are crying but you don't have any money. And the goats are usually milked to feed the baby."

Cattle-raiding here is as old as anyone can remember. That isn't new. But as the climate becomes drier, the cattle-grazing land shrinks. Rival tribes are pushed into greater competition to survive. Raids are more frequent, intense and deadly as a result. Newton is young, but he's already been in a number of lethal fights. In one recent raid he shot and killed someone. Others fired back. "The bullet came through here," he says, pointing to a scar on his leg.

In between the roots of the trees are narrow paths. Newton and his two friends crouch down and examine the pathway. "These footprints here belong to the Pokot," Newton says. "They were walking around here at midnight." This tracking is something that they do most days when they are moving the cattle around, three at the front looking for tracks and three at the back to guard the cattle. "It's as if they haven't left. You have to be ready to fight and shoot them. If they were to find you, they would kill you as well."

—

I wanted to see what the future of chaos looks like, so I have come to a place where the future has already arrived. I am here to look at perhaps the biggest disruptive force that is going to shape the rest of my lifetime: the impending climate crisis. We have already passed the various scenarios that would lead us to a manageable climate adjustment of 1.5 degrees Celsius. The rising temperature will unleash all kinds of chaos from the natural world: sea levels will rise and cities will be submerged, some farmland will freeze over and some will turn to desert, mosquitoes will head northwards to Europe and bring malaria, and dormant diseases, like smallpox, will awaken from Siberia's thawing ice. This chaos will, no doubt, disorder our society and our politics and lead to all kinds of new conflicts. A recent survey of climate experts in *Nature* predicted that a four-degree warming of the planet would cause armed conflicts to rise fivefold. But what does "conflict" mean? I had seen in Mosul, Ukraine, Greece and Venezuela a kaleidoscope of fractured lives. What chaos will climate change create? What is its engine? How can it be stopped?

I dug into the research. I discovered that it was in the depths of Pentagon bureaucracy that this question was first seriously posed, and the answer framed the climate debate for years to come. It started with a long-time maverick named Andrew Marshall. He had been appointed by Richard Nixon to propose a plan for how America could survive nuclear Armageddon. Fiercely intelligent, eccentric and impish in stature, he became known as the "Yoda" of the Pentagon. Over the decades, he built up a roster of outside thinkers to feed him blue-sky perspectives about the future of warfare. In 2002 he commissioned one to write a report on the security risks climate change will bring.

The man Marshall hired was Peter Schwartz. He was a professional futurist, a "scenario planner" who helped corporations prepare for the turbulent years ahead. He was also Hollywood's favourite sci-fi world builder and had just finished working with Steven Spielberg on *Minority Report*. His first Hollywood gig was, incidentally, a vision of how Pentagon scenario planning could, by itself, trigger the apocalypse. In the early 1980s he was asked to consult on a script about a young Stephen Hawking–type genius. "I guessed that the genius kids these days are playing computer games," Schwartz tells me. "I was in Palo Alto [at the Stanford Research Institute]. We were the earliest gamers. 'Pong' had just been invented." The film became *War Games*: a teenage Matthew Broderick hacks into a Pentagon computer in search of new games to play. The problem is, the artificial intelligence cannot tell the difference between simulation and reality, and tries to beat Broderick at a game of "Global Thermonuclear War" by starting a global thermonuclear war. Now Schwartz was gaming out a new scenario, one that replaced Cold War nukes with a twenty-first-century climate catastrophe.

Schwartz's first problem was political. George W. Bush was president. Climate change was officially not happening and not a problem. "There was a lot of debate about, 'Is climate change real?'" Schwartz says. "So what I decided to do was just take the actual climate event that actually occurred 8,200 years ago . . . The climate had cooled rather dramatically over about ten years." Together with his colleague Doug Randall, he ran through the consequences of a decade of extreme and abrupt climate change starting in 2010. Their report was subtitled "Imagining the Unthinkable." Their story began with the disappearance of the Gulf Stream and the transformation of North America and Northern Europe into a desolate tundra and ended with the collapse of human civilisation as we know it. At the centre of their climate prediction was an engine of chaos: "resources."

"Humanity would revert to its norm of constant battles for diminishing resources, which the battles themselves would further reduce even beyond the climatic effects," they wrote. "Once again warfare would define human life." Climate change would make water and food scarce. The competition for the very things needed to sustain life would turn violent, just as it had done thousands of years in the past. Schwartz and Randall drew on archaeological research that showed that once the food supply drops below what a given population needs, conflict breaks out. "Every time there is a choice between starving and raiding, humans raid." Too little food for too many people sets in motion a cascade of crisis: markets disintegrate, states collapse, wars erupt, millions flee. If this vision was a science-fiction movie, it would be *Mad Max*. A kind of stateless anarchy, a return to the Hobbesian nightmare of a war of all against all.

Their prophecy was deliberately extreme. Schwartz and Randall's goal was not an accurate prediction but to show how climate change could precipitate chaos, and how that chaos could cascade, spread, mutate and amplify. They wanted to show how food and water security could drive conflict in the years to come. They wanted to get the defence community thinking about climate change. And in 2007 they succeeded. "Economic and environmental conditions in already fragile areas will further erode as food production declines, diseases increase, clean water becomes increasingly scarce, and large populations move in search of resources," the Center for Naval Analysis (CNA) concluded in a groundbreaking report. The CNA authors didn't envision an apocalyptic scenario. They instead considered how small changes to the availability of food and water could have big effects. Crucially, they considered this kind of resource stress not so much as a new kind of conflict but as an amplifier of existing conflicts. There might not be water or food wars, but the wars that existed were going to get worse: they would be more lethal, last longer and generate more refugees. The CNA authors coined a phrase that would come to define how the defence community saw the climate–conflict connection. They called climate change a "threat multiplier."

Yet there was still much that the Pentagon didn't know about how this "multiplier" works. They could sketch out plausible scenarios for ways in which food and water could escalate conflicts, but how this was playing out in the complex messiness of reality remained unknown. The challenges of not understanding emerging threats were all too real at the Pentagon in 2008. The insurgencies in Iraq and Afghanistan were hobbling the American Goliath. Defense Secretary Robert Gates wanted to prevent such blunders in the future. He founded and poured hundreds of millions into the Minerva Initiative to fund research into the new forms of conflict that would define twenty-first-century warfare.

Cullen Hendrix was a young assistant professor when he got the

CONFLICT & RAINFALL
IN AFRICA

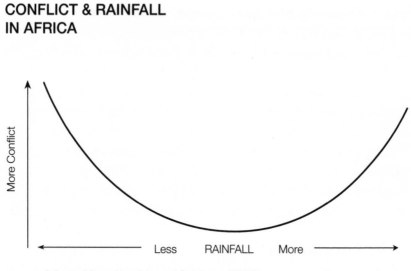

Adapted from Hendrix and Salehyan (2012)

news that the Initiative had given a group of political scientists an unprecedented grant of \$7.6 million to study the climate–conflict connection and he was one of them. The first question he asked was a simple one: what is a conflict? "We started thinking about things that might happen in response to wars breaking out, India and Pakistan going to battle over the Indus River. But we were also thinking that there were a lot of ways in which it could spark conflicts," Hendrix tells me. "What about herder conflicts? What about protests? What about strikes? What about communal conflicts?" Hendrix and his colleague Idean Salehyan hired a team of researchers to go through reports of clashes between herders, farmers, protestors, militias and governments across Africa. They found 6,000 conflicts, large and small. They then ran a statistical analysis to see if this chaos in the real world was correlated to chaos in the climate: whether extremes in rainfall—too much or too little—predicted these conflict events. "Lo and behold it does," Hendrix says. "You get a U-shaped curve where conflict increases substantially in periods of very little rainfall and then in periods of superabundant rainfall."

Peter Schwartz's "unthinkable" scenario was already happening. But there didn't need to be an abrupt or extreme weather event like a new ice age or superstorm. It turned out that many people who live off the land also live on the edge of chaos. These societies are highly sensitive. They are right on the boundary between order and disorder. And in many places, the climate-driven fight for resources was pushing societies over the threshold. It is already happening in Turkana, Kenya.

"I have seen the loss that a life of herding brings," Newton tells me. We're sitting under a tree as the midday sun beats down on the canopy. "It destroys the body, and you're hungry all the time. Plus, your cattle are stolen every day." Newton is optimistic, however. "When I get money, I can go to Nakuru for driving school. Learn about driving cars, instead of going into the forest all the time and being shot at by the Pokot." He hopes that once he saves up for driving school, he can become a taxi driver or drive trucks for the oil company Taro. He hopes that he can move somewhere safer, where he can live an orderly and stable life. He wants to move to a city.

I leave Turkana. I take the journey south to Kenya's capital, Nairobi, a journey that millions of other rural people are destined to take over the coming years. These climate refugees are feeding the growth of megacities around the world, from Mexico City and Guatemala City to Bangalore and Chennai, to Cape Town and Lagos. In Africa these cities are set to grow fourfold over the next three decades, and 40 per cent of this growth will come from rural dwellers no longer able to live off the land, like Newton. As my car makes its two-day journey south, I can see why. Much of the landscape is Martian, an open red plain of dust stretching to the horizon. Life isn't possible here. So it moves.

Many will move to Kibera. Sitting in the heart of Nairobi, it is Africa's biggest super-slum. A million people live here. The slum has grown through a kind of spontaneous order, improvised dwellings made from corrugated iron spread out like fractals around a train track that runs through its centre. The terracotta-earth streets unfold like a narrow web adorned with clothes lines and stalls with people cooking food, selling SIM cards or plastic items. There is no sewage system underneath this unplanned city and garbage is scattered everywhere. The future of climate change is not in Newton's place of forests and deserts and streams, but the incredible migration it will bring to super-slums like this one.

I meet Marta. She's twenty-two years old, has two kids and was born here. Her mother migrated from rural Kenya. "She thought that life is cheap in Kibera, but it turns out that's not the case," she tells me. "It's so much more expensive here than up in the country." The transition from rural to urban life is a profound one: it's the transition from living off the land to earning wages, from a subsistence economy to a market economy. Marta has two jobs. She cleans houses during the week and at the weekend she gets paid by an NGO to play soccer, provided her team wins. She normally spends over half her earnings on food for her family. The rest goes to her kids' school fees, charcoal for her stove and rent for her single-room home. And most of her food budget goes on a single item: maize flour, or *ugali* as it is known here. Her problem is that the price of *ugali* can change drastically from day to day. "It's hard to budget," she says, "you never know what the price is."

Small price rises of just a few shillings can have a big impact. When the prices are high, she and her kids are unable to eat. "They say, 'We can't sleep, we are hungry,'" Marta tells me, "so, we tell them, 'You just sleep, you'll get something tomorrow to eat.' And it makes me feel bad." This wave of hunger travels through the whole of Kibera. "So people will just start blaming the government. They are saying the government have taken their money." Protests erupt.

I'd come to Kenya looking for the future of chaos and I find myself back where I started. I was back to prices, the price of imported wheat and the anti-government protests that a global food price spike could trigger. I looked again at Schwartz and Randall's "unthinkable" scenario and the Center for Naval Analysis's "threat multiplier" report and found no mention of prices. Cullen Hendrix calls this first wave of thinking the "Malthusian" approach to the climate–conflict problem, a vision "where people are fighting over the underlying resources." This kind of direct competition happens without markets; it's what I saw in Kenya where cattle are directly stolen, or in *Mad Max* where the characters battle over buckets of water and oil. "Absolute scarcity," Hendrix says of this approach, "is the result of fundamental limits that are implied by our physical environment."

Scarcity, in the Malthusian model, comes down to two variables. On the one hand, there's the food produced. For each extra degree Celsius the climate warms, global yields of maize will decline by 7.4 per cent, wheat by 6 per cent and rice by 3.2 per cent. On the other hand, there's the human population this food needs to feed. And the world's population, according to the World Bank, is set to grow at approximately 1.1 per cent a year. It is these diverging trends—declining food productivity with a growing population—that will create absolute scarcity in the physical world. It is why four degrees of warming will ravage food supplies. It is why many neo-Malthusians believe that climate change will fuel conflict.

Just as this apocalyptic vision of the future was taking off, the Global Food Crisis of 2008 struck. At first, the crisis appeared to validate the fears that food and water were truly in short supply. Surging commodity prices, worldwide protests and two revolutions looked just like the cascading crisis these reports predicted. "But when I started looking at what really caused the 2008 Food Crisis," Hendrix says, "I realised that something doesn't need to be scarce in the absolute sense. There was more food produced by the international food system in 2007 than at any point in human history." Hendrix, and other researchers tackling the conflict–climate problem, realised they needed a different approach. "When we think about threats to the food system and global agriculture we think of the changing climate, desertification, increasing water stress," Hendrix says, "but the bigger issue is how these markets operate, are allowed to operate, and what happens when they break down."

This is a radical challenge to the Malthusian model, one that rejects the idea that hunger comes from too little food for too many people. Consider another resource, one we have already seen in the UK: housing. Do we have homeless people on the streets of London because we don't have enough houses? No. There are neighbourhoods where one in three houses is vacant. There are entire streets where lights are never turned on because nobody lives in any of them. The housing crisis is not caused by the lack of an absolute resource. There are plenty of houses. The problem is that the homeless people—and many others—simply cannot afford the price. If we wanted to put homeless people in the empty homes we could, but as a society we've chosen not to. We allocate homes using the "price system." The housing crisis doesn't come from an "absolute" lack of physical structures but from the rules of a social game. The same is true for food and famines.

It was this insight that earned Amartya Sen the Nobel Prize. He showed that, like with houses in London, modern famines are not caused by an absolute shortage of food. Such shortages only directly cause hunger for those living off the land, such as Newton in Turkana. Should his goats become sick, starve or be captured, then his family can no longer drink the milk they provide. But most people don't live off the land. They exchange something they make or provide for food. And most, like Marta in Kibera, live in market economies where this exchange is ordered by prices. What matters for her are not the Malthusian quantities of food and people, but the local price of food and the price at which she can sell her labour. Sen discovered that the major famines of the twentieth century were caused by a mismatch between these two prices. Physical food was usually available. But it was too expensive to be purchased on the wages most people received—that is, if they had wage-paying jobs at all. Famines were not made by climate shocks directly, but through elaborate rules of a social game we call the market.

It is this crucial insight that was missing from the Pentagon's conception of climate chaos. The resource wars they envisioned are already here and they are driving massive urban migration. These urban migrants have to buy food in markets and take up jobs to earn the wages to pay for it. It may well be that climate change does ultimately lead to an absolute shortage of food and societal collapse, where markets disappear, and we live in a *Mad Max*–style Armageddon. But in the decades ahead it looks like climate change is going to expand the international markets by adding urban dwellers to their ranks, rather than eroding them.

For Cullen Hendrix and others in the field, the study of climate change is also the study of prices. They soon discovered that the relationship between food productivity and global prices wasn't a straightforward one. "You start peeking under the hood on this kind of stuff and pretty soon, when you want to understand the real, fundamental drivers of a lot of this market volatility, it's often pretty hard to find an obvious climate signal or weather problem that's affecting it," Hendrix says. The chaos wasn't coming from the climate, but from finance. "It really started blowing my mind."

"We think about the food system like the world's largest factory," David Potere, the CEO and founder of TellusLabs says. "It's the largest factory on earth. It's 1.4 billion workers inside the factory, and it has no roof . . . Satellites are flying around the earth, 700km over the surface, orbiting from pole to pole . . . They can see through clouds, they can see colours that are way outside the human spectrum. All that information is coming into the satellite sensor." TellusLabs collects this data from NASA and the European Space Agency and feeds it into its artificial-intelligence machine. The AI has built a model based on twenty years of satellite data, which it uses to predict the future harvest from the current conditions.

Potere found three kinds of customers. Food manufacturers wanted advance warnings if their agricultural supply chains were going to be disrupted and if they should expect sudden changes in price. There were also growers, seed companies and buyers of grains. "We certainly found financial-market actors, hedge funds, asset managers, who are either directly, or for their clients, trying to create opportunity in the volatility that's coming inside the commodities markets," Potere says. But to his surprise he found that, unlike the food manufacturers, farmers and growers, they were less interested in the *real* harvests. Instead, they wanted Potere's team to predict what the official government reports would *say* they'd be.

"This was another real eye-opener for us. We've had a lot of surprises along the way, just in the last few years. We started getting interest right away from folks who were saying, 'You know, it's interesting, it's important on the fundamentals to know whether the US harvest is gonna be the largest harvest in the history of the country. But even if you're right, that it's gonna be the highest harvest ever, if along the way most of the market thinks it's a terrible year, I can blow up between here and there as a firm. And so what I need is, I need a bridge to get me from where I am to where you know the market is, or eventually the harvest, is gonna be. And that bridge is, I need to understand what the rest of the market is going to think about the harvest. Because that's the information that's actually moving the commodities market day to day.' And so we started getting customer interest in 'Can you model the government forecast each month? And can—'"

"So, sorry," I say, trying to get my head around what he's telling me, "that means you want to predict the government forecast?"

"Predict the government forecast."

"OK . . ."

"And so we found ourselves in this existential moment when we realised, 'OK, you understand we believe the harvest is going to be x this year. But you want us to tell you what we think the government thinks this harvest is gonna be and what they will publish? Because the rest of the world is gonna see not our forecast, but the government's forecast. And that's where the rational market reaction's gonna be.' So we find ourselves building two classes of model. One that we call a forecast of forecasts, which is essentially us trying to get inside the heads of the government prediction system as best we can. And then the second one, which is the applied science of, having seen the plants, and having seen how this movie plays out for twenty years, this is what we think will actually happen. And both are really important. And the difference between those two can be quite different from country to country."

The availability of this satellite data wasn't making the prices more accurate. This new technology does not undermine or negate the speculative game, it's merely a new weapon in the hedge funds' arsenal. A weapon that helps them obtain the emerging market orthodoxy—this time consecrated by the official crop reports—before their rivals. Because even having access to powerful predictive technology does not change the fact that markets are still, as they were in Keynes's times, beauty pageants. It is the collectively shared perception of reality, rather than reality itself, that drives prices.

Predicting official crop reports is just one deployment of this technology as a speculative weapon. But there's another one, one that struck me as potentially far more dangerous than the other drivers of food-price spikes I'd encountered: commodity-index investing and trend-following. A strategy that seemed uniquely engineered to exacerbate the human costs of climate change and fuel the climate wars for the years to come.

"The key thing about commodities is [filtering] what's relevant and what's not relevant," says Doug King, the Chief Investment Officer of RCMA Asset Management. "As a trader myself, there's so much stuff that's just absolutely not worth talking about . . . Around the world in commodities today, there's only a few countries that are relevant. In agriculture, you'd have Russia for wheat, North America and South America. That's it. Don't look at anything else . . . What you find is a lot of people will say, 'Wow! Look over there. It looks like there's a drought in Guatemala. There's a drought in Colombia.' Yes, they are producing some product. Yes, that is going to impact. But it isn't going to be particularly meaningful to a major surge or deficit in a particular commodity." The problem with satellite data, as King sees it, is that it detects slight fluctuations in local harvests that make little difference to the overall global supply. For a drought to impact supply significantly it needs to be a continental-scale event that doesn't require a satellite to learn about it. Nevertheless, data-driven hedge funds still buy and trade on this granular data. "These quant funds that are just looking for new data sources that they can program in. And if there's enough [funds] playing with [the data], it becomes relevant to the situation."

"As far as I understand it," I say, "the satellite data is not actually useful, but because enough of these funds are using this data, it becomes a self-fulfilling prophecy."

"Yes, totally," King says. Since quant funds are trading on satellite data, and quant funds know that other quant funds are trading on satellite data, they can anticipate their trades by also using satellite data, whether or not that data ultimately gives "relevant" descriptions of real-world supply. It's the same data-driven self-fulfilling "beauty pageant" phenomenon I had seen where algorithms trade on headlines, about Iraq or Anne Hathaway. Whether it is a war or a climate shock, these programs amplify small disturbances in the real world into major price spikes.

"The amount of trading on commodity markets through electronic trading platforms and traders has now reached its highest ever level in my opinion. Close to probably 75 per cent of all trades, or 80 per cent of all trades, are done by algorithmic-type trading strategies," King says. "The interesting thing is the real commodity hedgers have gone!" These "hedgers" are the real-world users of commodities, such as farmers and food manufacturers. The original purpose of the futures market was to give them security by guaranteeing a future price for their products. It was supposed to give them assurance that investments they made today would pay off tomorrow. But now these markets are themselves the source of uncertainty and these real-world users are abandoning them. "Coffee users won't hedge, rubber users won't hedge, so that side of hedging has gone. So you've lost a huge component that was utilising futures markets to manage budgets and manage their supply chains. What you're left with is programs against programs."

I had seen such a digital war before. It was the plot that Peter Schwartz suggested for the 1983 film *War Games*. In the film, the Pentagon hands over control of its nuclear arsenal to a computer named WOPR: War Operation Plan Response. It is powered by artificial intelligence designed to protect the US from a nuclear strike. The AI is trained to see such an attack as a move in a strategic game, to consider all the possible moves and counter-moves and launch the optimal response. But, of course, it doesn't turn out that way. WOPR was trained through conventional games such as chess and checkers and is unable to distinguish those from the real-world moves the US and the USSR make in a nuclear exchange. To the computer, both are games of ones and zeros, of strategies and probabilities. And when the computer tries to "win" the game called "Global Thermonuclear War," chaos breaks out.

Schwartz's prophecy of Armageddon triggered by artificial intelligence seemed to me an eerily prescient prediction of the climate wars to come. Far more so than his 2003 Pentagon report that imagined a *Mad Max*–style conflict over physical food and water. It is true that these resource conflicts are under way in rural Africa, as I had seen in Turkana. But as I had learnt from Newton, these conflicts represent the past, not the future. They are extinguishing themselves as rural dwellers flee to the cities. Climate change is fuelling this migration, and changing the nature of climate conflict itself. It is in these swelling megacities that the future of climate chaos lies for hundreds of millions of Africans. They no longer depend on the land but on the international markets for sustenance. Most, like Marta, spend over 50 per cent of their wages on food. They live on the edge of chaos, where even a small increase in international prices can trigger poverty and hunger, riots and revolution.

These prices are determined by another kind of conflict thousands of miles away: the speculative battle of "programs against programs." These "algos," like WOPR, see no difference between the digital world and the real one. They are trained solely to anticipate the moves of their opponents and launch a counter-attack, all in the blink of an eye. Their bets on the price of wheat and corn are just the means by which hedge funds raid each other's coffers. Each trade is a shot fired across the narrow streets of Lower Manhattan and the City of London, but the explosion is felt in lands far away.

The digital weapons they deploy both exploit and amplify climate chaos. The algos trading on granular satellite data are highly sensitive to even the smallest climate events. The dominance of algorithmic trading in the commodity markets means that the planet does not need to warm by two degrees or four degrees to disrupt food availability across the world. Such a disruption comes before there is too little food for too many people. It can just be a small climate shock. A shock that is read by a satellite, turned into a prediction, fed to an algo, which anticipates that another algo has the same prediction, which creates incentive for all the algos to trade. The ensuing digital battle increases global prices and pushes the burgeoning megacities of the developing world towards the edge of chaos. There, millions who had fled the climate conflicts of rural living find themselves ensnared in another one. A new kind of global climate war of programs battling programs.

"The challenges currently posed by climate change pale in significance compared with what might come," Mark Carney, governor of the Bank of England, told a crowd of insurance brokers in the Lloyds of London building on 29 September 2015. "The far-sighted amongst you are anticipating broader global impacts on property, migration and political stability, as well as food and water security." But, he explained, there was yet another class of risk that his audience of risk calculators had failed to consider. The very building blocks of the financial markets—from insurance to stocks to bonds—were also threatened. It was not just the world's poor who were at risk, but the world's financial capitals too. That evening, he sketched out the workings of a bomb built under their feet. A climate–finance doomsday device whose countdown had already begun.

His speech marked the beginning of a flurry of research among the world's financial firefighters. Economists deep inside the Bank of England, the European Central Bank, the Bank of International Settlements and the Commodity Futures Trading Commission prepared anticipatory war games. They charted their foe's line of attack from the changing physical environment to the real-world economy and then finally to the magical world of finance. They considered what would happen if the planet warmed by two or four degrees Celsius, when governments would be forced to intervene, and how the central banks could manage the ensuing fallout. These technocratic war planners largely ignored the lives of Newton and Marta and the millions of others in the developing world caught up in the climate conflicts already under way. Their focus was on the prices of intangible financial products and how their collapse would devastate the US and Europe.

For all generals who plan for the next war, the shadow of the last one looms large. Modern central banking has been forged out of the lessons of the 2008 Financial Crisis and thus placed its trigger—falling house prices—at the centre of its scenarios. The avalanche it anticipates begins with a warming planet and rising sea levels; this would cause coastal house prices to plummet and the insurance markets to freeze up. Mortgage-backed securities would fail and banks implode. But this rerun of the Financial Crisis would be just one crisis among many. Add in major disruptions to economic activity on America's coasts and you have disrupted the majority of US GDP. Add in the forced migrations, the drop in consumer spending, falling crop yields, the flooding of factories, the sinking of roads, the cutting of telecommunications and the destruction of industrial equipment and you add climate shock on top of climate shock to create a kind of economic super-shock never seen before. Mark Carney implored insurance brokers to consider shocks far beyond those of floods and droughts. "In addition," he said, "climate change could prompt increased morbidity and mortality from disease or pandemics." The cumulative detonation of these shocks will not tip over the house of cards that is the global financial system, but bury it in a crater deep underground.

This is only phase one of the technocrats' battle plan. They anticipate that another front will emerge, one potentially even more destructive. They predict that when governments are faced with the reality of climate change, they will rush to decarbonise the economy to stop it. The burning of fossil fuels would be drastically curtailed and even prohibited. The oil, coal and natural gas still in the ground would have to stay there. These "stranded assets" are currently valued at $28 trillion. They are already priced into the financial markets as the stocks and bonds of energy companies. These assets are the backbone of the financial system: a third of equity and fixed income assets belong to the energy and related sectors. They hold up the balance sheets of pension funds and banks. And as governments around the world try to stop the physical effects of climate change and order unused carbon to stay "stranded" in the ground, the price of these financial assets will be forced to $0. This balance-sheet black hole will trigger a second detonation of the climate–finance doomsday device. As Mark Carney warns, the "paradox is that *success is failure*."

The origin of this doomsday device, the Bank of International Settlements concludes, is prices. For centuries the global markets have priced carbon incorrectly. Fossil fuels are simply too cheap. Their price does not take into account the "external" costs passed on to other people in other places in other times. Yet these prices have coordinated the economy, nevertheless. By "telling us what we ought to do" they have created a spontaneous order that has brought environmental chaos. Even now, prices are failing to "price in" the very changes to the climate that they continue to coordinate. S&P Global Ratings estimates that the insurance industry is underpricing climate risks by as much as 50 per cent. The stock market, allegedly the most "efficient" market of all, is not, according to the IMF, accounting for the coming climate costs for carbon-related companies. In the few places where climate risks are priced in—such as flood insurance in parts of the UK or wildfire insurance in California—the markets have ceased to function. Climate risks are so great that they are uninsurable. The premium is too high for anybody to pay. Our magic risk mitigators have failed before the true climate calamity has even arrived.

But these technocratic reports make a fundamental error. They describe the financial system in passive terms: unthinking cogs in a preordained machine. In fact, financiers are active protagonists in this story. The European Central Bank found that banks have continued to lend to fossil-fuel and carbon-related industries without taking into account the ever-increasing risks. Since 2016, sixty major banks have invested over $3.8 trillion into the carbon energy sector, the four biggest investors being Wall Street banks: J.P. Morgan Chase ($317 billion), Citi ($238 billion), Wells Fargo ($223 billion) and Bank of America ($199 billion). They are lending to companies whose assets will soon be "stranded" in the ground. They are financing the very climate–finance doomsday device that will one day destroy them.

I had gone to Kenya in search of the climate wars and found

myself back in New York and London. I started off seeing climate change as a "threat multiplier" that would exacerbate existing conflicts. But then I came to understand that it was our financialised markets that are doing the multiplying. They are underpricing carbon, encouraging and coordinating its continued release into the atmosphere. They are amplifying the impact of climate shocks on food prices, bringing climate chaos to the very people who have fled it. They have integrated carbon into the modern economy so deeply that our attempt to build a green one will create a financial crisis all of its own. Finance has trapped us in the very crisis that it has created, a crisis whose human costs it multiplies.

There is another front in the climate wars that I had yet to consider. One that still saw prices deployed as a weapon but existed far away from the financial markets. These combatants first appeared to be operating not just in a different country but in a different universe. Yet the closer I got to them and their tactics, the more familiar they appeared. They used the same playbook as hedge funds. In fact, they were not just analogous, but fighting alongside each other in the same war. They were in Kenya's eastern neighbour, Somalia. They are the terrorist organisation Al-Shabaab.

Arbitrage: Al-Shabaab, the Terrorist Hedge Fund

As the plane descends, a row of perfect beaches comes into view. Despite their brilliant yellow sand they are all completely empty. Then I remember which coastline this is. It's a place where no tourists would ever dare go. The cityscape behind them is usually photographed with plumes of smoke rising from bombed-out buildings and burning cars. I look across the rooftops and see nothing untoward. I check my watch. It's only 8 a.m. in Mogadishu, and there's still plenty of time for Al-Shabaab to strike.

A representative from the hotel meets me at the airport. "There have been no terrorist attacks in the last two months," David tells me as I wait for my luggage.

"Weren't there three bombings here last week?" I ask.

"Yes," he says, nodding, "but last year they were every day." For a moment I'm reassured. Then I do the maths. It's from an attack every day to every other day—a 100 per cent improvement, admittedly, but not exactly the comforting reassurance that David thinks it is.

David drives me through the Mogadishu International Airport base (MIA). It's a sprawling military base that stretches two miles down the beach and houses the UN, various embassies and three hotels. The road is filled with white military vehicles with "UN" brandished on them in large black lettering. I pass tall concrete walls with barbed-wire fencing, and posters encouraging the base residents to be a "Good Peacekeeper." I pass by the main gate. It's a series of concrete barriers to stop suicide bombers entering. Last year a truck detonated before it could reach these walls and killed 587 people inside the city. Just as the gate slips out of view, I spot a herd of goats skipping over the barriers towards me. David says they live here and move about freely. I wonder if Al-Shabaab is cruel enough to use them as carriers for explosives. If people put bombs in shoes or underpants, why not goats?

We pull up to a steel gate flanked on either side by turrets. This is the hotel. Men stand around with their automatic weapons pointing downwards. They let us in. "If the base is safe, why is there another base inside the base?" I ask.

"I don't know," David replies with a shrug. The hotel is laid out in a U-shape. It's made from disused shipping containers stacked one on top of the other. They have been converted into hotel rooms. There are no other guests here.

An hour later I'm granted a short interview with Brigadier Paul Lokech of the Ugandan People's Defence Forces (UPDF). He's the military commander of the UN's peacekeeping mission in Somalia, AMISOM. An enormous map of the country covers an office wall. It's divided into sectors, each one assigned to a different African nation responsible for peacekeeping. "Sector 2 we have the Kenyans," the brigadier, in a green beret and camouflage uniform, says as he points to the map. "Sector 3 we have the Ethiopians, Sector 4 we have Djiboutians, Sector 5 we have Burundians, and Sector 1, of course, we have the Ugandan forces." This coalition is assembled under the umbrella of the UN and is paid for by Western nations, who have essentially outsourced the dirty work of peacekeeping to these African armies. The brigadier is Ugandan and Sector 1 is Mogadishu, a city that the brigadier helped to capture from Al-Shabaab in 2011 as the commander of two battle groups.

I tell the brigadier that I've come to Somalia to understand the future of the climate wars. That I've already seen how food can be fought over and food prices can trigger famines and riots. I've come here because I've heard that Al-Shabaab is using food as a weapon of war itself. That Somalia, like her neighbour Kenya, is already experiencing climate shocks of increasing frequency and severity. I want to know if this country offers a window into the contours of our conflicted future.

He tells me that the problem in Somalia, from the start of the civil war in 1991 to today, is the lack of security. "The government failed to give an umbrella of security," he says. "If the state fails in giving security to everybody, what happens then? People resort to finding ways of getting security. So it's the same thing with the Somalis. They were exposed to all these problems. Then later on, there was a vacuum created here. And that vacuum was occupied by extremists." Al-Shabaab has kept the war going for so long by maintaining that vacuum. "When they bring, for instance, a VIED—a vehicle packed with bombs—and then it explodes in the marketplace or it explodes in the centre of the city, that is creating terror, creating fear in the population. To make the population know that 'No, we are still in existence. The government is not in control. Even if they have their armies with them we can still penetrate their lines.'" It was a feedback loop: people turn to Al-Shabaab for the very security in an insecure country that Al-Shabaab has created.

I probe further. I try to push our conversation from physical security to food security. But, just as I had found with the Russian-backed separatist in Donetsk, I was inside a military operation: there is a single approved script that is repeated on a loop. There is no follow-up to be had, no deep dives into the question of military tactics and climate shocks. The brigadier offers an opening, however, a chance for me to break out of this military bubble on the airport base. He says I can join a convoy to a market town and talk to people myself.

My handler from AMISOM, Captain Charles Kabona, arrives at 8:30 a.m. As he steps out of the car, his green Ugandan beret and uniform sparkle through gusts of sand. He takes me to the AMISOM base. He hands me body armour and a helmet. Neither fit particularly well, but I clumsily work the straps to stop them from sliding off. A poster on the wall says, "STAY ALIVE." I look closer. It lists instructions on how to strap on a helmet and how to strap into an armoured personal carrier (APC). In the cartoonish graphic of an aeroplane safety card, it shows an APC hitting an IED and exploding. Below is a picture of a man in a green suit plastered against the vehicle wall with red blood splattered on either side of him like a swatted fly. Another shows a gun flying into his mouth and blood spurting out. The last shows a green bag falling from above and splitting his head open like a crimson coconut. I ask Captain Charles what risks the journey brings. "They plant IEDs on the roads so that they can hit our convoys as the main target," he says. "And another trick they apply is suicide bombers. Yeah, they also have a tactic about using suicide bombers who come in vehicles, VIEDs, and the vehicle explodes and of course causes destruction."

After three hours and several rounds of tea and biscuits, he takes me to the convoy. It is finally ready. Seven APCs line up in a row, each one large and metal and tan. Ugandan troops are filing into them. I crawl inside one. There is a driver in front, a soldier who mans a machine-gun turret right behind him, and at the back another soldier stands up outside with a pair of binoculars as lookout. I strap in.

We wait. And wait some more. After an hour we are told to get out of the APC. We would not be leaving today. The tow truck has broken down. Without the tow truck, the convoy can't move. Should one of the APCs run into trouble, they would be left out there in the darkness. Sitting ducks for Al-Shabaab. It was too late in the day for the engineers to fix it. We wouldn't be able to make it there and back by sundown. Tomorrow, they said, the truck should be fixed.

Bad news. The truck would not be ready today either. The engineers can't fix it in time. It will have to be tomorrow, Thursday, or maybe Saturday, possibly Monday. My shipping-container hotel room is expensive and this trip is already over-budget. I wonder if I should bail.

Two hours later: good news. The truck is fixed and Captain Charles is coming to pick me up, so I get my camera gear ready to go. Another two hours: I am in the convoy with my helmet and jacket on and the rusty armoured personnel carrier is finally moving. The whole thing rattles like a tin can. Just as the poster had warned, bags fly into the air. I suspect this APC is a vintage one without much suspension.

To my left is a man standing above, handling the machine gun, and to my right is a man standing lookout. Captain Charles, sitting opposite, is clearly relieved. "Do you want to see Mogadishu?" he asks.

"Can I?" I say.

"Stand up there," he says, pointing to the position for the lookout.

I stand up and clumsily walk over. As the APC bounces up and down, my helmet hits the roof and the camera slips from my shoulder. Charles gets up and steadies me towards the hole as the lookout soldier steps down.

As my head pokes up, I finally leave the base bubble and see the real Somalia for the first time. I see the convoy stretching out in both directions like a military invasion. There is not much of a road yet and the streets are packed on either side with donkeys and carts. It looks like the modern world never came here, as if the civil war had frozen this place in time. People stop and stare at me just as I stare back at them. I let go of the rim of the APC to balance my camera. The vehicle jerks violently. My midsection slams against the ridge. My foot twists and strains and a shooting pain ricochets through my leg. But I can't take my eyes off what is in front of me. I've been sent back in time and put in army formation barraging through the civilian population. I feel that I have to keep filming, but keeping the camera steady is impossible.

Banged again. I must get down.

The convoy continues to hurtle forwards. Through the small gaps in the armour plating I can see that we have left the city. The rural landscape appears underdeveloped. Every ten minutes or so we pass an "internal displacement camp" of bright-green and blue tents that house people this war has forced from their homes. After an hour, the convoy arrives at a forward operating base to pick up more soldiers. Twenty minutes later we finally get to a small market town.

Captain Charles tells me that thanks to AMISOM this area is

now safe. As we begin to walk, I look behind me. I see over fifty Ugandan troops and Somali police officers and four armoured personnel carriers. A soldier walking beside me appears to be carrying what I believe is a heavy-duty Uzi. I had not seen anything like this in Ukraine or Iraq. This is not the front line nor a battlefield, but a small market town where goats and camels are traded. And yet I have my own personal army.

I stop walking and frame up my camera to capture the scene. Within a second, a tap on my shoulder. "You cannot stand still," Captain Charles says. "You must keep walking." The situation sinks in. There could be an Al-Shabaab sniper or suicide bomber hiding in the crowd. Stopping made me an easy target. So, flanked by men with machine guns, I walk through the town. Standing by market stalls selling textiles or barbequed goat meat, the residents stare at me and the small army that rolls past them.

We arrive back at our APC. Today, it turns out, I would not be able to talk to anybody without a uniform. It is just too dangerous. I had left the bubble in only the most literal sense. I had learnt nothing. Only, perhaps, that Somalia remains an extraordinarily dangerous place. I had rolled the camera the entire time I had been walking. The whole excursion had lasted eleven minutes.

"We have captured a lot of good video," Captain Charles says, smiling as the APC starts rattling forwards. "The last time I came, with the BBC, they did not get the opportunity. We stopped five metres away from our defence." It turned out that our chaotic departure had given us a tactical advantage. "Last time, people had information that we are coming, and you could see their facial expression: they were not ready to talk to us. Now, our [visit] was a surprise."

The convoy rolls forwards. After half an hour our vehicle pulls over. We wait. Five minutes. Ten minutes. The sky begins to darken. We must be an hour away from the airport base at least. I then hear a distant rat-tat-tat. Machine-gun fire? My face flashes red. Panic.

"So, did you hear about the suicide bomber yesterday?" Captain Charles asks, attempting small talk to drown out the din.

"No. I didn't. Who did they attack?" I say.

"An Italian convoy, Italian vehicles that were moving. I think they lost people: two people died, four were injured. It was near the Ministry of Defence headquarters."

"Do they suicide-bomb a lot?"

"Yes. It was a VBIED: Vehicle-Borne Improvised Explosive Device. It is a suicide bomber, but in a vehicle. But they do not target our forces as such, just any convoy moving. They can target anybody."

"But they attacked a convoy yesterday," I say, wondering why he has decided to wait until the moment when we are stranded out in the middle of nowhere with the sound of gun battles raging, as the dark night sky descends, to tell me.

"It wasn't ours!" he retorts defensively, as if it is somehow unrelated to our current predicament. "It wasn't our convoy."

"I mean convoys in general," I say, trying to get him out of this defensive position.

"So common," he replies, relaxing a little. "That convoy is in town, it was other convoys in town. Not like these convoys."

I am not reassured that a stranded convoy was somehow safer than one inside a town, but thankfully the engines start up again and after half an hour we roll forwards.

I had come to one of the most dangerous parts of the world, and ultimately it was too dangerous for me to find out anything. I had risked my life for nothing. The next day I was scheduled to fly back to Kenya. Maybe there I'd be able to find Somalis who could tell me about Al-Shabaab.

"They say today a huge explosion took place in Somalia." Oh, by who? "By Arsenal," Mohammed, a Somali refugee living in the Kakuma refugee camp, tells me. "If they use the name Al-Shabaab, security members like police or others say, 'Why are you talking about the history of Al-Shabaab? Are you linked with Al-Shabaab?' So instead of saying Al-Shabaab they say Arsenal." Even here in Kenya, the shadow of Al-Shabaab looms over the lives of Somalis. Even in a refugee camp, a supposed island of safety, they must talk in code.

Soccer is a key part of popular culture here. Mohammed has a small TV with a rusty antenna where he can watch the sports news and get glimpses of the Premier League. He's a Chelsea fan and plays soccer most days a week. His TV is a portal to the outside world, somewhere that relates to neither where he's fled from nor the camp that he's lived in since 2012.

He grew up in rural Somalia. His family were pastoralists who owned camels and cows. In 2010, Somalia suffered a severe drought amid the civil war, then in its nineteenth year. The UN declared a famine in Southern Somalia: 3.5 million were at risk from hunger and starvation. Al-Shabaab controlled many of these southern regions, including Mohammed's home. One day, Al-Shabaab soldiers visited his family farm. They demanded that his father pay a tax and hand over much of his livestock. When he refused, the soldiers attacked him and his son. Mohammed escaped to Mogadishu.

There he started to work for an international aid agency that sent food supplies to camps filled with people displaced by famine and war. But Al-Shabaab was refusing to let them into the areas they controlled. They claimed that the agencies were spies for the West and the food delivered was not fit for human consumption. They highjacked convoys and burnt 2,000 tons of food aid. But many agencies sent food convoys anyway.

Mohammed was on one of them. "Then, as we were travelling, on the way Al-Shabaab militants attacked us and killed two of us," he says. "And they have looted all vehicles and all property that we are carrying to the displaced people." Shortly afterwards, Mohammed's name was read out on a target list on Al-Shabaab's radio station. They were telling their supporters to find him and others who were working for the NGOs and kill them. "I didn't have any choice but to leave Somalia."

"In Somalia, we tend to see drought or flood about every seven years," Judd Devermont tells me at the Center for Strategic and International Studies in Washington, D.C., where he directs the Africa Program. "But it only becomes a famine, or an international crisis, when it is man-made." Devermont was the national intelligence officer for Africa under Barack Obama when his administration recognised the Somali government for the first time. He tells me that the kind of attacks on food convoys that Mohammed had told me about in the Kakuma refugee camp is a common Al-Shabaab tactic. They frequently attack food convoys and aid organisations. The tactic is most effective, however, when famine strikes. And in 2010–11 a climate shock delivered the worst drought the country had seen for fifty years. This climate crisis was Al-Shabaab's opportunity.

The "hunger weapon" is as old as warfare itself. From the Spartan siege of Athens in 430 BC to the German U-boat attacks against the Allies in the Second World War, cutting off the enemy's food supply is an ancient military tactic. "[I]f the enemy is well fed, be able to starve him," advised Sun Tzu in *The Art of War*. Naval blockades are just one option. Retreating armies often destroy farms so that their enemies are deprived of the food the land would produce upon its recapture. Even if agricultural production is not directly targeted, wartime disruption to roads and rail cuts off supplies such as feed and fertiliser and stops the harvest from reaching the people who need it. As diverse as these problems are, they are all ones of absolute scarcity. They are Malthusian problems of food failing to reach people. In these wars, markets are largely suspended and the state steps in to organise food provision. But in Somalia, that's not the case. Al-Shabaab's wielding of the hunger weapon is different.

Somalia lacks a functioning government, but an informal market economy thrives nevertheless. Livestock accounts for up to 40 per cent of GDP; 60 per cent of households farm and many city dwellers earn their living through the trade and exchange of animals. When drought strikes, farmers face extra costs: the price of feed increases, and to access dwindling water sources they often have to pay additional transportation costs. There is no government support to help them. So, to cope with these rising costs, farmers sell more of their cattle. This increase in supply pushes down prices: in 2010–11 cattle prices in Southern Somalia dropped by 30–50 per cent. And just as incomes for Somalis were plummeting, Al-Shabaab seized on their vulnerability. As they had done to Mohammed's family, they confiscated livestock and taxed the transportation routes. They amplified the costs.

"Most people in Sub-Saharan Africa don't join groups that engage in violence because there's an ideological reason," Devermont explains, citing research by the United Nations Development Programme. "When we look at surveys on individuals who join extremist groups, for example, the number-one thing that they say is employment insecurity. And I think you can broaden that to talk about just your ability to survive. And when you don't have the ability to survive, then you're more likely to join groups that are going to help you. In fact, many people who have joined groups like Al-Shabaab or Boko Haram have talked about the salaries they get." Over half of the people surveyed in the UN study were from Al-Shabaab, the rest were from Boko Haram and ISIS. Despite being organisations best known for an extremist ideology, the majority of recruits said they had "limited" or "no understanding of religious texts." Instead, the researchers were told, "Employment is the most frequently cited 'immediate need' faced at the time of joining." Those with jobs and secure incomes didn't join because they didn't need to.

Many Somalis join Al-Shabaab because they are desperate, and they are desperate because of Al-Shabaab. They are desperate because Al-Shabaab has taken their cattle and taxed their transport, driven down their wages, only then to exploit their desperation as a tool for recruitment to their ranks. This is the cycle of hunger and violence, of how hunger fuels violence and violence fuels hunger. This cycle amplifies climate shocks. It is why, when cattle prices decline in Somalia by 6 per cent, there is an uptick in recorded conflict of 72 per cent.

Al-Shabaab deployed the hunger weapon through manipulating prices. They innovated the age-old tactic from a Malthusian problem of absolute scarcity to one that is deployed through markets. And the more I looked into Al-Shabaab, the more attuned to the markets I realised they are. A key source of revenue for them is commodity-trading: smuggling sugar and charcoal into neighbouring Kenya, thereby avoiding the tariffs and pocketing the difference. Indeed, this exploitation of two diverging prices is the most common of hedge-fund strategies. It's called arbitrage.

The more I thought about it, the more the tactics of Al-Shabaab and many hedge funds looked the same. It wasn't just arbitrage. Each sees chaos as an opportunity, as something to be exploited rather than ameliorated. And through their exploitation, they amplify the crisis and compound human suffering. The main difference is one of magnitude. Al-Shabaab is contained within the Horn of Africa. They are a militant group with guerrilla-army weapons of AK-47s and improvised bombs. By contrast, hedge funds are armed with state-of-the-art technology, from cutting-edge artificial intelligence to a global satellite surveillance network. Once fired, their weapons traverse the globe at the speed of light. Although these weapons exist in the digital realm, the fallout is profoundly human, altering the means of survival for all. Despite the hedge funds' superior weaponry, their business model is the same. Al-Shabaab was a terrorist hedge fund.

Al-Shabaab's war crimes have been condemned across the world. From human rights groups to the UN to the US State Department, their weaponisation of hunger is denounced as a violation of international law. "Intentionally using starvation of civilians as a method of warfare by depriving them of objects indispensable to their survival, including wilfully impeding relief supplies," is a war crime, as stated by the Geneva Conventions and the International Criminal Court. These rules of war allow for all kinds of murderous and destructive behaviour, but they carve out particular actions that can never be excused no matter the stakes. Even when the nation's survival is in question, there are some weapons that simply should never be used. The hunger weapon is one of them. Forced starvation and blocking food supplies can never be justified.

The effectiveness of Al-Shabaab's hunger weapon depends, however, on the economic environment. While their use of the tactic is routine, its most devastating deployment was during 2011. The drought was seen to be the key enabling condition, triggering an economic crisis that made an economic weapon all the more potent. "Though less publicised than the drought, of equal importance in triggering the famine was the simultaneous steep climb in the price of food globally," concludes a study published in *Global Food Security*. The prices of local cereals—such as wheat and maize, which most Somalis depend on—were pushed up by global prices of those internationally traded commodities. The drought depressed incomes by depressing livestock prices at precisely the same time as food prices were soaring. Somalis were trapped in a double economic bind, a bind that magnified the power of Al-Shabaab's food weapon and its humanitarian destruction.

The food-price spike of 2010 and 2011 was one I had already investigated at the beginning of my journey. Prices were pushed up by speculators, by those following an upward trend or viral narratives of Russia's failed harvest and quantitative-easing-driven inflation. I had traced how these high prices had triggered riots and revolutions in the Middle East. But in Somalia, the high prices had another effect: they enabled hunger to be weaponised in a brutal civil war. Hedge funds and Al-Shabaab did not just share similar tactics, they were working together to create one of the worst human catastrophes of the century. The hedge funds were operating at a global scale by driving up the price of food everywhere. On the ground, Al-Shabaab turned this impoverishment into an opportunity to bolster their bloody campaign.

There is an important difference, however. Al-Shabaab was denounced across the world: depriving civilians of food and essential goods is a war crime. Yet the financial speculators driving the price spike faced no such recriminations, blame or calls for justice.

If there were ever to be such an accounting, it would have to wait. The butterfly was still flying, I had to follow it. And this time chaos was returning to where it all began: the US.

Short: Coffee, *Coyotes*, Kids in Cages

A woman walks towards me clutching a machete. The blade looks at least a foot long. She lifts it up and plunges it into the slender gap between the door and the wall. She wiggles it back and forth.

"Why did you lock the door?" she asks me. "It's so safe here."

She hadn't given me a key for my hotel room and, not wanting my camera equipment stolen, I locked it from the inside. I assumed they'd have a key.

I should have known that this wasn't an ordinary hotel. When I first walked in, I saw a giant plastic deer standing on top of a similarly large 1990s TV. The lobby was large and empty, filled with rows of unused tables and chairs. In the middle, three women were carefully dividing up a roll of toilet paper. They sold each piece separately to travellers who wanted to use the hotel restroom. I picked up the local newspaper left on a chair. The headline read: "*Macheteó a su padre y le corta la cabeza*" ("He macheted his father and cut his head off"). I opened the paper and saw a photograph of a decapitated body. Page after page reports murder after murder. This shouldn't have surprised me: the hotel is in the few miles of no-man's-land between the Mexican and Guatemalan borders. Rival cartels are in the midst of a battle here to control the drug trade. This contested patch is called The Square.

The woman is struggling with her machete and the door. A co-worker shows up and uses her phone as a light. Another five minutes and the door swings open.

In the morning, over eggs, I casually discover that just two days ago a man was shot and killed on the hotel steps. I wonder if I've accidentally ended up in yet another war zone. But I hadn't come here to investigate the chaos of the cartels. I had come to investigate the origins of the US border crisis that had erupted into The Feed in the summer of 2019.

After years of declining, migration was suddenly surging. Photographs showed kids in cages, wrapped in Mylar foil, staring out through iron bars. Reports circulated of children sleeping in unwashed clothes, being forced to drink from toilets, barely surviving on a starvation diet and suffering outbreaks of chickenpox. Trump, who had promised to build a "beautiful wall" along the southern border, was suddenly faced with the very chaos he promised to end. He cycled through scapegoats to blame for this migrant "invasion"—Barack Obama, the Mexican government, the criminal gang MS-13—but knew that blaming others wouldn't work. "You are making me look like an idiot," Trump shouted at his aides. "I ran on this. It's my issue." He scrambled for solutions. "Privately, the president had often talked about fortifying a border wall with a water-filled trench, stocked with snakes or alligators," reported the *New York Times*. "He wanted the wall electrified, with spikes on top that could pierce human flesh . . . he later suggested that [soldiers] shoot migrants in the legs to slow them down."

While the debate erupted over Trump's cruelty theatre, few wondered what had caused this avalanche of migration to begin with. The surge was, in fact, unusual. Migration had been trending down. The recession had reduced American demand for migrant labour. Endemic violence in Honduras and El Salvador, another traditional driver of migration to the US border, was also trending downwards. And the country most represented at the border was not a traditional narco-state. It was Guatemala. What had caused this exodus?

I head a few miles north from Murder Hotel to an immigration checkpoint where buses of Central American migrants cross into Mexico. There are no barriers here, it is just a small building by the side of the road. There are four soldiers wearing camouflage jackets and holding semi-automatic weapons. The immigration officer is a middle-aged man in a white T-shirt and red cap. The atmosphere is relaxed. The buses roll in and the officer boards and takes a look. In between buses, he tells me how he spots migrants. He says Central Americans have a distinct accent, their faces look different from Mexicans' and they're shorter. If they fit this profile, he asks a few questions: where they're going to, where they're from, and if they can name any of Mexico's national holidays. If they stumble, he asks for their papers.

One large bus pulls up. He invites me inside to see him do an inspection. He walks up to two young men sitting next to each other. One is wearing a red cap.

"Where are you from, gentlemen?" he asks.

"We are . . . from here . . . Tuxt . . . from here . . ." the one in the red cap replies.

"Can you show me your IDs, please?"

"I don't have any."

"Where did you come from?"

"Over there in . . . what was the name of this place again?"

"From the north," his friend says.

"Tijuana?" red cap adds tentatively.

"Let's see, which way is north?" the officer says.

"I mean, to be really, really honest, I'm not from . . ."

"Let's get off the bus for a second, please take your things with you."

The officer leads them to a small white jail cell on the side of the road. Through the bars, the one in the red cap says he'll tell me his story but won't tell me his name. He says he's from Guatemala. His plan was to travel through Mexico to Tijuana and then cross the border to the US. He was going "to follow the American Dream." His family is poor, his dad is a coffee farmer, but the coffee industry back home has collapsed. "There's no money," he says. "Because the thing that really makes money is coffee." Without it, his family can't make ends meet. "My family has debts," he continues, "that's why I wanted to get out of the house, to help my family." His family didn't want him to leave, but he went anyway, saying that God would protect him. "I'm sad because I don't know if I'm coming back. Only God knows. If I come back today, tomorrow, the day after, or not at all. Or if I die in the truck, I don't know." He was travelling with a friend who has family in America. They are risking crossing the border by themselves. Neither one has the money to hire a smuggler—a *coyote*—to help them. "I came to work, to get by," he says. "But what a shame, I couldn't make my dreams come true."

I trace his journey back to the coffee plantations in Guatemala. I cross the border and head to Huehuetenango and then out towards a coffee cooperative at Todos Santos Cuchumatán. The car spirals up a mountain road into a white fog that submerges the roadside foliage. The air thins with the elevation, but the higher we climb the less I can see as the fog thickens. Behind the opaque clouds are coffee trees lining the hillside: a red, grape-sized berry fuels the economy here.

I get out of the car and walk along a dirt road. It's started raining and the water is now rolling down my cheeks. I meet a coffee farmer at his home. Gaspar Ramírez Torres, forty-seven, lives here with his wife and three children. It's a single room with a covered porch, where we sit. Around him are large buckets filled with coffee beans soaking in water. They are supposed to be drying out. This rain could ruin them. "It's the first time it has rained like this," he tells me.

He noticed the change in the weather about eight years ago; with it has come a persistent fungus on his coffee plants called *roya*, translated as rust. "And now, it strikes every year, even if we fumigate. The rust always damages the coffee." The chemicals to fumigate the coffee trees add to the already expensive loan that he has had to take out from local moneylenders to fund his crop. Using the deeds to his home and land as collateral, he is charged 10 per cent interest a month, or 120 per cent a year.

In 2018, he was no longer making a profit. The coffee prices were below his costs. This continued into 2019. Interest payments compounded and his debt grew unmanageable. If he failed to pay, he'd lose his land and his home. "So I travelled to the States because the coffee price was so low," he tells me. "We left from here and got on a truck, and from there we hopped on a train towards the border." He had heard that he'd be able to enter the US if he travelled with his seven-year-old son. But when they were caught, they were held in a detention centre for fifteen days. They slept outside. Torres was given a single meal a day. "It was always a little rough, but he hung in there with me because he's still young." They were returned to Guatemala. His debts remain. "If the coffee price remains low, I might try to cross again, to pay my debt."

I meet Sebastian Charchalac, an environmental engineer and consultant. He has advised coffee farmers like Torres for his entire career, helping them adapt to the changing climate. "Normally, it shouldn't be raining," he tells me as it continues to pour down all around us in this mountain town. "It's a time when farmers are drying their coffee," he says. "Now the farmers are starting to dry the coffee in their yards. They usually dry it on concrete patios on the roofs of their houses, and when an unexpected rain comes, well, nobody is expecting a rain. And if it lasts more days it's worse. Then they can have considerable losses, even the complete loss of their crop."

There are other problems: it has been frosting over when the coffee plants flower, and the wind has been damaging them as well. As Torres told me, rust is perhaps the most significant. It's the extreme fluctuations in temperature from hot to cold, from dry to damp, that help the fungus grow. "All these changes have been increasing," Charchalac says. "We are a perfect example of the effects of climate change."

I'm struck by how similar this is to the story that I heard in Kenya: the weather is making earning a living harder, and this is sending people to cities. Whereas in Africa I had seen how this trend was fuelling growing megacities inside countries, here it was driving people abroad. This is because as migrants flood the cities, the labour supply increases and wages drop. So, to find a living wage, they look outside their home country. This climate-induced international migration is forecast to reach staggering proportions in the years to come. By 2050, there could be up to a billion climate refugees heading for the US and Europe.

This exodus is already under way here in Guatemala. Everywhere, I see shops selling "American clothes," posters advertising American visas, and homes and graves painted with the stars and stripes to show gratitude to the place where they had been able to earn a decent living. Even now, walking around the foothills along the roads, new buildings are being built, their concrete shells emerging from the ground as men with hard hats drill and hammer away. These buildings, Charchalac tells me, are paid for from the remittances from those living in America. And while these remittances have become crucial to the Guatemalan economy, they have also weakened it.

Charchalac drives me deep into Guatemala's northern countryside to San Mateo Ixtatán to demonstrate. The houses here are scattered up the hillside like the keys on a typewriter. The white clouds move around the buildings, some still concrete shells, others pastel shades of red and yellow. But the roads that wind around them are largely empty. The fact that these homes were built with money from America is what earned this town the nickname "Ghost Town New York."

One street is busy, however, as women in traditional woven dresses bring their children to the market. "People meet every fifteen days because every fifteen days remittances arrive through agencies," Charchalac says. "They do all the grocery shopping and have changed their way of eating, now they buy a lot of packed things, they have stopped producing vegetables, the normal food they made." Migration has crippled the local economy. "The ghost towns are communities where they stopped doing agricultural practices because there are no longer men to work," he says. There are no men for the women to marry. The towns atrophy. Those abroad see little reason to come back. They leave the houses they paid for unfinished or abandoned. "This is distorting what a normal society is," he says. Just as I had seen from Mosul to Donetsk to Caracas, the ones left behind are living fractured lives.

Climate change is a long-term trend. In Guatemala, the climate has been radically changing for two decades. Back in 2010, the Global Climate Risk Index declared it the second-most vulnerable country in the world. So why was 2019 the year that migrants surged to the US?

After all, climate change had been steadily pushing up the cost of production year after year. But then prices dropped suddenly in 2018. Farmers lost money on their crop. They couldn't pay back their loans, and hundreds of thousands left for the US in the hope that they could earn enough to get themselves out of debt and hold on to their land.

This just raised another question: why did the prices fall so spectacularly? When I delved into the research, the first story I found was the most popular: Brazil and Vietnam were producing more coffee, and this increase in supply was pushing down the coffee price. But, as I had learnt from Shiller and the food and oil price spikes throughout my journey, while such a story may be grounded in fundamentals, the narrative also amplifies its own effects, turning a small change in the real world into a large price shock. Indeed, just as coffee prices began to drop, the *Financial Times* noted that their downward turn was being driven by speculators:

> The coffee market is struggling under a "big short" created by hedge funds that have built up record bearish positions. Expectations of a record crop in Brazil, the world's largest producer, and high inventories among importing countries have been weighing on arabica, the higher-quality bean. Prices last week hit the lowest level in two years of 115.30 cents a pound in New York, and, although they have bounced back, they are trading well below the cost of production for many coffee farmers. Hedge funds and other speculators have been increasingly bearish on arabica since the middle of last year, astonishing many in the market. The position size was "extraordinary," said James Hearn, co-head of agricultural commodities at brokers Marex Spectron. "When is enough, enough?" he asked.

Economists have long found bubbles in the coffee market, where speculators have pushed prices away from fundamental supply and demand. In 2018, this story of a glut of global coffee created yet another bubble whereby hedge funds pushed the prices down further than they ought to have been. Unlike previous bubbles, however, that pushed up prices, this one sent them downwards. It was the same kind of negative bubble I had seen in 2014 when similar narratives of abundance—booming shale oil, increased Saudi production and declining demand from China—went viral. All these stories were rooted in reality, but the market machine amplified the change in price from a modest correction to a sharp and devastating shock.

The butterfly had finally returned to the US in the form of chaos on the border. It had started its journey nearly two decades before when the Clinton administration deregulated the commodities markets. Its wings had sent tsunamis of chaos to every corner of the globe, but it had never created a crisis inside the US itself. In 2018, that changed. By pushing down the coffee prices, speculators forced Guatemala, a country already on the edge, past its critical threshold. Climate change had been making the core of its economy more precarious, more fragile, more sensitive to even a small shock in the international price of its core commodity. The result was a predictable one: a surge in migrants looking for a wage to survive on.

Yet, as had happened during the global refugee crisis that rocked Europe in 2015–16, the images of The Feed did not feature the financial speculators who caused the chaos. Instead I saw photo-friendly "caravans" of migrants, foreign invaders marching menacingly towards the border and greeted as a new weapon in a long-standing domestic culture war. Trump used their arrival as evidence that America's immigration laws were too lax and needed to be toughened. Trump critics decried his cruelty theatre of locking kids in cages as evidence that the laws were not just tough, but inhumane. As had happened in Europe, the true cause of the migrant surge was left unnoticed and unexamined. Few understood that it had been triggered by prices, and that these prices were set by speculators residing in New York and London.

In Mexico, however, I discovered an entire economy finely attuned to the role of prices in this crisis, and to one price in particular: the price of people.

"He left his crops, his land, his house, he left everything," a Mexican *coyote* tells me of a recent client. "For his whole life, he had grown coffee to survive, but nowadays climate change has come to that Guatemalan region and the people are forced to leave. And this person told me, sad and crying, that he regretted having left his land and having to emigrate to the US, having been forced to emigrate and not knowing if his future would be good." The idea of migration as a price war was not news to the *coyotes*. "If people had the means to survive, if they had a minimum wage to meet their needs, they wouldn't have to emigrate." And he's seen for himself the surge in migrants in the last two years as they've sought out his services.

"We have to change their clothes, dress them properly, bathe them, for us to cross them safely, and teach them some Mexican mannerisms so they can speak for themselves when an authority passes by," the *coyote* says. "Sometimes we even dress them as our wives." He accompanies them on the buses and guides them through the checkpoints. But the most important thing that he does is pay the bribes. The cartels along the border are in disarray, and the Mexican National Guard and police have replaced them as the gatekeepers. "What we used to pay to the Zetas and the Gulf cartels who controlled that area, we now have to pay to the Mexican authorities."

He worries about those who cannot afford to hire *coyotes* like him to cross safely. Some hitch a ride on top of the freight train known as "the Beast," as Torres did with his son. "The Beast has been a crucifix to many migrants," the *coyote* says. "Many have fallen from that monster and become crippled here in Mexico." The migrants are also preyed upon by criminal gangs and the cartels. They're ideal for kidnapping as the families cannot appeal to the authorities. Women face the added risk of rape and being forced into sex work by the cartels.

The price of a *coyote* isn't cheap. He charges around $4,000 per person, with nearly half of that going towards bribes and expenses. It's not his main gig; he also works in construction, farming and plumbing, but trafficking people is how he can afford to support his family. He makes around $30,000 a year from it, but it also comes with great personal risk. He can get caught in wars between cartels, be targeted by smaller gangs, and of course by the Mexican

authorities. He receives frequent calls from military and police officers threatening to expose him unless he pays a bribe. Usually he can
just discard his phone and get another, but not always. "I'm a father,
I have children, I have a family, I have a home, and that worries me
too, because I don't want to orphan my children someday," he says.
"But I also have the need to work in this business, because we have
to support them, we have to survive. And the money, the minimum
wage here in Mexico is not enough to meet our needs, to meet our
expenses."

The *coyote*, like the migrants, was being told what to do by prices.
The price of coffee, the price of labour in Guatemala and Mexico,
the costs of buses and bribes and the wages Americans pay undoc-
umented migrants are all "telling people what they ought to do."
Together these prices form a spontaneous order that has coordinated
mass migration from Guatemala to the US. The alternative order,
one preferred by both Trump and Obama, where falling wages in
Central America lead to foreign investment taking advantage of the
cheap labour available there, has yet to arrive. It may, in the long
run, but most Central Americans do not have the luxury of waiting. It is far faster to mortgage one's land, hire a *coyote* and cross the
borders. The spontaneous order of human-trafficking emerges far
faster than fresh capital arrives from abroad. These economic forces
continue to overwhelm the feeble political obstacles put in their way.
"The United States will always need migrants and human traffick-
ing will be unstoppable," the *coyote* says. "Donald Trump's policy is
a joke. He won't be able to stop it."

"A few years ago I went to the Davos meeting for the World Economic Forum," recalls Robert Johnson, a former managing director
at Soros Fund Management and now the president of the Institute
for New Economic Thinking. "There was a lot of awareness that
extremes of inequality created a more socially unsustainable, fragile society, and anger at those who were the winners. Some people,
not in the forums, not in the panels, but at private dinners, were
saying, 'This is not on a stable trajectory. This is getting more and
more scary.'" What scared Johnson's dinner companions working

in private equity and hedge funds—"the kind of people who make more than a billion dollars a year"—was not climate catastrophes or impoverishment or starvation. It was that "many of these people knew that they would not be, how do we say, viewed benevolently in the event of a widespread social breakdown."

They saw the silhouettes of pitchforks forming on the horizon. "Their fear for their families or themselves led to an escape plan," Johnson says. Over these Davos dinners, he heard the Masters of the Universe exchanging advice on how best to insulate oneself from the oncoming mob. Some were building bunkers in their Connecticut mansions complete with large storerooms filled with "tradable" items such as razor blades and tampons, in case paper currency becomes worthless. Others were following Peter Thiel's lead and acquiring large tracts of land in New Zealand on which to build fortress compounds complete with their own airstrips. An ordinary private plane on the ready from San Francisco or New York was inadequate. They told Johnson that it was essential to have not just a private plane, but "large enough planes so the pilot could take his whole family." Nothing would be worse than arriving at one's Gulfstream only to be held hostage by the pilot demanding that his or her family fly to a safe haven, too. Not only did the planes need to accommodate two families, the compounds did as well.

What struck Johnson was their fatalism. The Masters seemed to accept that nothing could be done. Yet they were, after all, powerful people adept at bending their world to their will. "I was sad because I would like to see those with wealth and power exercise what I would call their stewardship in making society more broadly prosperous," Johnson says. "My feeling was it was a bit tragic for society, but actually even tragic for these people who, at a time when wealth is supposed to create a sense of freedom and possibility, were hunkering down. They were getting into the equivalent of a psychological bomb shelter. And at some level—and some of these people are my friends, they're my neighbours—I felt sad because I felt, 'God, you guys live in a haunted house.'"

It isn't just poor Guatemalan coffee farmers who find themselves fleeing the consequences of climate change and finance capitalism. It is, strangely, the supposed winners of this system too. They can see all too clearly the chaos at the heart of our economic system, as well as their own culpability in creating it. And yet, despite sitting quite literally in the comfort of the clouds, they too see their only option as a flight to safety. They too need help, their own *coyotes* to pilot their planes and whose price must be paid. The galactic inequality between those two kinds of migrants, however, is more than just wealth. The Guatemalans' journey is criminalised, pushing them into the hands of gangs and cartels, onto decapitating trains and into sexual slavery, and, for the lucky ones who make it to the American border, having one's children taken away and locked in cages.

For certain Masters of the Universe, chaos is not just something to escape from. It's a financial opportunity. "I think of safe havens as just being payoffs," says Mark Spitznagel, Chief Investment Officer of Universa Investments. "Some people think of it as a place that you hide away, but to me it's a payoff." He's not talking about a fortress in New Zealand, but an investment that hedges risk in the event of chaos erupting. When the markets cratered in 2008, for instance, his hedge fund won big. He, along with his "Distinguished Scientific Advisor" Nassim Taleb, had bet on such a catastrophic "black swan" coming home to roost. He spent his winnings buying Jennifer Lopez's Bel-Air mansion, located a stone's throw from his hero Ronald Reagan's home.

Spitznagel's safe haven is built with derivatives. "Derivatives are weapons of mass destruction," he says. "If you're on the other side of one of my trades, it is a weapon of mass destruction. On the other side," that is, Spitznagel's side, "it provides you a cushion or safety net in a crash." Most of the people with whom he's entering into these derivative bets fail to appreciate this. "The explosiveness means that it's there, but most of the time you don't even know that it's there. It's like holding a net underneath a high-wire act that you're doing. It's there for the extreme detrimental occurrence that happens infrequently. The explosiveness is important and is really what makes a black-swan hedge a black-swan hedge."

"I'm confused by your answer," I say, lost in the jargon. "Do you mean explosive in terms of the money that you make in a black-swan event, or are the black-swan events themselves explosive?"

"I mean the money that the hedge makes in a black-swan event. So, this tiny investment that you make explodes and wakes up and provides a tremendous amount of cushion in terms of return on capital during that painful event."

"But the events themselves are explosive?"

"They're explosive. We can talk about explosive as being negative explosive or positive explosive. They're meant to balance each other out. The positive explosiveness of the black-swan hedge is there to counteract the negative explosiveness happening in your portfolio during the black-swan event."

But what exactly is "exploding"? I press him on the real-world risks he's talking about. "You could think about risk in terms of idiosyncratic risks, so that's us pinpointing various idiosyncratic things that can go wrong and hurt us personally. Then you can think of risk as being more systemic, so that would be more like a financial crisis that would impact many things. Now of course, the latter sort of subsumes the former: when you have these systemic risks, you see all other things go awry and all these correlations, for instance, all of a sudden go awry and the world looks very different. So, you can hedge these idiosyncratic risks by hedging systemic risks."

In other words, the financial world is a house of cards, and we do not need to know which individual card will be the first to fall to know that the whole stack will eventually crumble. It is the collapse of this "systemic" house that Spitznagel bets on.

"To me, risk mitigation is about setting things up such that you're agnostic to how things work out because you've got a plan, you've got a contingency for everything," he says. It doesn't matter if there's a climate catastrophe, a pitchfork insurrection, or another unimagined "black-swan" disaster. He and his clients will weather the storm. "I'm more *amor fati*, in Nietzsche's words: you're happy with what your fate is, it doesn't matter how it turns out. That's kind of the goal here."

PART IV

IMAGININGS

10

Covid-19: The Climate–Finance Doomsday Device Detonates

24 February 2020 was the day I panicked. I was scrolling through The Feed on my phone when I saw images of empty supermarkets in Italy. They were the very same images that I had seen in Venezuela. I had seen the chaos that came with barren shelves: the queues, the hoarding, the speculation, the desperation. I also knew that whatever virus was in Italy would soon be in London. I went to my local supermarket to stock up. I texted my friends: the lockdown, the shortages, the empty shelves are coming for us next, and God knows what else. They didn't believe me. That's not going to happen *here*, they said. I told them that was the very same answer I had heard in Iraq, Ukraine and Venezuela when I asked why they had stuck around when the apocalyptic horsemen were riding towards them in plain sight. They always said the same thing. *I never thought that it would happen to us.*

I remembered Donald Rumsfeld in the documentary *The Unknown Known* blaming America's great failure to foresee the 9/11 or Pearl Harbor attacks on "failures of the imagination." Although he lacked the self-awareness to apply this to his own catastrophic record, his insight resonated. Even as a mushroom cloud forms before our eyes, we assume there must be a bubble to protect us from the incoming blast.

This protective bubble of "normality" had already been pierced by Ebola and SARS. We didn't need to imagine anything. Back in 2008, a report published in *Nature* warned that viruses once contained in animal populations were increasingly "spilling over" to humans.

Viruses that have long circulated among bats are now infecting humans through intermediary animals such as pigs, camels or pangolins. These "spill-over events" are increasing as the natural barriers between species are eroded. New cities, infrastructure and climate change are all forcing animals to migrate to new places, exposing them to new species. China is going through the fastest urbanisation in history. Bat habitats have been destroyed and once-isolated forests are criss-crossed with roads. Something was going to spill over there, and in the autumn months of 2019 something did: SARS-CoV-19.

By March 2020, the pandemic had triggered the very kind of climate–finance doomsday that the Bank of England governor, Mark Carney, had once prophesied. In 2015 he warned that "climate change could prompt increased morbidity and mortality from disease or pandemics" and bring chaos to the financial markets. And although we do not yet know with certainty the origins of Covid-19, it is precisely this kind of natural shock that our warming planet will bring. This is not because climate change invents new viruses—no more than it invented floods or droughts—but because it is making such outbreaks more likely, increasing their frequency, turning them into a normal feature of a world where the climate has changed. It is this fast-growing class of risks that Carney implored his audience of risk calculators to price into the markets. But despite his warnings, the financial markets were just as fragile in the face of such a shock from the natural world as they were in 2015.

The avalanche had begun. The cascading crisis tumbled from lockdowns to unemployment to unprecedented government interventions paid for by countries selling their US Treasury holdings, the bedrock of the global financial system. This sudden sell-off pushed the magical world of finance to the brink of collapse as real-world poverty and hunger soared. A financial implosion threatened to make the tsunami of human suffering not a passing wave but a decade-long deluge.

"Rich Americans Activate Pandemic Escape Plans," announced Bloomberg, "Interest in New Zealand bunkers has surged." Private jets were in short supply as the Masters of the Universe sought physical safety. Those who had invested in Mark Spitznagel's "Black Swan Protection Protocol" fund found themselves with a staggering 3,612 per cent return in March alone. His derivative bets had "exploded" again and gauged windfalls from rival speculators on the other side of his black-swan trade. "These returns likely surpass any other investment that you can think of over the period you have been invested with us," Spitznagel wrote to his investors on 7 April. "Kudos to you for such a sound 'tactical' allocation to Universa."

The war between hedge funds fed off and exacerbated the crisis, in just the way my investigation of the turbulent 2010s had revealed again and again. The constellation of a climate shock, the financial amplification machine, and the Masters' escape plans and profiteering had aligned. It felt like the natural—if apocalyptic—conclusion to the chaotic decade, and the end of my journey.

But one piece of the story didn't fit. Despite the very real economic pain felt by ordinary people throughout 2020, the climate–financial doomsday device that the Bank of England had predicted seemed paradoxically to have both detonated and not detonated. The financial markets had exploded, but there was no wave of financial destruction in the West.

I began to wonder if there was something about the global market maze that I didn't understand. After all, I had seen previous explosions overthrow governments, fund wars and create an exodus of refugees. But that only happened outside the financial capitals. It seemed like the global maze had a different architecture in the West. An architecture built from different rules.

To understand why the detonation failed to disrupt the world's financial centres, I delved into the market's "rules of the game," as Milton Friedman put it, and the "umpire[s]" who "interpret and enforce the rules decided on." I discovered that these umpires and their interpretations were far more powerful than the rules themselves: that their rulings decided whether or not economic bombs were allowed to detonate, and who would be caught up in the blast. I began by looking into the first time these rules were written down: after a climate shock four centuries ago.

—

"I hear new news every day, and those ordinary rumours of war, plagues, fires, inundations, thefts, murders, massacres, meteors, comets, spectrums, prodigies, apparitions, of towns taken, cities besieged in France, Germany, Turkey, Persia, Poland," Robert Burton wrote in *The Anatomy of Melancholy.* He was describing The Feed of 1638, a "vast confusion" that would come to him every day through books, pamphlets, *corantos* and gossip. He too was living in a tumultuous time: wars, famines, epidemics and other horrors were ravaging the world. Behind this chaos was a climatic shock—now recognised as the Little Ice Age—that had devastated harvests across the globe. For two decades, crops had frozen, flooded and failed to ripen. Prices spiked, famine followed, riots broke out, monarchs were overthrown and long, bloody wars raged. Refugees fled in search of food and safety, bringing whatever disease they had with them to new places. And, facing starvation, many ate "famine foods"—rotten or unripe grains—which, along with the hunger, created widespread ill health. The result was a global apocalypse of death and disease. A witch-burning craze swept Europe as people searched for scapegoats. It was no wonder that one refugee from this chaos, Thomas Hobbes, who had fled the English Civil War to seek safety in France, concluded that life had become "solitary, poor, nasty, brutish, short."

This was a time in many ways parallel to our own: a climatic shock which became a price shock that triggered an avalanche of cascading catastrophes. It is now called the "General Crisis of the Seventeenth Century." It was also the beginning of the price revolution that led to the chaotic decade we have just lived through. It was from these tumultuous times that the Enlightenment emerged, with Thomas Hobbes as one of its first and foundational thinkers. It marked both the high point of witch-burning in Europe but also the start of its demise. Perhaps throwing fit men and women on burning pyres wasn't helping after all. Maybe the cause of chaos isn't supernatural but material, a result of the way in which mankind is organising itself. Intellectuals began replacing superstition with science.

By the end of the seventeenth century, some had begun to recognise that prices were at the root of the problem, and wondered if prices could be part of the solution too. Because even as the Little Ice Age ended, the high prices persisted. From 1720, Europe's population swelled. Farms could barely produce enough to meet the growing demand. France, in particular, teetered on the edge of chaos. Even the smallest change in the weather could cause prices to spike and riots to break out. "Long live the king, provided that the price of bread diminishes!" a bystander shouted at a young Marie Antoinette on a promenade through Paris in July 1774. The outburst worried her, as neither the monarchy nor anybody else could control the weather. And she was right to worry; we saw earlier how it turned out for Marie and King Louis. But we skipped over the part where the king turned to a prominent civil servant, M. Turgot, for help. "Inform M. Turgot immediately that I appoint him Comptroller-General of my finances," Louis instructed his staff. "Let M. Turgot come see me tomorrow and bring with him the memoir on grains."

M. Turgot was the administrator of the French backwater province called Limousin, east of Bordeaux. The province had been struck by drought, famine and speculation in 1769. He wrote a series of letters (or "memoir") on the grain trade the following year. He was sharply critical of France's system of regulating the grain trade into a number of regional markets, as well as of the government's obligations to regulate the price of bread. Turgot imagined changing the medieval "rules of the game" that committed the king as "baker of last resort" to his people. Under his new rules, the social contract would be shredded and a new "policy of freedom" would free the market and let prices reign. The medieval regulations would be abolished, and grain would flow freely throughout France and beyond her borders. He imagined a system where a failed harvest would push up the price of grain and merchants across Europe, upon seeing these high prices, would hurry in with fresh supplies, feeding the locals and profiting at the same time. He imagined that stable prices should spur farms to be more productive, which, in the long term, would increase the total supply of grain and benefit workers. It was the birth of *laissez-faire*.

Turgot's ideas were the accumulation of seventy years of Enlightenment thinking on the dilemma of climate shocks, famine and the fate of the monarchy. These Liberals imagined that the chaos of the Hobbesian nightmare could be banished by the superior and stable rule of prices. *Laissez-faire* was fast becoming their foundational belief. Most famous of these Liberals was Adam Smith, whose *The Wealth of Nations* popularised free-market ideas among English speakers. In Joseph Schumpeter's *History of Economic Analysis*, however, it is Turgot, the less famous of the two, who is credited as the true innovator. Schumpeter makes this case because Turgot, unlike Smith, was a civil servant who had the opportunity to try out his ideas in practice.

In 1774, Turgot used his new powers to repeal government regulations and set the merchants free. Order didn't last long. In March 1775 riots broke out. The harvest had been weak, and prices soared. Desperate peasants banded together to raid bakeries, monasteries, granaries and merchants' homes for grain. They had no fear. "Starving or being killed meant the same thing to them," one onlooker wrote. As always, they appealed to the king as the baker of last resort, for his administrators to intervene, to sell bread at a responsible price, search for stores of grain and stop speculators from hoarding. On Turgot's instructions, these appeals were rebuffed. In April, 300 riots rocked the Paris Basin and in May a mob raided 1,200 bakeries in the capital. To combat the unrest, Turgot became a military commander, deploying troops to quell the protests. His "policy of freedom" had turned violent. A crowd of 8,000 confronted King Louis in Versailles. As Marie Antoinette wept that her husband had to cancel that day's hunting trip, the king promised cheap bread for Paris. Turgot was furious. He rescinded the king's command. Louis fired him. Turgot's imagined free-market utopia had clashed with reality. During the hostilities, the rioting public called it the *guerre des farines*: the flour wars. It was the first price war created by the free market.

Louis XVI never did solve France's grain problem. When poor weather arrived in 1787, food prices rose and, on their highest day, Revolutionaries stormed the Bastille and before long his reign was over. It wouldn't be until well into the nineteenth century that Turgot's vision was fully realised on the global scale he had imagined.

The invention of the steamboat and the telegraph made international markets possible, and the British Empire used her imperial might to make it a reality.

Turgot appeared vindicated: free trade meant that grain would flow to where its price was highest, which usually meant the industrial urban centres of Europe. London saw the greatest drop in price as supply surged. Wheat prices in the capital fell by 35 per cent between 1870 and 1913. Enjoying the cheap imports from abroad, workers saw their real incomes rise. Socialist parties in Britain, Germany, Belgium, Italy and Switzerland became champions of free trade. A British Labour Party leaflet declared that tariffs were "to the advantage of the 'protected' capitalist, but to the injury of the worker." Turgot's free market had finally brought order to Europe. The chaos of the eighteenth-century price wars was over. Famines were a distant memory. Prices reigned.

In India, however, Turgot's utopia was struggling to be born. The subcontinent had joined the global market in 1869 with the opening of the Suez Canal. Yet famines weren't disappearing but becoming more frequent, more severe. The viceroy of the British Raj, Lord Northbrook, paid for grain imports to avert famine in 1873. Catastrophe was averted. There were only twenty-three recorded deaths. His successor, Lord Lytton, chose a less costly approach when famine struck again in 1876. "Turgot conceived, developed, and, in the face of great opposition, carried into effect views no less identical with those which have guided our own action," the new viceroy said. The government would not buy grain from abroad. Instead, Indian labourers would be forced to pay into a famine-relief fund to subsidise the construction of railways to facilitate the grain trade. Lord Lytton imagined that "India will eventually enjoy as complete an immunity from the worst results of scarcity as that which now exists throughout those regions of France where but a century ago such a result might have seemed as difficult of attainment as it now appears to be in many of our own provinces."

Instead, millions died; estimates vary between 5.5 million and 10 million. The road to Madras "bore almost the appearance of a battlefield," a British journalist wrote at the time, "its side being strewed with the dead, the dying, and those recently attacked." This "battlefield" was a new kind of price war: one that Turgot hadn't counted on. By creating a global market, labourers in India were now competing with labourers in London for the same wheat supply. Londoners' higher wages meant they could always pay more. The prices in London were always higher than in Bombay, Madras or Delhi, so that is where the grain went. The railways just made it cheaper for merchants to get the grain out of India to Europe. The free market was working, just as it was intended to. It just wasn't working to feed Indians.

This period of calamitous British Liberal rule became known as the "Age of Famines and Epidemics." Just as had happened during the General Crisis of the Seventeenth Century, Indians resorted to "famine food" and migration to survive, which, combined with overall malnutrition, created epidemics of diarrhoea, cholera and smallpox. The very Enlightenment ideas that were supposed to prevent such a Hobbesian nightmare from returning had in fact orchestrated a brand-new one on a continental scale. India suffered twenty major food crises between 1869 and 1910, killing between 18 million and 22 million people. In every year, India exported grain to Europe.

In 1914 the rule of prices unravelled. The First World War halted global trade. Britain was the world's largest importer of wheat, and when German U-boats aggressively targeted those shipments in 1916, the island nation was nearly starved into submission. The aftermath of the Great War was no less chaotic. European nations battled each other with trade wars. In 1924, the rising British intellectual John Maynard Keynes declared the "end of *laissez-faire*." Whatever was left of nineteenth-century Liberalism was soon decimated by the Wall Street crash of 1929 and the Great Depression that followed. Keynes saw how political chaos—wars, revolutions, fascists and communists—arose from economic chaos and he sought to provide a new framework for stability. At its centre was the need for full employment, the key ingredient for peace and prosperity. He advocated that it was imperative that the government intervene in the economy to ensure that everyone who wanted a job could get one.

The Second World War fundamentally changed the relationship between the citizen and the state. The Allied states had proved that they were capable of coordinating the economy to win the war. People did not have to imagine government providing jobs and bread for all; it had already just done it. And, having made great sacrifices for the nation, citizens expected the state to continue to provide these basic necessities. A new social contract emerged, one that would protect people from the volatile prices that had upended their lives in the decades before. It was not just in the West; revolutionary leaders leading independence movements against the colonial powers also promised to end the rule of prices. Whether it was Nehru's "Nationalism" in India or Nasser's "Arab Socialism" in Egypt, these revolutionaries used a mixture of food subsidies and wage guarantees to ensure that food would never again be too expensive. Politicians across the world looked to Keynes and a cabal of emerging "Keynesian" economists to fulfil the promise of these new social contracts. The rules of the game for economics—and the political possibilities they allowed—had changed for the West and much of the non-communist world.

Some, however, were unhappy with the Keynesian consensus. They were a motley bunch. There was Friedrich Hayek. He was born at the peak of the Austro-Hungarian Empire only to come of age as it crumbled, reduced to a resourceless and landlocked state. He imagined a new economic empire modelled on the empire of his youth, one with a "double government"—a federation enforcing Liberal free trade while delegating cultural issues to the subordinated individual states. Then there was Arthur Burns, a conservative economist at Columbia University who styled himself as Keynes's foremost American critic. One of his eager students was the young Alan Greenspan. He was called "the undertaker" by his hero, Ayn Rand, whose cult, "The Collective," instilled in him a lifelong objection to the very idea of government itself. It was in Burns's classes at Columbia where Greenspan learnt the economic rationale for his libertarian philosophy: "Excess government spending produces inflation." Milton Friedman was another of Burns's students, and Burns would later award him a grant to write his first book.

This group often fought and disagreed with one another. But what united them was their opposition to the post-war social contracts. The foundational text of their movement was Hayek's *The Road to Serfdom*, which radicalised Friedman from an academic economist to a political crusader. Hayek argued that the new social provisions the state guaranteed to ordinary people in the form of jobs and food may appear benign and beneficial. But the state would be forced to grow and grow, until the power of the individual disappeared and the populace was reduced to "serfs." To stop this inevitable slide to totalitarianism, it was necessary to return to the free-market principles of nineteenth-century Liberalism. This is why they called themselves "Neo-Liberals." Friedman imagined erasing the social contracts completely, and shrinking the provisions offered by the state to those that Lord Lytton had provided in imperial India. "[A]t the height of the British empire," Friedman said, "British government expenditure was 10 per cent of the national income . . . I've come to the conclusion that 10 per cent must be a pretty good number."

There was little interest in these utopian imaginings. The global economy was booming. Keynesian government interventions had cured the disease of mass unemployment that had rocked the world between the world wars. Deadly famines and pandemics had vanished from India. In 1965, *Time* magazine made Keynes its "Man of the Year." "Today, some 20 years after his death, his theories are a prime influence on the world's free economies," *Time* wrote. "In Washington, the men who formulate the nation's economic policies have used Keynesian principles not only to avoid the violent cycles of pre-war days but to produce a phenomenal economic growth and to achieve remarkably stable prices . . . We are all Keynesians now."

Prosperity eluded some. Salvador Allende was elected President of Chile in 1970 on a socialist platform. Soon there was economic chaos and runaway inflation, culminating in his overthrow in a *coup d'état* by General Augusto Pinochet. In a lecture in 1976, Milton Friedman trotted out the argument he had read in Hayek's *Road to Serfdom*, about how social spending escalates to totalitarian communism.

"The Government incessantly spread its influence giving rise eventually to the Allende regime, which threatened to bring about totalitarian rule of the left. The subsequent economic and social chaos led to a military takeover by the Junta which now governs Chile." At the heart of this economic chaos was government spending itself: Chile "reached a level of spending that came to be so large that it was impossible to finance it without producing substantial inflation." This is not, Friedman stresses, what any politicians wanted. "The downfall of freedom in Chile did not arise because evil people tried to do evil. The downfall of freedom in Chile arose from good people trying to do good, but trying to do good in the wrong way."

What Friedman neglects to mention is the US's economic war against Allende and the CIA's involvement in the Pinochet coup. When Allende was elected, President Richard Nixon told his staff that he wanted "a plan to make the economy scream." Kissinger obliged. A host of economic weapons were deployed: Chilean bank accounts were frozen, access to dollar credit was cut off, its exports were blocked not just to the US but to Europe as well, food shipments were cancelled and crucial manufacturing parts needed for the country's mining industry were embargoed. (It is, I recognised, the same playbook Trump would deploy against "socialist" Venezuela in 2017.) The economic chaos that resulted was not because of "good men trying to do good" but a foreign power set on destroying a regime cursed with an abundance of copper. Copper which had been mined by American companies until Allende nationalised them. Chile was the victim of a geopolitical price war, an economic shock created by American interests, not domestic economics. Yet this argument, that social spending causes inflation and inflation leads to chaos, would become a crucial narrative in the years to come, especially when another economic war broke out, this time across the entire world.

It started at 2 p.m. on Yom Kippur, 1973, when Egyptian and Syrian jets roared across Israel's border as its troops and artillery opened fire below. It was the start of the fourth Arab—Israeli War and the Israelis were on the defensive. Saudi Arabia warned President Nixon not to send supply planes to their beleaguered ally. "Goddamn it, send everyone we have," Nixon instructed Kissinger, "tell them to send everything that can fly!!" This was another Cold War proxy war: the Soviets were backing the Arab states and the US supported Israel. Saudi Arabia's warning, however, was not an idle threat. The US had just begun to import oil for the first time and Saudi Arabia led the newly confident oil cartel, OPEC. The question loomed over the White House: would OPEC use the "oil weapon" to win the war? The global economy was at stake. "We have to get the bloody Saudi [ambassador] in," Kissinger told his chief deputy. "I want to keep them from doing something crazy." The Saudi ambassador didn't meet with Kissinger. Within days, OPEC doubled the oil price. The next month they doubled it again. "We shall ruin your industries as well as your trade with the Arab World," Muammar Gaddafi, the thirty-one-year-old "Revolutionary Chairman" of Libya, said. "We are determined to hit America."

Kissinger was facing the very same economic warfare from OPEC that he had deployed against Chile three years before. Fearing shortages, Americans swamped their gas stations. Lines mushroomed, tensions rose. Gas attendants were run over, some were killed. "These people are like animals foraging for food," one gas-station dealer said. "If you can't sell them gas, they threaten to beat you up, wreck your station, and run you over with a car." Inflation soared. Nixon's America began looking like Allende's Chile. Stock markets around the world suffered the biggest crash since 1929. The global economy cratered.

Keynes's toolbox stopped working. Inflation and unemployment were rising at the same time. This was unprecedented. A new word had to be invented for it: "stagflation." It seemed immune to Keynes's prescriptions. "Economists are distinctly in a period of re-examination," the legendary Keynesian economist Walter Heller confessed at the end of 1973. "There are many things we really just don't know."

The Keynesian crisis was Friedman's opportunity. He repeated the same script he had used on Chile. "Inflation is produced in Washington, and it is produced by government," he said. "[T]he government blames inflation on Arab sheiks who raise the price of oil or on trade union leaders," he continued. "All of those are excuses and scapegoats. None has anything important to do with inflation."

It was a seismic change in thinking, but politicians across the political spectrum were desperate to end the chaos. In fact, politicians from the very same parties who had enacted the post-war social contracts were the first to abandon them and the economics that made them possible. "We used to think that you could spend your way out of recession," the British Labour prime minister, James Callaghan, said in 1976. "I tell you in all candour that that option no longer exists." Callaghan had come to believe that Friedman was right and government spending only created inflation. He abandoned the socialist platform he ran on. Jimmy Carter was next. He quashed the Congressional Democrats' plans for a government job guarantee and universal health care. He fought to cut back spending and balance the budget. He deregulated the airlines, trucking and finance.

The foundation of the social contracts that had shielded ordinary people from the rule of prices had fractured. People were told that the security they enjoyed was no longer sustainable, that it had to be subordinated to a high power: the need to control inflation. It appeared that Friedman's prophecy had come true. Government spending—on job creation, welfare, food and fuel subsidies—would all have to be sacrificed to appease this vengeful god. A new orthodoxy emerged in which deficits were demonised as the ultimate evil.

Strangely, it didn't seem to matter that it wasn't true. The onset of stagflation did not correlate to rising deficits or increased government spending. It had struck the advanced economies of the US, Western Europe and Japan simultaneously in 1973 and 1979—the two "oil-shock" years of the Arab–Israeli War and the Iranian Revolution. High oil prices fed inflation because the price of oil was factored into almost everything: from the costs of transporting goods, to powering factories and machines, to being a chemical ingredient in plastics and fertilisers. Keynes's prescriptions failed because they worked by manipulating demand: tinkering with government spending to control growth and inflation. Soaring oil prices was a supply shock imported from foreign economies over which domestic policymakers had little influence. That's why when oil prices declined in 1983, so too did inflation across the advanced economies simultaneously. Deficits had nothing to do with it. Indeed, under Ronald Reagan the federal deficit soared and inflation declined. Yet the notion that deficits create inflation stuck.

Friedman's theory would shape what was considered imaginable across the world for decades to come. It cemented the new rules of the game: rules that would define the relationship between the state and society, between capital and labour. Yet, in implementing these rules, Friedman's followers faced a persistent problem. The rules were unpopular. Cutting deficits usually meant gutting the post-war social contract. Turgot was empowered by an absolute monarch to enact his free-market experiment. Similarly, no Indian had ever voted for Lord Lytton; he was installed by imperial rulers thousands of miles away. Carter and Callaghan had moved in Friedman's direction, but neither was popular, nor had they brought the public around to their approach. But no matter. Soon, democratic politics would itself be marginalised. Prime ministers and presidents found themselves "dominated" by forces outside their control— forces that would bury the post-war social contracts and let prices reign once more.

"I have a young wife, I need the capital," Walter Wriston, the chairman of Citibank, explained as he turned down the position of US Treasury Secretary in 1974. And his bank was certainly acquiring a lot of capital. Citibank's branches in Saudi Arabia were the envy of Wall Street. Wriston not only attracted the oil windfall that OPEC's eye-watering prices were generating, he also found eager borrowers in the developing world, and Latin America in particular. These countries needed to borrow US dollars because their rapidly rising oil-import bills were priced in US dollars. Citibank led a stampede of British and American banks taking OPEC's new dollars as deposits and lending them out to the Third World. It was tremendously profitable business: soon half of Citibank's profits came from these loans. "Countries can't go bust," Wriston said.

But they could. In 1976, Peru was in trouble. The government couldn't pay the interest on the loans. The banks panicked. What if the countries began defaulting on their debts? It could bring down not just the banks but the entire American financial system. Arthur Burns, the anti-Keynesian conservative who taught Friedman and Greenspan, was now the chairman of the Federal Reserve. He came to Wall Street's rescue and pledged to restore order. "We need to develop the rule of law in this field, and the only instrument for this is the IMF," he said in February 1977. "Unless we have the rule of law, we will have chaos." The IMF would become the worldwide debt enforcer for the British and American banks.

This, Burns argued, would be for everybody's benefit. "Bankers are not alone in wanting to see countries in deficit pursue adjustment policies more diligently," Burns said. "This interest, in fact, is widely shared by economists and other thoughtful citizens who see an urgent need for healthier and more prosperous economic conditions around the world. The interests of the international economy and of private lenders thus converge and point to the need for a much more active role by the Fund." He acknowledged that their crushing debts came from OPEC's extortionate oil prices, but nevertheless, he continued, these countries "are going to have to practice some fiscal and monetary restraint, either of their own volition or because they find it obligatory to do so." Translation: indebted countries would have to pay back banks in New York or London no matter what. The loans would not be renegotiated at the expense of the banks and their shareholders. If that meant crippling austerity measures, the gutting of the welfare state and breaking their social contracts, so be it. Burns was writing the new rules of the game, rules that aligned financial interests with conservative austerity.

When the second oil shock came in 1979 with the Iranian Revolution, the new chairman of the Federal Reserve, Paul Volcker, aggressively hiked US interest rates to fight rising inflation. By 1982, interest rates had risen to 20 per cent. Anyone with a loan in US dollars faced crippling interest payments. That included many developing countries who had borrowed dollars from Citibank and other

Wall Street firms to pay for their US dollar–dominated oil imports. They couldn't service the loans. It triggered the global default known as the Third World Debt Crisis.

In country after country, the IMF stepped in to restore order just as Burns had imagined. The IMF demanded that the national budget be slashed along with job guarantees and subsidies to food and fuel. As the social contracts were torn up, political chaos broke out. Between 1976 and 1992, there were 146 major anti-austerity riots. Most were violently repressed, but many regimes were toppled or fatally weakened. The governments of Peru, Brazil, Argentina, Mexico, Jamaica, Venezuela, Philippines, Panama, Sudan and Haiti were eventually either voted out or overthrown. Bread riots engulfed the Middle East: they led to the downfall of Sudan's government and crippled Bourguiba's regime in Tunisia. As the IMF imposed Friedman's "Neo-Liberalism" on these nations, the price wars of nineteenth-century Liberalism returned.

The embattled politicians tried to reinstate the social contracts, to bring back the subsidies the IMF had forced them to cut. Even those who were successful rarely returned the provisions in full. Everywhere they were cut, compromised or abolished. This is because the IMF installed a fundamental check against the governments inside those governments. Its "structural-adjustment" programmes demanded that the government's existing central bank be made "independent" from politicians' orders. At the time, central banks were integrated into the government machinery of individual nations and were used to finance infrastructure and development projects and to secure full employment. But now these newly independent central banks served a single mandate: to fight inflation and ensure "price stability."

Under the new rules, central banks were to be pure expressions of technocratic power: ignoring the will of the electorate or even a populist dictator in order to keep inflation in check and, by doing that, inspire the confidence of the market. And since, as Friedman had argued, government spending creates inflation, then government spending—and the welfare state—had to be curtailed. The post-war social contracts were simply economically unsound and must be relegated to the realm of the unimaginable. "There is No Alternative" became the mantra of the day. And, should governments try to deny the "unpleasant arithmetic" of economic reality, then central bankers could serve as benevolent umpires by punishing them through raising interest rates, thus cutting growth and making borrowing more expensive.

The advocates of this radical new social arrangement called it "monetary dominance." Hayek had dreamt of a "double government" like this, an economic federal union that dominated subordinate "cultural" states. But in the arrangement now emerging, the "double government" existed inside the state itself: central bankers set the rules the formal government had to play by. The globalisation of this government inside the government was sometimes coerced by the IMF, but often it was embraced enthusiastically by politicians such as Tony Blair and Gordon Brown who, upon their election in 1997, voluntarily gave up control of the Bank of England. They sincerely believed that the newly empowered technocrats would hold down inflation and encourage investment, and that economic prosperity would follow.

There was, however, an unexpected critic of this arrangement: Milton Friedman. He had never believed in the enlightened rule of technocrats or government officials: he called for the IMF to be abolished and the chairman of the Federal Reserve to be replaced by a computer. He found the idea of an "independent" central bank an anathema, that "in a democracy to have so much power concentrated in a body free from any kind of direct, effective political control" was dangerous. He believed that this body would be captured by interest groups, especially by the financial sector from which such banker-administrators were sure to be drawn. They would not be neutral umpires of the market. Indeed, he saw the IMF's loans to indebted countries as just covert subsidies to Wall Street. "Banks made loans to the debtor countries at terms they considered profitable, taking full account of the risks involved," Friedman wrote in *Newsweek*. "Had all gone well, they would have reaped the profits.

If any loans go sour, the banks (i.e., their stockholders) should bear the loss, not the taxpayers." Friedman's imagined utopia of a truly neutral free market was slipping away.

"I've been governor of a small state for twelve years," a boyish Bill Clinton said during the 1992 presidential debate. "I see middle-class people whose services have gone down while the wealthy have gotten tax cuts. When people lose their jobs, there is a good chance I know them by their name. If the factory closes, I know the people who ran it." This was his empathetic "I feel your pain" pitch to a nation sliding into recession. He presented himself as a populist to win back the Reagan Democrats. At the centre of his campaign was a 10 per cent tax cut for the middle class. It was "The economy, stupid."

His victory met with a frosty reception on Wall Street. Bond traders began selling US Treasuries, causing the long-term interest rate on government debt to rise. The French president, François Mitterrand, had suffered such a speculative "attack" by bond traders in 1983 and it forced him to abandon his socialist programme in favour of market-friendly policies. That year, a Wall Street economist named Edward Yardeni christened them the "bond vigilantes" for their extra-judicial good works. He later explained that should a government pursue inflationary spending, "the vigilantes can step in to restore law and order to the markets and the economy." Now they had their sights on Clinton, an economic populist and the first Democratic president since 1981.

There was panic in the air. Fed chairman Alan Greenspan went to the president-elect in Arkansas. The price of these bonds, he explained, could seal the fate of his presidency. While the Federal Reserve set short-term interest rates, the long-term interest rates paid on mortgages, car loans and business loans were determined by the bond traders. If Clinton wanted the economy to grow, he needed to keep the long-term interest rate low, and that meant winning their confidence. These traders believed, like Greenspan and Arthur Burns did, that government borrowing caused inflation, and if inflation wasn't kept in check the president would lose their confidence. Greenspan told Clinton that he had no choice but to cut spending, balance the budget and appease the bond traders. If he did, interest rates would fall and the economy would boom, but if he didn't, then the vigilantes would force interest rates up, sparking recession. Greenspan presented himself as a neutral technocrat and the president's personal economics coach: these were just the Hard Facts of Economic Life, the rules of the game he'd have to play by. Clinton would have to shrink his imagination. There was no alternative.

Clinton's team was divided. Robert Reich and James Carville encouraged Clinton to stick to his populist promise to the middle class. "I always ask the question: why does a dog lick his dick?" Carville said to Clinton. "Because he can. Why don't we balance the budget? Because we can't." To this political operative, Greenspan's aspirations were politically absurd. But the rest of Clinton's team sided with Greenspan. "We help the bond market," Clinton said in frustration, "and we hurt the people who voted us in." Any objections that Reagan and Bush ran enormous budget deficits to finance the military and issue tax cuts without meeting the wrath of the bond vigilantes were ignored. Greenspan won. He helped Clinton's team draft the next budget and personally oversaw the cuts. "I used to think that if there was reincarnation, I wanted to come back as the president or the pope or as a .400 baseball hitter," Carville lamented. "But now I would like to come back as the bond market. You can intimidate everybody."

When Clinton heard that the bond markets responded positively to his pivot from populism, he went on TV to boast that he had won over "the most conservative and skeptical critics of all, those who run our financial markets." In a case of ideological Stockholm Syndrome, Clinton embraced his captors. "It's a wonderful time to be a bond trader," the *New York Times* reported. Clinton is "enamoured of the bond market in ways that no recent President has been." The financial markets had gone from being a profound limitation on his imagination to the fuel for it. The day after the World Trade Center was bombed in 1993, most were wondering who had carried out this unusual attack—the Iranians? The Serbians? Pablo Escobar? But Clinton had another thing on his mind. He turned to a *Wall Street Journal* reporter and asked: will the bond market be affected?

From then on, Clinton did everything in his power to empower the markets. He signed the North American Free Trade Agreement, gutted welfare and, with Greenspan's personal help, deregulated the derivatives markets and removed restrictions on the size of investment banks. It was an incredible testament to "monetary dominance" over the popular will. In addition to influencing elected lawmakers, Greenspan had his own levers of power. He aggressively cut interest rates, throwing fuel on the fire of the rocketing stock market. And every time the financial markets faltered, Greenspan would cut rates and reinflate them. It became known on Wall Street as the "Greenspan put option," finance-speak for effectively guaranteeing a price: namely, the price of financial assets. He continued the policy of his mentor Arthur Burns: letting prices reign for ordinary people, while the Fed would intervene for finance.

Greenspan is often cast as the "maestro" or the "wizard"—a singular force who remade American capitalism. But the more I looked into central bankers across the world, the less remarkable Greenspan became. In fact, researchers have found mini-Greenspans everywhere. Like him, they used their "monetary dominance" over elected politicians to force market deregulation, subsidies for finance and cuts to government spending. But not just any spending: specifically spending by left-wing governments, spending that redistributed wealth, tried to correct inequalities and provide basic economic security. Just as Greenspan and the bond vigilantes had tolerated Reagan and Bush Sr. running up enormous deficits to fund the Pentagon, so too did central bankers in seventy-eight countries tolerate borrowing by right-wing governments. When left-wing governments came to power, the bankers raised interest rates to slow down the economy and make borrowing more expensive, which, combined, starved them of cash to spend on social programmes. Greenspan's disciplining of Clinton's early left-wing populism was the global norm.

Central bankers were not behaving as impartial umpires solely concerned with fighting inflation. They interpreted the rules of the market game to the advantage of finance, favouring conservative austerity budgets and undermining left-wing governments. They had been captured, exactly as Friedman had feared in 1962, by the interests of the financial firms that staffed them. The rotating door between private banks and central banks oriented these banker-bureaucrats to their past and future employers. Alan Blinder, Greenspan's deputy at the Fed and a lifelong academic, acknowledged that even those uninterested in a Wall Street career still looked to please the financial markets. "Central bankers are only human," Blinder said, "they want to earn high marks—from whomever is handing out the grades . . . the markets provide a kind of giant biofeedback machine that monitors and publicly evaluates the central bank's performance in real time. So central bankers naturally turn to the markets for instant evaluation—or have the evaluation thrown in their faces." Central-bank independence means "independence" from democratic politics, not from the markets they are supposed to govern.

In 2008, the housing market crashed and Greenspan's world collapsed. His personal crusade to deregulate derivatives and prop up asset prices by slashing interest rates had fuelled the real-estate bubble. The most prominent central banker in the world had failed to deliver the only thing he was supposed to deliver: "price stability." Barack Obama won a landslide victory by daring the American people to have the audacity to imagine a better future. His slogan was "Yes We Can."

Shortly after the votes were tallied, Peter Orszag visited the president-elect in Chicago. Orszag was a veteran Democratic economist, having served on Clinton's Council of Economic Advisers. He came to visit his new boss to deliver the same talk about the Hard Facts of Economic Life that Greenspan had delivered to Clinton in Arkansas almost exactly sixteen years earlier. He told Obama that if he drove up the deficit, inflation would rise, the bond vigilantes would attack, and another recession would ensue. It was an extraordinary statement: the global economy was crashing, unemployment was soaring, prices were falling, inflation was nowhere in sight.

George W. Bush had just run up deficits to pay for wars and tax cuts and there was no bond-vigilante strike, no inflation, no spike in interest rates. Yet Orszag's message was the same: Obama would have to rein in his imagination. The markets would tell him: No He Can't.

As the Financial Crisis unfolded, governments across the world—regardless of their beliefs about deficits—faced a blunt choice: bail out the banks or risk a Great Depression. Overnight, governments borrowed sums not seen since the Second World War to absorb bank losses. Deficits everywhere ballooned. Yardeni, the famed economist of the bond vigilantes, warned that a speculative attack was coming and interest rates would be forced to rise. Orszag prepared to battle the bond vigilantes.

Only the assault never came. The Federal Reserve and the Bank of England simply bought up their own government's debt. The bond traders were apoplectic: the central banks had replaced them. They were outgunned. Their mantra became "Don't Fight the Fed." It is "next to impossible for the vigilantes to ply their trade," Yardeni complained. This trick wasn't new. The Federal Reserve had bought bonds to control the long-term interest rates during the world wars. The Bank of Japan did it in 2002 and gave it its awkward, literally translated name: quantitative easing.

People struggled to understand what was happening. The markets, which for decades had pushed around governments, were suddenly neutered. When Fed chairman Ben Bernanke appeared on *60 Minutes*, the interviewer was perplexed at how the Hard Facts of Economic Life could be suspended so easily. "The banks have accounts with the Fed, much the same way you have an account in a commercial bank," Bernanke explained, "so to lend to the bank we simply use the computer to mark up the size of the account they have with the Fed. It's much more akin—although not exactly the same—it's much more akin to printing money than it is to borrowing." In other words, Bernanke pressed a button and the money appeared. This money could buy government debt or worthless mortgage-backed securities. Indeed, as Greenspan himself had explained in his showdown with Brooksley Born in 1998, the benefit of financial products is that they do not exist in the real world. "Government securities," he said, "are being continuously replenished." They are just pieces of paper or pixels on a computer screen. Greenspan had just chosen never to do the replenishing, to press the button as Bernanke had done. If the Wall Street speculators were the Masters of the Universe, the central bankers were the Masters of the Masters of the Universe. Deficit spending had been possible all along.

European Central Bank president Jean-Claude Trichet, however, did not cooperate with the EU's elected governments in the way that the Bank of England and the Federal Reserve had done. Instead, he played a game of brinkmanship: demanding austerity in return for pushing the money button. In the summer of 2011, his finger hovered above it as he watched the so-called vigilantes wreak havoc on the struggling Eurozone countries. The sell-off priced Italian sovereign debt as even riskier than Egypt's, which was in the midst of the Arab Spring revolutions. He sent secret ransom notes to the premiers of Italy, Ireland and Spain; the one to the Italian prime minister, Silvio Berlusconi, was leaked to the press. In it, Trichet demanded "large-scale privatizations," "balanced budget in 2013, mainly via expenditure cuts," cuts to pensions, the weakening of unions, "reducing wages" of public-sector employees, "automatic deficit-reducing clause should be introduced," and they should bypass the democratic process and enact them "as soon as possible with decree-laws" to be followed by "constitutional reform tightening fiscal rules" further insulating them from democratic accountability. The Eurozone debt crisis was a crisis of choice, and it only ended once the integrity of the euro itself was threatened. "The role of bond markets in relation to the ECB and the dominant German government was less that of a freewheeling vigilante, than of state-sanctioned paramilitaries delivering a punishment beating whilst the police looked on," writes Adam Tooze, a leading economic historian at Columbia University.

The Bank of England governor, Sir Mervyn King, made similar public threats ahead of the 2010 election in the UK when he declared that "fiscal policy too will have to change," to develop a "clear plan to show how prospective deficits will be reduced." He didn't need to release his paramilitaries because an ally to austerity, David Cameron, won the election. Obama joined him. In January 2010, Obama declared in his second State of the Union address that reducing the deficit took priority over jobs. And in 2014, once Wall Street ceased to benefit from quantitative easing, Bernanke took his finger off the money button while unemployment remained historically high.

Wall Street, the City of London and the central bankers got their way. The banks were saved, the stock market soared once more, austerity reigned and wages remained depressed. But this victory had come at a great cost. The central bankers had been forced to show their hand: they were in charge and the bond vigilantes were nothing more than a paramilitary force at their disposal. The central bankers had shown, too, that they were not politically neutral, technocratic economists delivering the Hard Truths. And their central job, "price stability," to fight a war against inflation, was antiquated. Inflation had not been a problem for decades. Nor had the enormous rise in deficit spending led to a spike in interest rates or to another recession, as Orszag had warned Obama and Greenspan had warned Clinton. Despite record borrowing, interest rates hovered around zero. The "unpleasant arithmetic" that drove the dismantling of the post-war social contracts no longer added up. Voters across the West were beginning to wonder if there was an alternative: if they could again imagine a scenario where the governments sought to boost wages rather than the profits of financiers.

By 2016, there were plenty of characters—many of them quite literally unimaginable even at the time—who were promising to do just that. On the left, Bernie Sanders and Jeremy Corbyn promised to bring back the post-war social contracts their parties had abandoned in the mid-1970s. Trump promised to fight a trade war with China to bring back well-paying manufacturing jobs to the Midwest. Boris Johnson and Nigel Farage claimed that leaving the EU would reduce immigration, boost wages and bring down the high cost of living.

This pivotal moment collided with chaos created by the other bubbles Greenspan had unleashed in the commodities markets.

These lesser-known bubbles, the bubbles I spent two years following around the world, would be instrumental in determining which of these futures voters would pick. When the chaos returned to the West as the global refugee crisis, it was the populist right whose imagined future resonated. The anger with austerity, with globalist banks and condescending elites collided with images in The Feed of outside "invaders." Trump did start a trade war and Johnson did leave the EU. But they also integrated their administrations into the world of finance, both appointing former Goldman Sachs bankers to run their Treasuries. Prices still reigned.

"I think that's a problem that's going to go away," Trump said at a press conference in New Delhi on 25 February 2020. The novel coronavirus was spreading, and a pandemic seemed inevitable. "But we lost almost 1,000 points yesterday on the market, and that's something." Just as Bill Clinton had responded to the World Trade Center bombing by asking how the bond market was doing, Trump too was seeing the crisis through the prism of prices. When Greenspan's deputy, Alan Blinder, remarked that central bankers graded their performance by market moves, he was describing a distortion in the governing elite's imagination that stretched well beyond the technocrats all the way to Trump. His administration prioritised the markets over public health: they blocked early efforts to organise mass testing and purchase ventilators because they worried that such headlines would "spook the markets." When the state governors ordered lockdowns, Trump pushed back hard to reopen the economy as soon as possible. "Today, as you probably saw, the Dow surged over 2,100 points," he said at a White House briefing on 23 March. "I think a very big part of it is they see that we want to get our country opened as soon as possible."

Trump wasn't alone. His populist brethren agreed. On 3 February, Boris Johnson railed against nations needlessly locking down their economies to deal with the overblown threat of Covid-19. Britain would take no such measures and, when the phoney crisis ended, would be uniquely positioned to "take off its Clark Kent spectacles and leap into the phone booth and emerge with its cloak flowing as the supercharged champion." Privately, his Svengali Dominic Cummings described the government's strategy as: "herd immunity, protect the economy and if that means some pensioners die, too bad." In Brazil, Jair Bolsonaro similarly defended his refusal to curtail the economy by claiming that Brazilians "never catch anything. You see some bloke jumping into the sewage, he gets out, has a dive, right? And nothing happens to him."

I recognised in these statements what I had been following for the last two years: the rule of prices, the fear of the markets, the fear of what the speculators might do. It was clear from the outset that the economy could not operate during a public-health emergency. Workers would be sick; consumers would refuse to spend. But this connection between the real world and the financial world had long been forgotten. The human beings who make up real-world markets had been scrubbed from them. People had been purged from our imaginations as everything became reduced to Arabic numerals fronted by the symbols £ $ €. The result of such a distortion was catastrophe.

As I had seen time and time again, from the Enlightenment through the British Empire to the Wall Street crash to the Financial Crisis, the rule of prices is chaotic. And when that chaos did arrive in March 2020, those very same policymakers were forced to respond with policies that only days earlier they believed were unimaginable, policies that had even been resisted through the worst periods of the 2008 Financial Crisis. Governments everywhere stepped in to guarantee basic incomes. Wage guarantees, boosts to unemployment benefits and directly paying companies' payrolls were so expansive that many called the intervention "war communism." For the first time since the mid-1970s, the post-war social contracts had returned. Security was once again guaranteed by the state.

True to form, the central bankers declared that these extraordinary measures still had to abide by the rules of the game. The Bank of England governor, Andrew Bailey, took to the pages of the *Financial Times* on 5 April to remind the government and his readers that despite the crisis there was no escaping the Hard Truths of Economic Life. He pledged that Britain's central bank would not print money to fund the government's new spending commitments—a step beyond quantitative easing known as "monetary financing." Such a step, he warned, would lead to "runaway inflation." As the UK economy was falling into its worst economic recession in three centuries, he declared that his singular "goal is to ensure that borrowing costs and spending are consistent with achieving the inflation target." A thousand Britons were dying a day. Unemployment soared, poverty exploded, millions went hungry. Yet the crisis Bailey feared was one that didn't exist and hadn't existed in Britain for decades: high inflation. It was an incredible statement: an admission of the mythology that had gripped not just Britain but central bankers across the world for forty years. They were fighting OPEC's ghosts in the midst of a global catastrophe. But the mythology couldn't fend off reality for long. Just four days later it crumbled. As the *Financial Times* reported, "The UK has become the first country to embrace the monetary financing of government to fund the immediate cost of fighting coronavirus."

This real-world crisis of unemployment and hunger was only one front that central bankers were fighting on. The other was far larger and, in their minds, far more dangerous. It was one that Bailey's predecessor, Mark Carney, had warned about back in 2015: the detonation of the finance—climate doomsday device. In March, the Covid-19 crisis had exploded the bedrock of the global financial system: the US Treasury market. At first, it seemed as if the chaos was caused by a worldwide "dash for cash" as governments sold their Treasury Bills to access hard US dollars. But then in April the Bank of International Settlements reported that much of the selling was by hedge funds caught up in a speculative "basis trade" gone wrong. This type of trade had originally profited from exploiting the difference between the prices of Treasury bonds and Treasury futures. Since the differences were small, the hedge funds leveraged themselves to create big profits. But as Treasury prices declined, this trade created enormous losses and banks demanded the hedge funds put up collateral. They had to sell, pushing prices down, triggering yet more collateral calls, creating a downward doom spiral.

Once again, financial speculators had constructed a doomsday device deep inside the financial markets, one that would amplify a shock into a catastrophe. And, just as before, the central banks would suspend the rules of the game to prop up the financial markets and save the speculators. This time, the scale of the interventions dwarfed those that had come before. Fed chairman Jerome Powell upgraded the money button into a "bazooka" launching "QE Infinity," pledging "unlimited asset purchases" to shore up the markets. He declared the Fed would do "whatever we can, for as long as it takes." By the end of March, the Fed had bought a trillion dollars' worth of US Treasuries. The markets stabilised.

The financial doomsday was averted because it only existed in the digital world of finance. The wheat crisis in 1770s France or 1870s India or the oil crisis of the 1970s were all rooted in a finite supply of a physical commodity. There was only so much wheat and oil in the world. But if I have learnt one lesson in writing this book, it is that financial alchemy is not constrained by the physical world. It is instead a social game of theoretical IOUs that is supposed to organise the flow of physical things more efficiently, whether it be labour, land, commodities or manufactured goods. Mark Carney's climate–finance doomsday device existed entirely inside this intangible realm. It would only detonate if the umpires chose to keep the rules of the game in place. Indeed, Carney's successor, Andrew Bailey, tried to, even as the mushroom cloud was forming. But changing the rules is far easier than managing the fallout, as these umpires had discovered in 2008. Once again, they swiftly scrapped their rules and printed money to buy bonds. Defusing the bomb was straightforward. They just had to choose to do so.

They justified their reluctance in the name of fighting their ultimate foe: inflation. The rules needed to be enforced to contain this monster. But despite their quantitative easing and monetary financing to fund government spending and bail out corporations, "runaway inflation" never appeared. In the US, Western Europe and Japan, inflation stayed stubbornly below the 2 per cent target throughout 2020. The central banks had pushed the real interest rates below zero, effectively making the bond vigilantes pay the government for the privilege of lending to them. With neither the threat of inflation nor soaring interest rates, even the IMF was forced to admit that the Hard Facts of Economic Life no longer limited government spending. Austerity was revealed to be not a necessity, but a choice.

Conservatives recognised this threat immediately. Paradoxically, the success of their economic interventions posed a threat to their governing philosophy. In the UK, the Conservative government tried desperately to return to austerity before voters became "addicted to the scheme," as one Tory apparatchik put it. Johnson's finance minister, Rishi Sunak, hastily ended the job-support scheme right as the pandemic's second wave was taking off. He launched a PR campaign instructing unemployed ballet dancers to retrain for a job in "cyber." He was forced to reverse course days later as the cresting second wave demanded a national lockdown. His problem was that Bank of England–financed government spending was working. "If we think borrowing is the answer to everything, that debt rising is fine, then there's not much difference between us and the Labour Party," Sunak confided to the sympathetic *Spectator* magazine. He scrambled for reasons to denounce his own policy. He resorted to making nonsensical claims, such as that taxpayers had a "sacred duty" to repay the money that the Bank of England had printed.

American conservatives saw the threat in apocalyptic terms. "I promise you over our dead bodies will this get reauthorized," said Republican Senator Lindsey Graham of the CARES Act, the $2.2 trillion Covid-19 support package. Stopping further income support became their number-one priority. As the summer months rolled on, many wondered why Republicans were working so hard to reject popular policies to help people during a crisis, right on the eve of a national election. Something else was at work beyond political incentives, public health and economic reality. There seemed to be a moral imperative at stake. Shock-jock radio host Glenn Beck believed that offering ordinary people security was such an affront to his patriotism that "I would rather die than kill the country." Another shock-jock, Rush Limbaugh, spoke admiringly of the early settlers, who had to "turn to cannibalism" to survive and "didn't complain about it." To outsiders, it was bizarre to invoke such apocalyptic imagery as a very real catastrophe was gripping the nation. Perhaps, for these conservatives, "it is easier to imagine an end to the world than an end to capitalism," as the political theorist Fredric Jameson put it.

But what exactly was "ending"? No government was enacting large wealth taxes or nationalisations. Modest interventions in the market economy to provide jobs and secure sustenance had gone hand in hand with capitalism for decades following the Second World War. Those interventions did, however, curtail the power of prices. With income support, prices were no longer "telling people what to do." Without the threat of hunger and homelessness, people were freed—if only by an incremental amount—from market discipline.

This discipline is central to Anglo-American conservative morality. It is through the market that the good are rewarded and the undeserving are punished. The market is both the mechanism for maintaining an unequal social order and the justification for it. To undermine this system is to risk rewarding the losers and taking the rightful winnings from the winners. It is to undermine the very idea of morality itself.

On 28 August 2020, conservative fears were confirmed. Jerome Powell announced that the Federal Reserve was reinterpreting its mandate. The economy's umpire was changing the rules, and not just as a temporary crisis-fighting measure but permanently. "Forty years ago, the biggest problem our economy faced was high and rising inflation," Powell said in a press conference. But now, he claimed, the problem the US and the other advanced economies faced was stubbornly low inflation. He announced that the 2 per cent target was no longer a ceiling but an average. "Many find it counterintuitive that the Fed would want to push up inflation," Powell said. "However, inflation that is persistently too low can pose serious risks to the economy." Besides, it was a risk worth taking to tackle the nation's biggest problem: unemployment. "[O]ur revised statement emphasizes that maximum employment is a broad-based and inclusive goal. This change reflects our appreciation for the benefits of a strong labor market, particularly for many in low- and moderate-income communities."

Each sentence was a nail in the coffin for conservative politics. Admitting that inflation was no longer a threat removed the pretext for austerity. Embracing full employment promised an active role in the labour market that would provide security and meaningful choices for workers. And, perhaps worst of all, it meant helping low-income communities, the "undeserving" losers of the market game. Conservatives had lost their anti-democratic ally in the hunger games of austerity.

From 1977 onwards, Arthur Burns, Paul Volcker and Alan Greenspan served as the chief architects of the financial maze that had constrained the choices—both real and imagined—of voters and politicians alike. As the power behind the throne, they fused together conservative austerity budgets, free markets for workers and unlimited support for finance. The result was forty years of soaring inequality and financial instability. Explosive boom-and-busts detonated with increasing frequency and severity. But each time the umpires would rewrite the rules in such a way that protected finance from the fallout. Everyone else, especially those living outside the world's financial capitals, in the developing world, was left to experience the full force of the mushroom cloud. From the Fed-IMF–imposed Third World Debt Crisis of the 1980s through Greenspan's bubbles and the tumultuous 2010s, the global market maze was built and rebuilt to protect the very interests powering the chaos. The paradox of the climate–finance doomsday device simultaneously exploding and not exploding is the result of this unequal geography. Yet, as the Covid crisis went on, the new rules did make a difference. For the first time, conservatives had been sidelined from their long-standing alliance with financiers and central banks.

This seismic shift in court politics reminded me of the Egyptian Arab Spring. President Hosni Mubarak had come to power in 1981. He served at the pleasure of a power behind the throne: the military. In 2011, the generals changed their allegiance as bread riots rocked the country, allowing him to fall. Across the world, people imagined a new Middle East led by a free and democratic Egypt. But the dream didn't last long. As the newly elected government floundered, the generals took back power and jailed the president. The game had not fundamentally changed: they had never relinquished control.

Revolutions are tales of monsters vanquished. They are moments when we can imagine a benevolent rather than beastly creature at the helm. But revolutionary tales tend to be tragedies. It turns out that the very structure that contained and produced the last nightmare is still in place. The walls of the maze never changed. And, despite all the apparent changes during the pandemic, we still live in a world dictated by unelected umpires in the central banks. They remain the undemocratic and unaccountable power behind the throne.

Their motivation for splitting from conservative orthodoxy is currently unknown. It is noteworthy that after Powell gave his landmark speech on 28 August, the stock market rallied. Throughout the crisis, the central banks remained in lockstep with financial interests, firmly pointing the monetary bazookas their way. Perhaps the financiers, as Robert Johnson told me, fear the repercussions of austerity and the instability it foments. On Biden's inauguration, the financial markets rallied once more at the prospect of a $1.9 trillion Covid relief bill packed with income support for ordinary Americans. Financiers may profit from chaos, but not the kind of chaos that threatens the social fabric upon which their personal security depends. A moderate safety net may be just enough to keep the Masters of the Universe in their sunny Bel-Air mansions rather than their rainy New Zealand compounds. They prefer that the hunger games stay out of 90210.

Conclusion

Markets and Madness

There's one story I can't stop thinking about. It's by one of the first anthropologists of cargo cults, Peter Worsley. The white colonists, he writes, believed that the Melanesians refused to accept the idea of a modern economy beyond their shores because they'd never seen it. They'd never laid eyes on a factory that made the tinned goods and cigarettes they had come to enjoy. They could not imagine the vast global supply chains because they were disconnected from them. Yet, Worsley says, the Melanesians' "problem" was precisely the opposite. They refused to believe in the tales of a vast global economy governed by prices, not because they did not have experience of it but because they did.

Many Melanesian men worked to grow and harvest copra. It's the kernel of a coconut that can be used to make coconut oil or livestock feed. Copra was an internationally traded commodity whose price had swung wildly from highs of £70 to lows of £2. These swings brought chaos to the islands. When the prices were high, young men could earn more than their elders and challenge the village hierarchy. When prices were low, they were unemployed and destitute. The fate of their society was decided by prices, a force over which they had no control.

Their subjection to this absolute and seemingly arbitrary number "made White society appear more mysterious and irrational to the islander," Worsley writes. They struggled to believe that these dramatic changes in fortune were the result of a deliberate man-made system. They refused to believe that human beings would design such an engine of chaos. Such a force, they reasoned, had to be supernatural in origin. "This underlying irrationality of European society not only created great hardships, it undermined confidence in rational activity, it created frustrations, and it sapped morale more than mere ignorance of productive process could."

The cargo cultists of Melanesia are held up as totems of wrongness. They were so extremely wrong that they appeared to outsiders as collectively insane. But, reading Worsley's account, it occurs to me that not only were they sane, they had been right all along. Perhaps the Melanesians could see the reality of prices in ways that we, who have lived and breathed them for so long, cannot.

My journey had taken me deep into the mythology that empowers prices as the ruler of our world. I had seen how radical intellectuals had tried to create a rational system based on these all-powerful digits. The system begins by pricing ordinary things that you can touch and hold and burn and eat and expands to the future prices of those tangible things, and moves on to the celestial realm where those intangibles have prices that are bundled, insured, leveraged, shorted and arbitraged. I heard again and again how this mathematical magic would produce an orderly world of "peace and harmony." And yet, the greater this financial order was allowed to grow, the more chaotic the world became: a world of monsters and apocalyptic horrors.

The wreckage looks like the wrath of an angry god. A god who wields awe-inspiring power that plunges nations into famine, revolution and war with childlike ease. A god whose tempers are inscrutable, cloaked behind a deliberate "non-transparency" that leaves us mortals guessing at which sin might have angered him. Our bottomless fear compels us to "appease the markets" and offer whatever human sacrifices are necessary to win back his favour. He may then, we pray, send us cargo once again.

Yet the Melanesians got a crucial part of the story wrong. The magical forces that govern the price system are not supernatural. There is no god at the heart of the market, only prices, and they are man-made. But their seemingly irrational nature does not reflect the madness of mankind: our "irrational exuberance," "popular delusions" or the "madness of crowds." Their irrationality serves a rational interest. It is how those who sit atop the market pyramid are able to transfer wealth from others to themselves. It is precisely prices' inefficiencies and inaccuracies, their ability to manipulate, hide, amplify and narrate that makes them engines of enrichment as well as engines of chaos. Explosive prices make an explosive world with the opportunities for explosive profits.

The Melanesians got this wrong, perhaps, because they were in the grip of a similar mythology themselves. The business of cargo cults relied upon a ritual that transferred wealth from the laity to the prophet and destroyed the community's shared wealth in the process. They too failed to see what was happening in front of their eyes. Even when the planes filled with cargo never arrived, many cultists declared the rituals successful. They blamed the outsiders— the white colonisers—who they claimed had intercepted their cargo en route.

The market mythologisers have deployed the same tactic. As I had seen again and again, migrants had played a pivotal role in keeping the would-be reformers at bay. The Feed, filled with the "rapist hordes" and "invading caravans," served up ready-made scapegoats, deflecting attention from inscrutable financial alchemy to the photofriendly "barbarians at the gate." But their appearance was not an accident. They were products of the chaos the markets had created.

Not all the chaos the market creates strengthens its grip. The Davos set recognise that ever-increasing inequality, financial instability and climate change are pushing us to the ultimate edge of chaos. This edge is not just another crisis that the populists will exploit and the central banks will resolve. It will be an event horizon: a threshold that, once crossed, plunges us into a black hole from which there is no escape. The Masters of the Universe see this horizon clearly and are preparing their own personal escape from its grasp. These plans are public admissions that the basis of their wealth is little different from a cargo-cult myth. It is a system that proclaims it makes us all richer but is leading to the destruction of all we hold dear.

There is one aspect of the market mythology that still blinds them: the belief that little pieces of paper stamped with the symbols £ $ € are worth anything in an uninhabitable earth. This is, ultimately, the irrationality inside their rationality. The Minotaur at the heart of the global labyrinth. The true madness in the markets.

Acknowledgements

This book couldn't exist without the generous help of its subjects. I thank each of them, as well as the translators and fixers who put us in touch and made communication possible. I also thank Helen Spooner and Jacob Kushner for keeping me alive and sane in some dangerous and insane places. I thank India Woods for her support from beginning to end. Without my accomplice Ignacio Marin, there are many places I wouldn't have gone to, and I thank him that we did. I'm not sure the project would have started or finished without the unflinching support of my two lifelong friends. Camilla Hall was my first guide in navigating the financial labyrinth. William Salaman diligently researched every topic in this book. I also thank Jørgen Juel Andersen, Gerald Epstein, Rana Foroorah, Devlin Kuyek, Ted Schmidt, Russell-Dudley Smith, Quinn Slobodian, Adam Tooze and Barbara Walter for helping me navigate the world of political economy. I also thank my two editors, Jenny Lord at Weidenfeld and Nicolson and Kris Puopolo at Doubleday, as well as my agents Andrew Gordon and George Lucas, for their work on helping me through my first book. All the errors are, of course, my own.

Notes

Introduction: Monsters and Mazes

3 "'**Brexit plus plus plus**'": Lizzie Dearden, "Donald Trump Says Election Victory Would Be 'Brexit plus plus plus' in Final Push for Voters," *Independent*, 8 November 2016, www.www.independent.co.uk.

3 **These legendary "chaos theorists" discovered:** Here I am drawing on Robert May's discussion of chaos; see Chapter 2.

6 **These prices harmonise the global supply chain:** This is not, of course, my own original definition. I am paraphrasing what "prices" are ideally supposed to do under the conditions of perfect information and competition, as I discuss in greater detail in Chapter 2.

Chapter 1: Chaos: Why Societies Boil at 210

11 **"For me, the problem is the thousands":** Alexander Stille, "How Matteo Salvini Pulled Italy to the Far Right," *Guardian*, 9 August 2018, www.theguardian .com.

11 **a million migrants come to Europe:** UNHCR, "Global Trends: Forced Displacement in 2015," www.unhcr.org.

11 **Right-wing populists declared:** Melissa Eddy, "German Lawmaker Who Called Muslims 'Rapist Hordes' Faces Sanctions," *New York Times*, 2 January 2018, https://www.nytimes.com. Karolina Tagaris, "Far-Right Golden Dawn Exploits Darker Side of Greece's Discontent," Reuters, 11 September 2015, https://www.reuters.com. Enes Vayrakli and Farid Hafex, "European Islamophobia Report 2017," *European Islamophobia Report*, 2017, http://www .islamophobiaeurope.com. "Wilders Tells Dutch Parliament Refugee Crisis Is 'Islamic Invasion,'" *Newsweek*, 10 September 2015, https://www.newsweek .com.

11 **"a total and complete shutdown of Muslims entering the United States":** Jenna Johnson, "Trump Calls for 'Total and Complete Shutdown of Muslims Entering the United States,'" *Washington Post*, 8 December 2015, https://www .washingtonpost.com.

11   **The Vote Leave campaign distributed leaflets:** Amanda Garrett, "The Refugee Crisis, Brexit, and the Reframing of Immigration in Britain," *Europe Now*, https://www.europenowjournal.org, accessed 14 January 2021.

12   **"Give us back France, damn it!":** Anne-Sylvaine Chassany and Harriet Agnew, "Le Pen Steps Up Anti-Immigration Rhetoric Ahead of French Election," *Financial Times*, 18 April 2017, https://www.ft.com.

12   **The accompanying headlines framed migrants:** Esther Greussing and Hajo Boomgaarden, "Shifting the Refugee Narrative? An Automated Frame Analysis of Europe's 2015 Refugee Crisis," *Journal of Ethnic and Migration Studies*, 43(11) (August 2017).

12   **Their xenophobic message finally resonated:** For quantitative studies on the impact of refugees and migration on the rise of right-wing populism, see: Dominik Hangartner, Elias Dinas, Moritz Marbach, Konstantinos Matakos and Dimitrios Xefteris, "Does Exposure to the Refugee Crisis Make Natives More Hostile?," *American Political Science Review*, 113(2) (May 2019), pp. 442–55. Elias Dinas, Konstantinos Matakos, Dimitrios Xefteris and Dominik Hangartner, "Waking Up the Golden Dawn: Does Exposure to the Refugee Crisis Increase Support for Extreme-Right Parties?," *Political Analysis*, 27(2) (April 2019), pp. 244–54. Andreas Steinmayr, "Did the Refugee Crisis Contribute to the Recent Rise of Far-right Parties in Europe?," *ifo DICE Report*, 15(4) (2017), pp. 24–7. Matthew Goodwin and Caitlin Milazzo, "Taking Back Control? Investigating the Role of Immigration in the 2016 Vote for Brexit," *British Journal of Politics and International Relations*, 19(3) (August 2017), pp. 450–64.

13   **Salvini closed down refugee camps in Italy:** Lorenzo Tondo and Angela Giuffrida, "Vulnerable Migrants Made Homeless After Italy Passes 'Salvini Decree,'" *Guardian*, 7 December 2018, http://www.theguardian.com.

15   **The theory began on a routine winter day in 1961:** This account is drawn from Edward Lorenz, *The Essence of Chaos* (Seattle: University of Washington Press, 1993), and James Gleick, *Chaos: Making a New Science* (London: Sphere Books, 1987).

18   **Populists held rallies denouncing their arrival, which the media covered and the algorithms powering Facebook and Twitter promoted:** Max Schaub and Davide Morisi, "Voter Mobilisation in the Echo Chamber: Broadband Internet and the Rise of Populism in Europe," *European Journal of Political Research*, 59(4) (December 2019), pp. 752–73.

21   **Bak, Wiesenfeld and Chang called this phenomenon:** Per Bak, Chao Tang and Kurt Wiesenfeld, "Self-Organized Criticality," *Physical Review A*, 38(1) (1988), p. 364.

21   **One of the most productive applications of their theory was on earthquakes:** Zeev Olami, Hans Jacob Feder and Kim Christensen, "Self-Organized Criticality in a Continuous, Nonconservative Cellular Automaton Modelling Earthquakes," *Physical Review Letters*, 68(8) (February 1992), pp. 1244–7.

22   **Between 2005 and 2008, global food prices:** Anuradha Mittal, "The 2008

Food Price Crisis: Rethinking Food Security Policies," in *G-24 Discussion Paper Series*, 56(1) (UNCTAD, June 2009), https://unctad.org/.

22 **over 155 million people were pushed into poverty and 80 million into hunger:** Rafael De Hoyos and Denis Medvedev, *Poverty Effects of Higher Food Prices: A Global Perspective* (Washington, D.C.: World Bank, 2009). USDA, *Food Security Assessment, 2008–09* (US Department of Agriculture: Economic Research Service, 2009), https://www.ers.usda.gov/. Raj Patel and Philip McMichael, "A Political Economy of the Food Riot," *Review* (Fernand Braudel Center), 32(1) (2009), pp. 9–35.

24 **A Tunisian blog had found it:** Marwan Kraidy, *The Naked Blogger of Cairo* (Cambridge, MA: Harvard University Press, 2016), p. 33.

24 **"Whether it's cash, services, land, property":** Wikileaks, "Corruption in Tunisia: What's Yours Is Mine," 23 June 2008, https://wikileaks.org/.

24 **"The dinner included perhaps":** Wikileaks, "Tunisia: Dinner with Sakher El Materi," 27 July 2009, https://wikileaks.org/.

24 **More and more people were going hungry:** A Gallup World Poll survey found that in Jordan, Egypt and Tunisia people were increasingly struggling to feed themselves. Joana Silve, Victoria Levin and Matteo Morgandi, "Inclusion and Resilience: The Way Forward for Social Safety Nets in the Middle East and North Africa," 2012, https://worldbank.org.

24 **Waving baguettes in the air:** Roula Khalaf, "Tunisia: After the Revolution," *Financial Times*, 6 May 2011, https://www.ft.com.

24 **The police responded with live ammunition:** "Baguette-Wielding Superhero Is Facebook Sensation," 19 July 2011, https://www.france24.com.

24 **Outraged, even more took to the streets:** Jane Harrigan, *The Political Economy of Arab Food Sovereignty* (Basingstoke: Palgrave Macmillan, 2014), p. 108.

25 **"We don't want bread or anything else":** Mark Tran, Matt Wells and Paul Owen, "Tunisia Crisis: As It Happened," *Guardian*, 14 January 2011, https://www.theguardian.com/.

25 **A viral Facebook post:** Kraidy, *The Naked Blogger of Cairo*, p. 46.

25 **What was first called the *thwart el-Khobz*:** Ibid., p. 47.

25 **In Jordan, the "day of rage":** Canadians for Justice and Peace in the Middle East, "Factsheet III: Protests in Jordan," February 2011, https://www.cjpme.org. Harrigan, *Political Economy of Arab Food Sovereignty,* p. 108. "Jordan Rally Targets Government," BBC News, 22 January 2011, https://www.bbc.co.uk.

25 **Yemenis took to the streets:** Washington Post Foreign Service, "Inspired by Tunisia and Egypt, Yemenis Join in Anti-Government Protests," *Washington Post*, 27 January 2011.

26 **They mapped out the twin eruptions:** Marco Lagi, Yavni Bar-Yam, Karla Z. Bertrand and Yaneer Bar-Yam, "The Food Crises: A Quantitative Model of Food Prices Including Speculators and Ethanol Conversion," *arXiv:1109.4859*, 21 September 2011.

26 **This social contract was part:** Eva Bellin, "The Robustness of Authoritarian-

ism in the Middle East: Exceptionalism in Comparative Perspective," *Comparative Politics*, 36(2) (January 2004), pp. 139–57.

27 **GRAPH: RIOTS & FOOD PRICES:** Adapted from Marco Lagi, Yavni Bar-Yam, Karla Z. Bertrand and Yaneer Bar-Yam, "The Food Crises: A Quantitative Model of Food Prices Including Speculators and Ethanol Conversion," *arXiv:1109.4859*, 21 September 2011.

27 **"democracy of bread":** Larbi Sadiki, "Towards Arab Liberal Governance: From the Democracy of Bread to the Democracy of the Vote," *Third World Quarterly*, 18(1) (March 1997), pp. 127–48.

27 **It's the source of 35 per cent:** Harrigan, *Political Economy of Arab Food Sovereignty*, p. 19.

28 **spend between 35 and 55 per cent of their income on food:** Ronald Albers and Marga Peeters, "Food and Energy Prices, Government Subsidies and Fiscal Balances in South Mediterranean Countries," *Economic Papers*, 437 (Brussels: European Commission, 2011).

28 **From the late 1970s:** This is discussed in detail in Chapter 10.

28 **By 2010, unemployment was soaring:** Mehran Kamrava, "The Rise and Fall of Ruling Bargains in the Middle East," in *Beyond the Arab Spring: The Evolving Ruling Bargain in the Middle East*, ed. Mehran Kamrava (London: Hurst & Company Limited, 2014), pp. 17–45.

28 **Bakers in Cairo:** Annia Ciezadlo, "Let Them Eat Bread," *Foreign Affairs*, 23 March 2011.

28 **announcing new subsidies and government jobs:** World Bank, "Investing for Growth and Jobs," *Middle East and North Africa Region: Economic Developments & Prospects, September 2011* (Washington, D.C.: World Bank, 2011), https://openknowledge.worldbank.org/.

28 **Only those regimes that offered:** Jack Goldstone, "Bringing Regimes Back In: Explaining Success and Failure in the Middle East Revolts of 2011," in *The Arab Revolution of 2011: A Comparative Perspective*, ed. Saïd Amir Arjomand (Albany, NY: SUNY Press, 2015), pp. 53–74.

30 **over 10 million forced from their homes:** Data collected from www.unrefugees.org, https://www.unicef.org, https://www.crf.org.

31 **Peasants normally spent:** Richard Brace, "The Problem of Bread and the French Revolution at Bordeaux," *American Historical Review*, 51(4) (1946), pp. 649–67.

31 **News of the banquet scandalised Paris:** Antonia Fraser, *Marie Antoinette* (London: Weidenfeld and Nicolson, 2002), p. 348.

31 **"Kill! Kill!":** Nancy Barker, " 'Let Them Eat Cake': The Mythical Marie Antoinette and the French Revolution," *Historian*, 55(4) (1993), pp. 709–24.

31 **These "October days" were a turning point:** Ian Davidson, *The French Revolution: From Enlightenment to Tyranny* (London: Profile Books, 2016), p. 46.

31 **"More often than not the queen appeared":** Barker, " 'Let Them Eat Cake,' " p. 718.

31 **She kept a harem of lesbian lovers:** Ibid., p. 723.

32 **Maximilien Robespierre tried imposing a "maximum" price of bread:** R. B.

Rose, "18th-Century Price-Riots, the French Revolution and the Jacobin Maximum," *International Review of Social History*, 4(3) (December 1959), pp. 432–45.

32 **As he was marched to the guillotine:** Ibid.

32 **France's bread problem was larger than any of these personalities:** Louise A. Tilly, "The Food Riot as a Form of Political Conflict in France," *Journal of Interdisciplinary History*, 2(1) (1971), pp. 23–57. Louise A. Tilly, "Food Entitlement, Famine, and Conflict," *Journal of Interdisciplinary History*, 14(2) (1983), pp. 333–49. Steven L. Kaplan, *Bread, Politics and Political Economy in the Reign of Louis XV* (2nd edn., London: Anthem Press, 2015).

33 **GRAPH: FOOD PRODUCTION & FOOD PRICES:** Source: UNFAO, http://www.fao.org/.

34 **both years had seen the most food produced in history:** FAO Food Production Index, https://data.worldbank.org/.

Chapter 2: Magic: Fairy Tales, Financial Alchemy and the
Business of Cargo Cults

35 **100 million starved:** Olivier de Schutter, *The State of Food Insecurity in the World* (New York and Geneva: FAO, 2009). Harvey Morris, "UN Task Force to Tackle Global Crisis," *Financial Times*, 29 April 2008, https://www.ft.com/.

37 **"Look at this lead pencil":** PBS, "Free to Choose: Part 1 of 10 The Power of the Market," https://www.youtube.com/watch?v=D3N2sNnGwa4, accessed 18 January 2021.

38 **He viewed prices as information-gathering machines:** Friedrich Hayek, "The Use of Knowledge in Society," *American Economic Review*, 35(4) (1945), pp. 519–30.

38 **"The function of prices":** Friedrich Hayek, "Nobel Prize–Winning Economist Oral History Transcript," *Oral History Program* (University of California, Los Angeles, 1983), http://archive.org/.

39 **Only it didn't remain a mere "hypothesis" for long:** For an accessible overview of the rise of the Efficient Market Hypothesis in economics, see Justin Fox, *The Myth of the Rational Market: A History of Risk, Reward, and Delusion on Wall Street* (London: HarperCollins, 2009).

39 **"A political system, in which you decide":** Milton Friedman, "The Fragility of Freedom," in *Milton Friedman in South Africa*, eds. Meyer Feldberg, Kate Jowell and Stephen Mulholland (Cape Town and Johannesburg: Graduate School of Business of the University of Cape Town, 1976), pp. 3–10.

39 **"The existence of a free market":** Milton Friedman, "Capitalism and Freedom," in *Essays on Individuality*, ed. Felix Morley (Philadelphia: University of Pennsylvania, 1958), pp. 168–82.

40 **"If somebody says to me":** Quotes from the testimony come from the official transcript. US House of Representatives, "H.R. 4062—THE FINANCIAL DERIVATIVES SUPERVISORY IMPROVEMENT ACT OF 1998 AND H.R. 4239," 17 July 1998, http://commdocs.house.gov.

41 **The notional value of these new financial products had tripled:** Commodity Futures Trading Commission, "Concept Release CFR Parts 34 and 35, Over-the-Counter Derivatives" (Washington, D.C.: CFTC, 1998).

41 **"I have thirteen bankers in my office":** Manuel Roig-Franzia, "Brooksley Born, the Cassandra of the Derivatives Crisis," *Washington Post*, 26 May 2009, https://www.washingtonpost.com/.

41 **When Chicago became the grain capital of North America:** This account is drawn from Ted Schmidt, *The Political Economy of Food and Finance* (London: Routledge, 2015).

42 **In 1875, the *Chicago Tribune* estimated:** William Cronon, *Nature's Metropolis: Chicago and the Great West* (New York: W. W. Norton & Company, 2009), p. 126.

42 **Speculators tried to rig the futures prices:** Thomas Hieronymus, *Economics of Futures Trading* (New York: Commodity Research Bureau, 1971).

44 **Greenspan co-authored a report with Larry Summers:** Lawrence Summers, Alan Greenspan, Arthur Levitt and William Rainer, *Over-the-Counter Derivatives Markets and the Commodity Exchange Act* (Washington, D.C.: US Department of the Treasury, 1999), www.treasury.gov.

44 **"I found a flaw":** Brian Naylor, "Greenspan Admits Free Market Ideology Flawed," NPR, 24 October 2009, https://www.npr.org.

44 **"weapons of financial mass destruction":** Warren Buffett, "2002 Annual Report," *Berkshire Hathaway Inc.*, 2002, p. 15, http://www.berkshirehathaway.com.

44 **The notorious "credit default swaps":** James Crotty, "Structural Causes of the Global Financial Crisis: A Critical Assessment of the 'New Financial Architecture,'" *Cambridge Journal of Economics*, 33(4) (July 2009), pp. 563–80.

44 **These "behavioural economists" had run experiments:** For an accessible introduction to behavioural economics, see Michael Lewis, *The Undoing Project: A Friendship That Changed Our Minds* (New York: W. W. Norton & Company, 2017).

45 **"This 'Madness' is not confined to any one area":** N. M. Bird, "Is There Danger of a Post-War Flare-Up Among New Guinea Natives?," *Pacific Islands Monthly*, 16(4) (November 1945), pp. 69–70.

45 **They would periodically bubble up:** Peter Lawrence, "Cargo Cult and Religious Beliefs among the Garia," in *Melanesia: Readings on a Culture Area*, eds. L. L. Langness and John C. Weshler (London: Chandler Publishing Company, 1971), pp. 295–314.

46 **In one typical episode:** Peter Worsley, *The Trumpet Shall Sound: A Study of "Cargo" Cults in Melanesia* (2nd edn., London: MacGibbon & Kee, 1968), p. 112.

46 **If the seeds failed to sprout:** Lawrence, "Cargo Cult and Religious Beliefs among the Garia."

46 **When the Europeans told them:** Peter Lawrence, "Cargo Cults and Politics," in *Papua New Guinea: Prospero's Other Island*, ed. Peter Hastings (Sydney: Angus & Robertson, 1971), pp. 106–20.

46 **It can be tempting to read accounts:** This has long been a problem in anthropological writing: the presentation of a "foreign" society as some kind of total unit where the inhabitants are uniform "cultural dopes," lacking the critical faculties of the (Western) anthropologist. More recent anthropological approaches emphasise how culture and identity are constantly contested, that things described as "culture" or "hierarchy" are, in fact, in a state of negotiation, challenge and flux. My own reading of cargo-cult phenomena emphasises the contestation of "culture" and how such contestations form strategies of self-enrichment and exploitation.

47 **"Kaum of Kalina claimed to have been killed":** Lawrence, "Cargo Cult and Religious Beliefs among the Garia."

49 **Before the Financial Crisis Donald MacKenzie:** Donald MacKenzie and Taylor Spears, "'The Formula That Killed Wall Street': The Gaussian Copula and Modelling Practices in Investment Banking," *Social Studies of Science*, 44(3) (2014), pp. 393–417. Donald MacKenzie and Taylor Spears, "'A Device for Being Able to Book P&L': The Organizational Embedding of the Gaussian Copula," *Social Studies of Science*, 44(3) (2014), pp. 418–40.

51 **As house prices rose, the quants' formulas calculated:** Scott Patterson, *The Quants: The Maths Geniuses Who Brought Down Wall Street* (London: Random House, 2012), p. 197.

51 **generated the majority of the banks' profits:** Adam Goldstein and Neil Fligstein, "Financial Markets as Production Markets: The Industrial Roots of the Mortgage Meltdown," *Socio-Economic Review*, 15(3) (2017), pp. 483–510.

53 **paper published by two Yale economists:** Gary Gorton and K. Geert Rouwenhorst, "Facts and Fantasies about Commodity Futures," *Financial Analysts Journal*, 62(2) (1 March 2006), pp. 47–68.

54 **One study estimated:** Yiqun Mou, "Limits to Arbitrage and Commodity Index Investment: Front-Running the Goldman Roll," *Social Science Research Network*, 2010.

54 **By another quirk of how these contracts were written:** For a detailed account of the economics of the "cash and carry" trade, see Ted Schmidt, *The Political Economy of Food and Finance* (London: Routledge, 2015).

54 **During the commodity boom of the 2000s:** Saule T. Omarova, "The Merchants of Wall Street: Banking, Commerce, and Commodities," *Minnesota Law Review*, 98 (2014), pp. 266–355.

54 **Morgan Stanley, for instance:** US Senate, "Wall Street Bank Involvement with Physical Commodities" (Washington, D.C.: Committee Reports, US Government Printing Office, 2014).

55 **It means that the prices of commodities:** Ke Tang and Wei Xiong, "Index Investment and the Financialization of Commodities," *Financial Analysts Journal*, 68(6) (2012), pp. 54–74.

56 **GRAPH: FINANCIALIZED ASSET PRICES:** Adapted from Marco Lagi, Yavni Bar-Yam, Karla Z. Bertrand and Yaneer Bar-Yam, "The Food Crises: A Quantitative Model of Food Prices Including Speculators and Ethanol Conversion," *arXiv:1109.4859*, 21 September 2011.

57 **"They were still enamoured with"**: CTA stands for Commodity Trading Advisor. It's a regulator designation applied to those entities—be they managed money, hedge funds, mutual funds and so forth—trading commodity futures contracts, options and swaps. Economists and financial analysts often use reports of CTA activity in the markets as a proxy for speculators, i.e., those who will not ultimately be taking delivery of physical commodities. While CTAs have varied trading strategies, trend-following is among the oldest and the most common.

58 **"Trend-following has produced substantial riches"**: G. Meyer, "Diversification adds to funds' appeal," *Financial Times*, 25 November 2009, https://www.ft.com.

58 **it was by no means new**: One of the earliest studies to analyse stock prices in terms of trends was Robert Edwards and John Magee, *Technical Analysis of Stock Trends* (Springfield, MA: Stock Trend Service, 1948).

59 **"The so-called chaotician"**: Robert Kahn, "Prospects for Nonlinear Education: Reflections from Lord (Robert) May," in *Chaos, Complexity, Curriculum and Culture: A Conversation*, ed. M. Jayne Fleener, William E. Doll, Donna Trueit and John St. Julien (New York: Peter Lang, 2005), p. 183.

59 **May was all too familiar**: Robert May, "Simple Mathematical Models with Very Complicated Dynamics," *Nature*, 261(5560) (1976), pp. 459–67.

60 **GRAPH: FEEDBACK & BOOM-BUSTINESS:** Adapted from James Gleick, *Chaos: Making a New Science* (London: Sphere Books, 1987).

61 **"People who argue that speculation is generally destabilising"**: Milton Friedman, *Essays in Positive Economics* (Chicago: University of Chicago Press, 1953).

62 **The Victorians had unwittingly killed off their only natural predators:** David Peacock and Ian Abbott, "The Role of Quoll (*Dasyurus*) Predation in the Outcome of Pre-1900 Introductions of Rabbits (*Oryctolagus Cuniculus*) to the Mainland and Islands of Australia," *Australian Journal of Zoology*, 61(3) (2013), pp. 206–80.

62 **Introducing new predators:** David Peacock and Ian Abbott, "The Mongoose in Australia: Failed Introduction of a Biological Control Agent," *Australian Journal of Zoology*, 58(4) (2010), pp. 205–27.

62 **This young economist and his colleagues:** J. Bradford De Long, Andrei Shleifer, Lawrence H. Summers and Robert J. Waldmann, "Positive Feedback Investment Strategies and Destabilizing Rational Speculation," *Journal of Finance*, 45(2) (1990), pp. 379–95. Andrei Shleifer and Lawrence H. Summers, "The Noise Trader Approach to Finance," *Journal of Economic Perspectives*, 4(2) (1990), pp. 19–33. Fox, *The Myth of the Rational Market*.

63 **speculators feared the Federal Reserve's bond-buying:** Ted Schmidt, "Financialization of Commodities and the Monetary Transmission Mechanism," *International Journal of Political Economy*, 46(2–3) (2017), pp. 128–49.

63 **trend-following capital was now poised to amplify:** Lagi et al., "The Food Crises."

63 **Nor was there a global shortage of wheat:** Klaus von Grebmer, Maximo

Torero, Tolulope Olofinbiyi, Heidi Fritschel, Doris Wiesmann, Yisehac Yohannes, Lilly Schofield and Constanze von Oppeln, *2011 Global Hunger Index: The Challenge of Hunger: Taming Price Spikes and Excessive Food Price Volatility* (Washington, D.C.: International Food Policy Research Institute, 2011).

Chapter 3: Perception: Pricing ISIS in Iraq

68 **Psychologists have found that:** Paul Slovic, David Zionts, Andrew K. Woods, Ryan Goodman and Derek Jinks, "Psychic Numbing and Mass Atrocity," in *The Behavioral Foundations of Public Policy*, ed. Eldar Shafir (Princeton, NJ: Princeton University Press, 2013), pp. 126–42.

74 **splintered into 1,000 independent militias and 3,250 smaller brigades:** Christopher Phillips, *The Battle for Syria: International Rivalry in the New Middle East* (New Haven, CT, and London: Yale University Press, 2016), p. 127.

75 **The US-led coalition:** This account is drawn from Joby Warrick, *Black Flags: The Rise of ISIS* (London: Transworld, 2015).

75 **The city's Sunni majority offered a strategic opportunity:** Tallha Abdulrazaq and Gareth Stansfield, "The Enemy Within: ISIS and the Conquest of Mosul," *Middle East Journal*, 70(4) (2016), pp. 525–42.

76 **Then ISIS sleeper cells let off bombs across the city:** Warrick, *Black Flags*.

77 **Such abject cruelty shouldn't happen in civil wars:** Barbara Walter, "The New New Civil Wars," *Annual Review of Political Science*, 20 (2017), pp. 469–86.

77 **bringing in between $1 million and $2 million a day:** David E. Sanger and Julie Hirschfeld Davis, "Struggling to Starve ISIS of Oil Revenue, U.S. Seeks Assistance from Turkey," *New York Times*, 13 September 2014, https://www.nytimes.com.

77 **Political scientists and economists have filled libraries:** Michael L. Ross, "What Have We Learned about the Resource Curse?," *Annual Review of Political Science*, 18(1) (2015), pp. 239–59.

79 **"Iraq violence lights fuse to oil-price spike":** Neil Hume, "Iraq Violence Lights Fuse to Oil Price Spike," *Financial Times*, 20 June 2014, https://www.ft.com.

80 **Even Bush's 2003 full-scale invasion of Iraq:** Robert E. Looney, "Oil Prices and the Iraq War: Market Interpretations of Military Developments," *Journal of Energy and Development*, 29(1) (2003), pp. 25–41.

80 **"Its price today should be $100":** Bin Laden quotes come from Mark S. Williams and Paul Williams, "The Weaponization of Oil in the Messages of Osama Bin Laden," *Journal of Military and Strategic Studies*, 10(2) (Winter 2007–08).

80 **He had calculated:** Mahmoud A. El-Gamal and Amy Myers Jaffe, *Oil, Dollars, Debt, and Crises: The Global Curse of Black Gold* (Cambridge, UK: Cambridge University Press, 2009), p. 67.

81 **Shiller is famous for his Nobel Prize–winning work on economic bubbles:**

To read more about Shiller's theory, see Robert Shiller, *Narrative Economics: How Stories Go Viral and Drive Major Economic Events* (Princeton, NJ: Princeton University Press, 2019).

83 **One summer's day in 1973, Marshall Applewhite and Bonnie Nettles:** This account is drawn from Robert W. Balch, "Waiting for the Ships: Disillusionment and the Revitalization of Faith in Bo and Peep's UFO Cult," in *The Gods Have Landed: New Religions from Other Worlds*, ed. James Lewis (Albany, NY: State University of New York Press, 1995), pp. 137–66.

84 **"The closing of the canon":** Max Weber, *Economy and Society: An Outline of Interpretive Sociology*, ed. Guenther Roth and Claus Wittich, vol. 1 (Berkeley: University of California Press, 1978), p. 459.

86 **When Anne Hathaway hosted the Oscars:** Dan Mirvish, "The Hathaway Effect: How Anne Gives Warren Buffett a Rise," *Huffington Post*, 3 February 2011, https://www.huffpost.com.

89 **El-Gamal predicted in 2013:** Mahmoud El-Gamal and Amy M. Jeff, "Oil Demand, Supply, and Medium-Term Price Prospects: A Wavelets-Based Analysis," Institute of Transportation Studies, Working Paper Series (Davis, CA: Institute of Transportation Studies, UC Davis, 2013). Hany Abdel-Latif and Mahmoud El-Gamal, "Financial Liquidity, Geopolitics, and Oil Prices," *Energy Economics*, 87 (2019).

91 **Yaneer Bar-Yam and his colleagues estimated:** Roozbeh Daneshvar, Marco Lagi and Yaneer Bar-Yam, "The Impact of Speculation on Oil Prices: A Quantitative Model" (Cambridge, MA: New England Complex Systems Institute, 2014).

Chapter 4: Contagion: Typhoons, Trump, Brexit, Brazil, Belt and Road

92 **"Last week I was in Tripoli":** David Cameron, "Prime Minister's First Speech to the UN General Assembly" (United Nations, New York, 22 September 2011), https://www.gov.uk/government/speeches/prime-ministers-first-speech-to-the-un-general-assembly.

92 **flogging another hundred to the Gulf:** Christopher Hope and Angela Monaghan, "David Cameron Promotes Typhoon Fighter Jets in Middle East," *Daily Telegraph*, 5 November, 2012, https://www.telegraph.co.uk.

92 **"We have one of the strictest regimes":** Nicholas Watt and Ian Black, "David Cameron Arrives in Gulf on Arms Trade Trip," *Guardian*, 5 November 2012, https://www.theguardian.com.

93 **"They eat camel":** Boris Johnson, "We Can't Afford to Ignore Our Dynamic Friends in the East," *Daily Telegraph*, 21 April 2013, https://www.telegraph.co.uk.

93 **Venezuela's Hugo Chávez ran for re-election:** Rory Carroll, *Comandante: Hugo Chávez's Venezuela* (London: Penguin Books, 2014), p. 283. Raul Gallegos, *Crude Nation: How Oil Riches Ruined Venezuela* (Lincoln: University of Nebraska Press, 2016), p. 160.

93 **steal money, reward allies, embolden the military:** Jørgen Juel Andersen,

Niels Johannesen, David Dreyer Lassen and Elena Paltseva, "Petro Rents, Political Institutions, and Hidden Wealth: Evidence from Offshore Bank Accounts," *Journal of the European Economic Association*, 15(4) (1 August 2017), pp. 818–60. Jørgen Juel Andersen and Silje Aslaksen, "Oil and Political Survival," *Journal of Development Economics*, 100(1) (2013), pp. 89–106. Egil Matsen, Gisle J. Natvik and Ragnar Torvik, "Petro Populism," *Journal of Development Economics*, 118 (2016), pp. 1–12. Keisuke Okada and Sovannroeun Samreth, "Oil Bonanza and the Composition of Government Expenditure," *Economics of Governance*, 22 (2021), pp. 23–46.

94   **It is as if the plundering of foreign riches:** Vanessa Ogle, " 'Funk Money': The End of Empires, the Expansion of Tax Havens, and Decolonization as an Economic and Financial Event," *Past & Present*, 249(1) (2020), pp. 213–49. Vanessa Ogle, "Archipelago Capitalism: Tax Havens, Offshore Money, and the State, 1950s–1970s," *American Historical Review*, 122(5) (2017), pp. 1431–58.

94   **During this digital dance, guns were delivered:** El-Gamal and Jaffe, *Oil, Dollars, Debt, and Crises: The Global Curse of Black Gold*.

94   **poorer education and worse health care:** Lara Cockx and Nathalie Francken, "Extending the Concept of the Resource Curse: Natural Resources and Public Spending on Health," *Ecological Economics*, 108 (2014), pp. 136–49. Lara Cockx and Nathalie Francken, "Natural Resources: A Curse on Education Spending?," *Energy Policy*, 92 (2016), pp. 394–408. Simon Wigley, "The Resource Curse and Child Mortality, 1961–2011," *Social Science & Medicine*, 176 (2017), pp. 142–8.

94   **It was not even a week after the bombing began:** David Wearing, "A Shameful Relationship: UK Complicity in Saudi State Violence" (London: Campaign Against the Arms Trade, April 2016), https://www.caat.org.uk/.

95   **"Let me be clear: leaving Europe":** "Read David Cameron's Full Referendum Announcement," *Independent*, 20 February 2016, http://www.independent.co.uk.

95   **pushing up house prices by 19 per cent:** Filipa G. Sa, "The Effect of Foreign Investors on Local Housing Markets: Evidence from the UK," *CEPR Discussion Paper* no. DP11658 (November 2016).

95   **"There would be a hit to the value of people's homes":** Rowena Mason and Hilary Osborne, "House Prices Could Fall by 18% if Britain Quits EU, Says George Osborne," *Guardian*, 21 May 2016, https://www.theguardian.com.

96   **"What the fuck was that?":** Tim Shipman, *All Out War: The Full Story of How Brexit Sank Britain's Political Class* (London: William Collins, 2016), p. 246.

96   **"My disabled mother missed out":** Martin Robinson, "Woman in Brexit Row Says Her Mother Was Rejected for SIX Bungalows," *Daily Mail*, 27 May 2016, https://www.dailymail.co.uk/.

96   **granular geographic breakdown of the island nation:** Ben Ansell, "Housing, Credit and Brexit," *Conference on Europe and the Credit Crisis, April 2017* (7 April 2017). Ben Ansell and David Adler, "Brexit and the Politics of Housing in Britain," *Political Quarterly*, 90 (2019), pp. 105–16.

97   **GRAPH: BREXIT & HOUSE PRICES:** Adapted from Ben Ansell and

David Adler, "Brexit and the Politics of Housing in Britain," *Political Quarterly*, 90 (2019), pp. 105–16.

97 **home ownership is a similar source of security:** Ben Ansell, "The Political Economy of Ownership: Housing Markets and the Welfare State," *American Political Science Review*, 108(2) (2014), pp. 383–402. John S. Ahlquist and B. W. Ansell, "Taking Credit: Redistribution and Borrowing in an Age of Economic Polarization," *World Politics*, 69(4) (2017), pp. 640–75.

97 **And rising house prices meant that the only alternative:** Ahlquist and Ansell, "Taking Credit," pp. 640–75.

98 **In the US, Ansell and his colleague David Adler:** David Adler and Ben Ansell, " 'I Love Bad Markets': Housing and the Politics of Place in the 2016 Presidential Election," unpublished manuscript.

98 **Much of the rise in prices came from oil money:** For research on commodity prices and surges in capital inflows, see Carmen M. Reinhart, Vincent Reinhart and Christoph Trebesch, "Global Cycles: Capital Flows, Commodities, and Sovereign Defaults, 1815–2015," *American Economic Review*, 106(5) (2016), pp. 574–80. For the research on oil prices, petrodollars and rising house prices, see El-Gamal and Jaffe, *Oil, Dollars, Debt, and Crises: The Global Curse of Black Gold*. For trade imbalances and house prices, see Ben W. Ansell, Lawrence Broz and Thomas Flaherty, "Global Capital Markets, Housing Prices, and Partisan Fiscal Policies," *Economics & Politics*, 30(3) (2018), pp. 307–39.

99 **A turboprop plane:** Michael McDonald, "Can Timber Rebuild Harvard's Endowment?," Bloomberg, 20 September 2012, https://www.bloomberg.com.

99 **Banks, hedge funds, university endowments, pension funds:** "Wall Street Bank Involvement," US Senate, 2014.

100 **"I can almost hear the camel bells":** Xi Jinping, "Promote Friendship Between Our People and Work Together to Build a Bright Future," Speech at Nazarbayev University, Kazakhstan, 7 September 2013, https://www.fmprc.gov.cn.

100 **Xi Jinping would go on a tour of the other Central Asian states:** Qishloq Ovozi, "How Far Will China Go in Central Asia," *Radio Free Europe*, 8 June 2015, https://www.rferl.org.

100 **not just Asia but Africa as well:** David Pilling, "Chinese Investment in Africa: Beijing's Testing Ground," *Financial Times*, 13 June 2017, https://www.ft.com.

100 **There were local fears that these investments:** Nick Van Mead, "China in Africa: Win-win Development, or a New Colonialism?," *Guardian*, 31 July 2018. Anthony Kleven, "Belt and Road: Colonialism with Chinese Characteristics," *Interpreter*, 6 May 2019, https://www.lowyinstitute.org.

101 **Harvard University created chaos:** This section is drawn from GRAIN and *Rede Social de Justiça e Direitos Humanos*, "Harvard's Billion-Dollar Farmland Fiasco," September 2018, https://www.grain.org.

101 **Even in the US, California farmers:** Michael McDonald, "Harvard Spent $100 Million on Vineyards. Now It's Fighting with the Neighbors," Bloomberg, 15 November 2018, https://www.bloomberg.com/.

101 **The World Bank warned investors in 2011:** World Bank, "Project Document,

Piaui: Pillars of Growth and Social Inclusion Project" (P129342), December 2015, http://documents.worldbank.org.

101 **Brazil is now the world's leader in land-grab murders:** "At What Cost? Irresponsible business and the murder of land and environmental defenders in 2017," *Global Witness*, 2018.

101 **Protests break out periodically in Central Asia:** Abdujalil Abdurasulov, "Kazakhstan's Land Reform Protests Explained," BBC News, 28 April 2016, https://www.bbc.co.uk. "China-led $280 Million Kyrgyzstan Project Abandoned After Protests," Reuters, 18 February 2020, https://www.reuters.com/.

101 **In Pakistan, Baloch rebels:** Jon Boone and Kiyya Baloch, "A New Shenshen? Poor Pakistan fishing town's horror at Chinese plans," *Guardian*, 4 February 2016.

101 **Many of China's "investments":** Iain Marlow and Dandan Li, "How Asia Fell Out of Love with China's Belt and Road Initiative," Bloomberg, 10 December 2018, https://www.bloomberg.com.

101 **The most extreme case was Sri Lanka:** Maria Abi-Habib, "How China Got Sri Lanka to Cough Up a Port," *New York Times*, 25 June 2018, https://www.nytimes.com.

101 **The western province of Xinjiang:** Frances Eve, "China Is Committing Ethnic Cleansing in Xinjiang—It's Time for the World to Stand Up," *Guardian*, 3 November 2018, https://www.theguardian.com.

Chapter 5: Boom: Putin's Chestiness Engulfs Ukraine

106 **Surkov isn't your run-of-the-mill propagandist:** Peter Pomerantsev, *Nothing Is True and Everything Is Possible: Adventures in Modern Russia* (London: Faber & Faber, 2017).

106 **Their support for Europe:** J. Feder, "The Russian Plot to Take Back Eastern Europe at the Expense of Gay Rights," *BuzzFeed News*, 9 November 2013, https://www.buzzfeednews.com.

106 **Social media lit up:** " 'Gay-titushki' Organized 'LGBT Community' Pride," National LGBT Portal of Ukraine, 11 January 2014, https://www.lgbt.org.ua.

107 **according to an investigation by the Ukrainian army:** Daniel McLaughlin, "Kiev Blames Putin Aide for Maidan Square Killings by Snipers," *Irish Times*, 21 February 2015, www.irishtimes.com.

107 **"There are many uniforms":** Timothy Snyder, *The Road to Unfreedom: Russia, Europe, America* (London: Tim Duggan Books, 2018), p. 183.

109 **great for ratings:** Peter Pomerantsev, "How Vladimir Putin Is Revolutionizing Information Warfare," *Atlantic*, 9 September 2014, https://www.theatlantic.com/.

113 **"[Putin] gave us notice":** Fox News Channel, 3 March 2014.

113 **"When the history books are written":** Evan Osnos, David Remnick and Joshua Yaffa, "Trump, Putin, and the New Cold War," *New Yorker*, 6 March 2017.

113 **Putin started his career as a KGB operative in East Germany:** Snyder, *The Road to Unfreedom*, p. 44.

114 **Yegor Gaidar, one of Russia's foremost economists:** Yegor Gaidar, *Collapse of an Empire: Lessons for Modern Russia*, translated by Antonina W. Bouis (Washington, D.C.: Brookings Institution Press, 2010).

114 **constructed a web of pipelines:** This paragraph is drawn from Randall Newnham, "Oil, Carrots, and Sticks: Russia's Energy Resources as a Foreign Policy Tool," *Journal of Eurasian Studies*, 2(2) (2011), pp. 134–43.

115 **GRAPH: RUSSIAN PIPELINES:** Adapted from Samuel Bailey, "Map of the Major Existing and Proposed Russian Natural Gas Transportation Pipelines in Europe" (15 November, 2009), under the Creative Commons Attribution 3.0 Unported license, https://commons.wikimedia.org/wiki/File:Major_russian _gas_pipelines_to_europe.png.

116 **has enjoyed essentially free gas from Putin:** Belarus does not even have to pay its heavily subsidised gas bills. In 2007, Lukashenko announced that he would not pay the $1.3 billion gas bill owed to Russia, and Putin cancelled the debt.

116 **However, as the 2000s went on Putin tussled with both regimes:** Newnham, "Oil, Carrots, and Sticks."

117 **Russia supplied 39 per cent of the EU's natural gas:** Szilvia Batkov, "Russia's Silent Shale Gas Victory in Ukraine," *Euractiv*, 2 September 2015, https:// www.euractiv.com/.

117 **Russia tried to negotiate access:** Stanley Reed, "Ukraine Signs Drilling Deal with Shell for Shale Gas," *New York Times*, 24 January 2013.

117 **Ukraine would become a net exporter to Europe:** Batkov, "Russia's Silent Shale Gas Victory."

120 **He found that the higher the oil price:** Cullen S. Hendrix, "Oil Prices and Interstate Conflict," *Conflict Management and Peace Science*, 34(6) (2017), pp. 575–96.

121 **GRAPH: CONFLICT & OIL PRICES:** Adapted from Cullen S. Hendrix, "Oil Prices and Interstate Conflict," *Conflict Management and Peace Science*, 34(6) (2017), pp. 575–96.

122 **Russia earned $53 billion a year from oil exports:** Adnan Vatansever, "Energy Sanctions and Russia: What Comes Next?," (Washington, D.C.: Atlantic Council, 2015), https://www.atlanticcouncil.org.

122 **Yaneer Bar-Yam estimates:** Daneshvar, Lagi and Bar-Yam, "The Impact of Speculation on Oil Prices."

122 **"Without outside help":** Anton Zverev, "Moscow Is Bankrolling Ukraine Rebels: Ex-Separatist Official," Reuters, 5 October 2016, https://www.reuters .com/.

124 **Russia's oil production continued to grow:** Bud Coote, "Impact of Sanctions on Russia's Energy Sector" (Washington, D.C.: Atlantic Council, 2018), https://www.atlanticcouncil.org.

126 **"We are special forces from the GRU":** Snyder, *The Road to Unfreedom*, p. 169.

Chapter 6: Bust: Venezuela's Fractal Apocalypse

134   **I discover that for her it is:** Reuters in Caracas, "Venezuela Crisis: Sterilizations Soar as Couples Count the Cost of Children," *Guardian*, 3 August 2016, http://www.theguardian.com.

136   **"negative financial bubble":** Den Fantazzini, "The Oil Price Crash in 2014/15: Was There a (Negative) Financial Bubble?," *Energy Policy*, 96 (September 2016), pp. 383–96.

136   **Harvard's commodity investment lost the endowment $1 billion:** Michael McDonald and Tatiana Freitas, "Harvard Blew $1 Billion in Bet on Tomatoes, Sugar, and Eucalyptus," Bloomberg, 1 March 2018, https://www.bloomberg .com/.

141   **a paper that said the coastline of Britain:** Benoit Mandelbrot, "How Long Is the Coast of Britain? Statistical Self-Similarity and Fractional Dimension," *Science*, 156(3775) (1967), pp. 636–8.

142   **how the resource curse could inflict economic pain:** Michael Bruno and Jeffrey Sachs, "Energy and Resource Allocation: A Dynamic Model of the 'Dutch Disease,'" *Review of Economic Studies*, 49(5) (1 December 1982), pp. 845–59. See also Jeffrey D. Sachs and Andrew M. Warner, "The Curse of Natural Resources," *European Economic Review*, 45(4) (1 May 2001), pp. 827–38.

143   **The farms were in disrepair:** Marta Kulesza, "Inflation and Hyperinflation in Venezuela (1970s–2016): A Post-Keynesian Interpretation," working paper (Berlin: Institute for International Political Economy, 2017).

143   **one of their most effective adversaries:** For example, Naomi Klein, *The Shock Doctrine: The Rise of Disaster Capitalism* (London: Macmillan, 2007).

143   **The last cycle started with the 1973 Arab–Israeli War:** This account is drawn from Raul Gallegos, *Crude Nation: How Oil Riches Ruined Venezuela* (Lincoln: University of Nebraska Press, 2016).

143   **When the oil price cratered in the early 1980s:** Kulesza, "Inflation and Hyperinflation in Venezuela (1970s–2016)."

144   **He warned of the dangers of black gold:** Hugo Chávez, "Discurso del Comandante Presidente Hugo Chávez ante la 54 Asamblea Anual De Fedecámaras," transcript from http://www.todo-chavez.gob.ve.

145   **"He set a good tone for a very ambitious agenda":** Clifford Krauss, "New Chief to Battle Venezuela's 'Cancer,'" *New York Times*, 3 February 1999.

145   **Clintonworld was impressed:** Diana Jean Schemo, "Venezuelan Leader Plans to Cut Spending to Pare Deficit," *New York Times*, 18 February 1999.

145   **"You haven't touched a single hair":** Rory Carroll, *Comandante: Hugo Chávez's Venezuela* (London: Penguin Books, 2014), p. 70.

145   **"Washington might green-light a coup against Chávez":** Jon Lee Anderson, "The Revolutionary," *New Yorker*, 3 September 2001.

146   **Discussion had long been taking place:** Christopher Marquis, "Bush Officials Met with Venezuelans Who Ousted Leader," *New York Times*, 16 April 2002. Juan Forero, "Documents Show C.I.A. Knew of a Coup Plot in Venezuela,"

New York Times, 3 December 2004. Ed Vulliamy, "Venezuela Coup Linked to Bush Team," *Guardian*, 21 April 2002.

147 **He finally took decisive control of PDVSA:** Carroll, *Comandante*, p. 102.

147 **Chávez now called himself a "socialist":** Cristina Marcano and Alberto Barrera Tyska, *Hugo Chávez*, translated by Kristina Cordero (New York: Random House, 2004), p. 22.

147 **But studies into his social programmes:** Michael Penfold-Becerra, "Clientelism and Social Funds: Evidence from Chávez's Misiones," *Latin American Politics and Society*, 49(4) (2007), pp. 63–84. Just as loyalists were rewarded, people who supported the opposition were also economically sanctioned, e.g., Chang-Tai Hsieh, Edward Miguel, Daniel Ortega and Francisco Rodriguez, "The Price of Political Opposition: Evidence from Venezuela's Maisanta," *American Economic Journal: Applied Economics*, 3(2) (2011), pp. 196–214.

147 **a strategy known as "clientelism":** Allen Hicken, "Clientelism," *Annual Review of Political Science*, 14(1) (2011), pp. 289–310.

147 **workers are surveilled by the managers:** Timothy Frye, Ora John Reuter and David Szakonyi, "Vote Brokers, Clientelist Appeals, and Voter Turnout: Evidence from Russia and Venezuela," *World Politics*, 71(4) (2019), pp. 710–46.

147 **Putin and his cronies raid:** Philip Hanson, *Reiderstvo: Asset-Grabbing in Russia* (London: Chatham House, 2014).

147 **hand over $100 billion:** Stephen Kalin and Katie Paul, "Saudi Arabia Says It Has Seized over $100 Billion in Corruption Purge," Reuters, 30 January 2018, https://www.reuters.com.

148 **the average Venezuelan lost twenty-four pounds:** Vivian Sequera, "Venezuelans Report Big Weight Losses in 2017 as Hunger Hits," Reuters, 21 February 2018, https://www.reuters.com.

148 **sanctions inflicted 40,000 deaths:** Mark Weisbrot and Jeffrey Sachs, "Economic Sanctions as Collective Punishment: The Case of Venezuela" (Washington, D.C.: Center for Economic and Policy Research, 2019).

149 **GRAPH: VENEZUELAN & COLOMBIAN OIL PRODUCTION:** Adapted from Mark Weisbrot and Jeffrey Sachs, "Economic Sanctions as Collective Punishment: The Case of Venezuela" (Washington, D.C.: Center for Economic and Policy Research, 2019).

155 **Five million have already fled:** International Organization for Migration, "Venezuelan Refugee and Migrant Crisis," 10 October 2019, https://www.iom .int/venezuela-refugee-and-migrant-crisis.

Chapter 7: Multiply: Climate Chaos in Kenya from *Mad Max* to *War Games*

160 **East Africa is supposed to be getting wetter:** David P. Rowell, Ben B. B. Booth, Sharon E. Nicholson and Peter Good, "Reconciling Past and Future Rainfall Trends over East Africa," *Journal of Climate*, 28(24) (2015), pp. 9768–88.

160 **Raids are more frequent:** Carol R. Ember, Teferi Abate Adem, Ian Skoggard

and Eric C. Jones, "Livestock Raiding and Rainfall Variability in Northwestern Kenya," *Civil Wars*, 14(2) (2012), pp. 159–81.

161   **The rising temperature will unleash all kinds of chaos:** David Wallace-Wells, *The Uninhabitable Earth: A Story of the Future* (London: Penguin, 2019).

161   **A recent survey of climate experts in *Nature*:** K. J. Mach, C. M. Kraan, W. N. Adger, H. Buhaug, M. Burke, J. D. Fearon, C. B. Field, C. S. Hendrix, J. F. Maystadt, J. O'Loughlin, P. Roessler, J. Scheffran, K. Schultz and N. von Uexkull, "Climate as a Risk Factor for Armed Conflict," *Nature*, 571 (2019), pp. 193–7.

162   **"Humanity would revert to its norm of constant battles for diminishing resources":** Peter Schwartz and Doug Randall, "An Abrupt Climate Change Scenario and Its Implications for United States National Security" (2004), www.iatp.org.

163   **"Economic and environmental conditions in already fragile areas":** *National Security and the Threat of Climate Change* (Washington, D.C.: Center for Naval Analyses, 2007).

164   **GRAPH: CONFLICT & RAINFALL IN AFRICA:** Adapted from Cullen S. Hendrix and Idean Salehyan, "Climate Change, Rainfall, and Social Conflict in Africa," *Journal of Peace Research*, 49(1) (2012), pp. 35–50.

164   **They then ran a statistical analysis:** Cullen S. Hendrix and Idean Salehyan, "Climate Change, Rainfall, and Social Conflict in Africa," *Journal of Peace Research*, 49(1) (2012), pp. 35–50.

167   **global yields of maize will decline by 7.4 per cent:** Chuang Zhao, Bing Liu, Shilong Piao, Xuhui Wang, David B. Lobell, Yao Huang, Mengtian Huang, Yitong Yao, Simona Bassu and Philippe Ciais, "Temperature Increase Reduces Global Yields of Major Crops in Four Independent Estimates," *Proceedings of the National Academy of Sciences*, 114(35) (2017), pp. 9326–31.

167   **grow at approximately 1.1 per cent a year:** World Bank, "Population Growth (Annual %)" (Washington, D.C.: World Bank Group), retrieved from https://data.worldbank.org/indicator/SP.POP.GROW.

168   **He showed that, like with houses in London, modern famines:** Amartya Sen, "Famines as Failures of Exchange Entitlements," *Economic and Political Weekly*, 11(31/33) (August 1976), pp. 1273–80.

170   **Because even having access to powerful predictive technology:** See Chapter 3.

174   **"The challenges currently posed by climate change":** Mark Carney, "Breaking the Tragedy of the Horizon—Climate Change and Financial Stability," Speech at Lloyd's of London, 29 September 2015.

174   **a flurry of research among the world's financial firefighters:** Patrick Bolton, Morgan Després, Luiz Awazu Pereira da Silva, Frédéric Samama and Romain Svartzman, *The Green Swan* (Basel: Bank of International Settlements, 2020). Robert Litterman, Clark E. Anderson, Nathaniel Bullard, Ben Caldecott, Martina L. Cheung, John T. Colas, Robert Coviello, Peter W. Davidson, Jeffrey Dukes and Hervé P. Duteil, *Managing Climate Risk in the US Financial System* (Washington, D.C.: Commodity Futures Trading Commission, 2020).

175 **disrupted the majority of US GDP:** Litterman, Anderson, Bullard, et al., *Managing Climate Risk in the US Financial System.*

175 **"climate change could prompt increased morbidity":** Carney, "Breaking the Tragedy of the Horizon."

175 **valued at $28 trillion:** Adam Tooze, "Why Central Banks Need to Step Up on Global Warming," *Foreign Policy*, 20 (2019), https://foreignpolicy.com/.

176 **"paradox is that *success is failure*":** Mark Carney, "Resolving the Climate Paradox," Arthur Burns Memorial Lecture, Berlin, 22 September 2016.

176 **underpricing climate risks by as much as 50 per cent:** S&P Global Ratings, "Effects of Weather Events on Corporate Earnings Are Gathering Force," *Resilience Economics*, 11 June 2018, pp. 1–23.

176 **The stock market, allegedly the most "efficient" market:** International Monetary Fund, *Global Financial Stability Report* (Washington, D.C.: International Monetary Fund, 2020).

176 **flood insurance in parts of the UK:** Bret Christophers, "The Allusive Market: Insurance of Flood Risk in Neoliberal Britain," *Economy and Society*, 48(1) (2 January 2019), pp. 1–29.

176 **The European Central Bank found that banks:** European Central Bank, "Financial Stability Review, November 2020," 25 November 2020, https://www.ecb.europa.eu.

176 **sixty major banks have invested over $3.8 trillion:** *Banking on Climate Change: Fossil Fuel Finance Report 2021* (San Francisco: Rainforest Action Network, 2021), https://www.ran.org/.

Chapter 8: Arbitrage: Al-Shabaab, the Terrorist Hedge Fund

185 **3.5 million were at risk from hunger and starvation:** Daniel Maxwell and Merry Fitzpatrick, "The 2011 Somalia Famine: Context, Causes, and Complications," *Global Food Security*, 1(1) (2012), pp. 5–12. Ken Menkhaus, "No Access: Critical Bottlenecks in the 2011 Somali Famine," *Global Food Security*, 1(1) (2012), pp. 29–35.

186 **The "hunger weapon" is as old as warfare itself:** J. Cribb, "War and Hunger," in *Food or War* (Cambridge, UK: Cambridge University Press, 2019), pp. 26–31.

186 **Livestock accounts for up to 40 per cent of GDP:** Jean-François Maystadt and Olivier Ecker, "Extreme Weather and Civil War: Does Drought Fuel Conflict in Somalia through Livestock Price Shocks?," *American Journal of Agricultural Economics*, 96(4) (2014), pp. 1157–82.

187 **citing research by the United Nations Development Programme:** UNDP, *Journey to Extremism in Africa: Drivers, Incentives and the Tipping Point for Recruitment* (New York: Regional Bureau for Africa United Nations Development Programme, 2017).

187 **when cattle prices decline in Somalia by 6 per cent:** Maystadt and Ecker, "Extreme Weather and Civil War."

188 **"Intentionally using starvation of civilians":** Statute of the International

Criminal Court, adopted by the UN Diplomatic Conference of Plenipotentiaries on the Establishment of an International Criminal Court, Rome, 17 July 1998, UN Doc. A/CON.183/9, Article 8(2)(b)(xxv).

188 **"Though less publicised than the drought"**: Maxwell and Fitzpatrick, "The 2011 Somalia Famine."

189 **The drought depressed incomes**: Maystadt and Ecker, "Extreme Weather and Civil War."

Chapter 9: Short: Coffee, *Coyotes*, Kids in Cages

191 **"You are making me look like an idiot"**: Michael D. Shear and Julie Hirschfeld Davis, "Shoot Migrants' Legs, Build Alligator Moat: Behind Trump's Ideas for Border," *New York Times*, 1 October 2019, https://www.nytimes.com.

191 **"Privately, the president had often"**: Ibid.

191 **Endemic violence in Honduras and El Salvador**: UNDOC Staff, "Global Study on Homicide" (Vienna: United Nations Office on Drugs and Crime, 2019). Also, World Bank Data, data.worldbank.org.

194 **as migrants flood the cities, the labour supply increases**: Mathilde Maurel and Michele Tuccio, "Climate Instability, Urbanisation and International Migration," *Journal of Development Studies*, 52(5) (3 May 2016), pp. 735–52.

194 **By 2050, there could be up to a billion climate refugees**: Anouch Missirian and Wolfram Schlenker, "Asylum Applications Respond to Temperature Fluctuations," *Science*, 358(6370) (December 2017), pp. 1610–14.

195 **Global Climate Risk Index declared it the second-most vulnerable country**: Research Program on Climate Change, Agriculture, and Food Security, "Guatemala," https://ccafs.cgiar.org/regions/latin-america/guatemala.

196 **"The coffee market is struggling"**: Emiko Terazono, "Coffee Market Struggles under 'Big Short' Position," *Financial Times*, 25 April 2018, https://www.ft.com.

196 **Economists have long found bubbles in the coffee market**: Kai-Hua Wang, Chi-Wei Su, Ran Tao and Lin-Na Hao, "Are There Periodically Collapsing Bubble Behaviours in the Global Coffee Market?," *Agrekon*, 59(1) (2020), pp. 65–77.

201 **He spent his winnings buying Jennifer Lopez's Bel-Air mansion**: Antoine Gara, "How a Goat Farmer Built a Doomsday Machine That Just Booked a 4,144% Return," *Forbes*, 13 April 2020, https://www.forbes.com.

Chapter 10: Covid-19: The Climate–Finance Doomsday Device Detonates

205 **a report published in *Nature* warned**: Kate E. Jones, Nikkita G. Patel, Marc A. Levy, Adam Storeygard, Deborah Balk, John L. Gittleman and Peter Daszak, "Global Trends in Emerging Infectious Diseases," *Nature*, 451(7181) (2008), pp. 990–93.

206 **These "spill-over events" are increasing**: Colin J. Carlson, Gregory F. Albery, Cory Merow, Christopher H. Trisos, Casey M. Zipfel, Evan A. Eskew, Kevin

J. Olival, Noam Ross and Shweta Bansal, "Climate Change Will Drive Novel Cross-Species Viral Transmission," *BioRxiv*, January 2020.

206 **China is going through the fastest urbanisation:** Andreas Malm, *Corona, Climate, Chronic Emergency: War Communism in the Twenty-First Century* (London and New York: Verso Books, 2020), p. 65.

206 **the pandemic had triggered the very kind of climate–finance doomsday:** See Chapter 7.

206 **"climate change could prompt increased morbidity":** Mark Carney, "Breaking the Tragedy of the Horizon—Climate Change and Financial Stability," Speech at Lloyd's of London, 29 September 2015.

206 **making such outbreaks more likely:** Caroline Buckee, Elena Shevliakova, Andrew J. Tatem, William R. Boos, Daniel M. Weinberger and Virginia E. Pitzer, "Identifying Climate Drivers of Infectious Disease Dynamics: Recent Advances and Challenges Ahead," *Proceedings of the Royal Society*, 284 (August 2017), p. 20170901.

206 **"Rich Americans Activate Pandemic Escape Plans":** Olivia Carville, "'We Needed to Go': Rich Americans Activate Pandemic Escape Plans," Bloomberg, 19 April 2020, https://www.bloomberg.com.

206 **Private jets were in short supply:** Rupert Neate, "Super-Rich Jet Off to Disaster Bunkers Amid Coronavirus Outbreak," *Guardian*, 11 March 2020, http://www.theguardian.com.

207 **3,612 per cent return:** Gara, "How a Goat Farmer Built a Doomsday Machine That Just Booked a 4,144% Return."

207 **"These returns likely surpass any other investment":** Ibid.

207 **I delved into the market's "rules of the game":** As discussed in Chapter 2.

208 **"I hear new news every day":** Robert Burton, *The Anatomy of Melancholy* (Project Gutenberg, 2004), https://www.gutenberg.org.

208 **Behind this chaos was a climatic shock:** David D. Zhang, Harry F. Lee, Cong Wang, Baosheng Li, Qing Pei, Jane Zhang and Yulun An, "The Causality Analysis of Climate Change and Large-Scale Human Crisis," *Proceedings of the National Academy of Sciences*, 108(42) (October 2011), pp. 17296–301.

208 **For two decades, crops had frozen:** Geoffrey Parker, *Global Crisis: War, Climate Change and Catastrophe in the Seventeenth Century* (New Haven, CT, and London: Yale University Press, 2013), p. 9.

208 **"solitary, poor, nasty, brutish, short":** Thomas Hobbes, *Leviathan* (London: Penguin Classics, 1982).

208 **a climatic shock which became a price shock:** Parker, *Global Crisis*.

208 **some had begun to recognise that prices were at the root:** Karl Gunnar Persson, *Grain Markets in Europe, 1500–1900: Integration and Deregulation* (Cambridge, UK: Cambridge University Press, 1999).

209 **Farms could barely produce enough:** David Hackett Fischer, *The Great Wave: Price Revolutions and the Rhythm of History* (Oxford, UK: Oxford University Press, 1996), p. 120.

209 **Even the smallest change in the weather:** Cédric Chambru, "Environmental Shocks, Religious Struggle, and Resilience: A Contribution to the Eco-

nomic History of Ancien Régime France," PhD thesis (Geneva: University of Geneva, 2019).

209   **"Long live the king"**: Steven L. Kaplan, *Bread, Politics and Political Economy in the Reign of Louis XV* (2nd edn., London: Anthem Press, 2015), p. 661.

209   **"Inform M. Turgot immediately"**: Ibid.

209   **a new "policy of freedom"**: A.R.J. Turgot, "Extracts from 'Letters to the Contrôleur-Général (AbbéTerray) on the Grain Trade' (1770)," in *The Economics of A.R.J. Turgot*, ed. P. D. Groenewegen (The Hague: Springer Netherlands, 1977), pp. 164–88.

210   **In Joseph Schumpeter's** *History of Economic Analysis*: Joseph Schumpeter, *History of Economic Analysis* (London: G. Allen & Unwin, 1955), p. 238.

210   **"Starving or being killed meant the same thing"**: Cynthia Bouton, *The Flour War: Gender, Class, and Community in Late Ancien Régime French Society* (University Park, PA: Penn State Press, 2010).

210   **In April, 300 riots rocked the Paris Basin**: Ibid.

210   **As Marie Antoinette wept that her husband**: Kaplan, *Bread, Politics and Political Economy*, p. 661.

210   **He rescinded the king's command**: George Rudé, *The Crowd in History: A Study of Popular Disturbances in France and England, 1730–1848* (New York: Wiley, 1964), p. 27.

210   **rioting public called it the** *guerre des farines*: Bouton, *The Flour War*, p. xx.

210   **on their highest day, Revolutionaries stormed the Bastille**: Fischer, *The Great Wave*, p. 147.

211   **Wheat prices in the capital fell by 35 per cent**: Kevin O'Rourke, "The European Grain Invasion, 1870–1913," *Journal of Economic History*, 57(4) (1997), pp. 775–801.

211   **Socialist parties in Britain, Germany, Belgium**: Paul Bairoch, "European Trade Policy, 1815–1914," in *The Cambridge Economic History of Europe*, ed. Peter Mathias and Sydney Pollard (Cambridge: Cambridge University Press, 1989), p. 136.

211   **There were only twenty-three recorded deaths**: Rune Møller Stahl and Mikkel Thorup, "The Economics of Starvation: Laissez-Faire Ideology and Famine in Colonial India," in *Intellectual History of Economic Normativities* (New York: Palgrave Macmillan, 2016), pp. 169–84.

211   **"Turgot conceived, developed"**: Lady Betty Balfour, *The History of Lord Lytton's Indian Administration, 1876 to 1880* (London: Longmans, 1899), pp. 235–6.

211   **Instead, Indian labourers would be forced to pay**: Stuart Sweeney, "Indian Railways and Famine 1875–1914: Magic Wheels and Empty Stomachs," *Essays in Economic & Business History*, 26(1) (2012).

211   **"India will eventually enjoy"**: Balfour, *The History of Lord Lytton's Indian Administration*, p. 235.

211   **estimates vary between 5.5 million and 10 million**: Mike Davis, *Late Victorian Holocausts: El Niño Famines and the Making of the Third World* (London and New York: Verso Books, 2002), p. 7.

211 "bore almost the appearance of a battlefield": William Digby, *The Famine Campaign in Southern India 1876–1878* (London: Longmans, Green and Co., 1878), p. 26.

212 The railways just made it cheaper for merchants: Ajit Kumar Ghose, "Food Supply and Starvation: A Study of Famines with Reference to the Indian Sub-Continent," *Oxford Economic Papers*, 34(2) (1982), pp. 368–89.

212 killing between 18 million and 22 million people: Arup Maharatna, *The Demography of Famines: An Indian Historical Perspective* (Delhi: Oxford University Press, 1996).

212 Britain was the world's largest importer of wheat: Margaret Barnett, *British Food Policy During the First World War (RLE The First World War)* (London: Routledge, 2014).

212 European nations battled each other with trade wars: Adam J. Tooze, *The Deluge: The Great War, America and the Remaking of the Global Order, 1916–1931* (London: Viking, 2014).

212 "end of *laissez-faire*": John Maynard Keynes, "The End of Laissez-Faire," in *Essays in Persuasion*, ed. J. M. Keynes (London: Palgrave Macmillan, 2010), pp. 272–94.

212 Keynes saw how political chaos: Zachary D. Carter, *The Price of Peace: Money, Democracy, and the Life of John Maynard Keynes* (New York: Random House Publishing Group, 2020).

213 He was born at the peak: Quinn Slobodian, *Globalists: The End of Empire and the Birth of Neoliberalism* (Cambridge, MA: Harvard University Press, 2018).

213 styled himself as Keynes's foremost American critic: Wyatt C. Wells, *Economist in an Uncertain World: Arthur F. Burns and the Federal Reserve, 1970–78* (New York: Columbia University Press, 1994), p. 12.

213 "Excess government spending produces inflation": Justin Martin, *Greenspan: The Man Behind Money* (New York: Basic Books, 2001), p. 29.

214 radicalised Friedman from an academic economist to a political crusader: Milton Friedman and Rose D. Friedman, *Two Lucky People: Memoirs* (Chicago: University of Chicago Press, 1999), p. 333.

214 Hayek argued that the new social provisions: Friedrich A. Hayek, *The Road to Serfdom* (London: Routledge & Kegan Paul, 1962).

214 This is why they called themselves "Neo-Liberals": Milton Friedman, "Neo-Liberalism and Its Prospects," *Farmand*, 17 February 1951, pp. 89–93.

214 "[A]t the height of the British empire": Milton Friedman, "The Milton Friedman View," in *Milton Friedman in South Africa*, eds. Meyer Feldberg, Kate Jowell and Stephen Mulholland (Cape Town and Johannesburg: Graduate School of Business of the University of Cape Town, 1976), pp. 42–52.

214 In 1965, *Time* magazine made Keynes: Nicholas Wapshott, *Keynes Hayek: The Clash That Defined Modern Economics* (London: W. W. Norton & Company, 2011), p. 239.

215 "The Government incessantly spread": Milton Friedman, "The Fragility of Freedom," in *Milton Friedman in South Africa*, eds. Feldberg, Jowell and Mulholland, pp. 3–10.

215 **"a plan to make the economy scream":** Jussi M. Hanhimaki, *The Flawed Architect: Henry Kissinger and American Foreign Policy* (Oxford: Oxford University Press, 2004), p. 103.

215 **A host of economic weapons were deployed:** Steven L. Spiegel, *The Other Arab–Israeli Conflict: Making America's Middle East Policy, from Truman to Reagan* (Chicago: University of Chicago Press, 2014), p. 255.

216 **"We have to get the bloody Saudi [ambassador] in":** TELECON, Cisco/Kissinger, 11 October 1973.

216 **"We shall ruin your industries":** Rüdiger Graf, "Making Use of the 'Oil Weapon': Western Industrialized Countries and Arab Petropolitics in 1973–1974," *Diplomatic History*, 36(1) (2012), pp. 185–208.

216 **"These people are like animals":** Allen J. Matusow, *Nixon's Economy: Booms, Busts, Dollars, and Votes* (Lawrence: University Press of Kansas), p. 263.

216 **"Economists are distinctly in a period of re-examination":** Soma S. Golden, "Federal Policies Puzzle Economists," *New York Times*, 29 December 1973.

216 **"Inflation is produced in Washington":** Milton Friedman, "Is Inflation a Curable Disease?," Alex C. Walker Memorial Lecture, 5 December 1974.

217 **"We used to think that you could spend":** James Callaghan, "Leader's Speech," Blackpool Labour Party Conference, 1976, http://www.britishpoliticalspeech .org/.

217 **Jimmy Carter was next:** Daniel Stedman Jones, *Masters of the Universe: Hayek, Friedman, and the Birth of Neoliberal Politics* (Princeton, NJ: Princeton University Press, 2014).

217 **The onset of stagflation did not correlate to rising deficits:** Michael Bruno and Jeffrey Sachs, *Economics of Worldwide Stagflation* (Cambridge, MA: Harvard University Press, 1985).

218 **"I have a young wife, I need the capital":** Nomi Prins, *All the Presidents' Bankers* (New York: Nation Books, 2015), p. 293.

218 **Citibank's branches in Saudi Arabia were the envy of Wall Street:** Phillip L. Zweig, *Wriston: Walter Wriston, Citibank, and the Rise and Fall of American Financial Supremacy* (New York: Random House Value Publications, 1997).

218 **half of Citibank's profits came from these loans:** Raúl L. Madrid, *Overexposed: US Banks Confront the Third World Debt Crisis* (London: Routledge, 1992), p. 46.

218 **"Countries can't go bust":** Judith Stein, *Pivotal Decade: How the United States Traded Factories for Finance in the Seventies* (New Haven, CT, and London: Yale University Press, 2010), p. 94.

219 **"We need to develop the rule of law in this field":** Barbara Stallings, *Banker to the Third World: US Portfolio Investment in Latin America, 1900–1986* (Berkeley: University of California Press, 2018), p. 283.

219 **"Bankers are not alone":** Arthur F. Burns, "The Need for Order in International Finance" (New York: Columbia University Graduate School of Business, 12 April 1977).

220 **Between 1976 and 1992, there were 146 major anti-austerity riots:** John K. Walton and David Seddon, *Free Markets and Food Riots: The Politics of Global*

Adjustment (Hoboken, NJ: John Wiley & Sons, 2008). John Walton and Charles Ragin, "Global and National Sources of Political Protest: Third World Responses to the Debt Crisis," *American Sociological Review*, 55(6) (1990), pp. 876–90. John Bohstedt, "Food Riots and the Politics of Provisions in World History," *IDS Working Papers*, no. 444 (2014), pp. 1–31.

220 **Its "structural-adjustment" programmes demanded:** Andreas Kern, Bernhard Reinsberg and Matthias Rau-Göhring, "IMF Conditionality and Central Bank Independence," *European Journal of Political Economy*, 59 (2019), pp. 212–29.

220 **At the time, central banks were integrated:** Gerald Epstein, "Central Banks as Agents of Economic Development," *WIDER Research Paper No. 2006/54* (Helsinki: United Nations University World Institute for Development Economics Research, 2006).

221 **advocates of this radical new:** Thomas J. Sargent and Neil Wallace, "Some Unpleasant Monetarist Arithmetic," *Federal Reserve Bank of Minneapolis Quarterly Review*, 5(3) (1981), pp. 1–17.

221 **"in a democracy to have so much power":** Milton Friedman, "Should There Be an Independent Central Bank?," in *Dollars and Deficits: Inflation, Monetary Policy and the Balance of Payments* (Englewood Cliffs, NJ: Prentice Hall, 1968).

221 **"Banks made loans to the debtor countries":** Milton Friedman, "'No' to More Money for the IMF," *Newsweek*, 14 November 1983.

222 **"I've been governor of a small state for twelve years":** Presidential candidates debate, "Presidential Candidates Debates," C-SPAN, 15 October 1992, https://www.c-span.org/.

222 **Bond traders began selling US Treasuries:** Victor F. Zonana, "Bond Market Packs a Punch Clinton Is Already Feeling," *Los Angeles Times*, 21 November 1992, https://www.latimes.com.

222 **"the vigilantes can step in to restore law and order":** Ibid.

222 **Fed chairman Alan Greenspan went to the president-elect:** Bob Woodward, *Agenda: Inside the Clinton White House* (London: Simon & Schuster, 1994).

223 **"I always ask the question: why does a dog lick his dick?":** Ibid.

223 **"the most conservative and skeptical critics of all":** Jonathan Fuerbringer, "Clinton Plan's Economic Drag Cited," *New York Times*, 5 August 1993.

223 **"It's a wonderful time to be a bond trader":** Floyd Norris, "Bond Traders Love Clinton, and Vice Versa," *New York Times*, 14 March 1993.

223 **Clinton is "enamoured of the bond market":** Jonathan Fuerbringer, "Bond Market Shows Doubt Over Clinton," *New York Times*, 28 April 1993.

224 **He turned to a *Wall Street Journal* reporter:** Norris, "Bond Traders Love Clinton, and Vice Versa."

224 **they used their "monetary dominance" over elected politicians:** Cristina Bodea and Masaaki Higashijima, "Central Bank Independence and Fiscal Policy: Can the Central Bank Restrain Deficit Spending?," *British Journal of Political Science*, 47(1) (2017), pp. 47–70. For other evidence of this phenomenon, see Thomas R. Cusack, "Partisanship in the Setting and Coordination

of Fiscal and Monetary Policies," *European Journal of Political Research*, 40(1) (August 2001), pp. 93–115.

225 **The rotating door between private banks and central banks:** Christopher Adolph, *Bankers, Bureaucrats, and Central Bank Politics: The Myth of Neutrality* (Cambridge, UK: Cambridge University Press, 2013).

225 **"Central bankers are only human":** Alan S. Blinder, *Central Banking in Theory and Practice* (Cambridge, MA: MIT Press, 1999), p. 61.

225 **deliver the only thing he was supposed to deliver:** Some central banks, including the Federal Reserve, have more than one official goal. The Fed has a dual mandate of price stability and full employment, but ever since Paul Volcker's tenure, the Fed has focused first and foremost on price stability. This is because the Fed, like most "independent" central banks, sees price stability as the key to economic growth and full employment.

225 **Peter Orszag visited the president-elect in Chicago:** Reed Hundt, *A Crisis Wasted: Barack Obama's Defining Decisions* (New York: Rosetta Books, 2019), p. 27.

226 **Yardeni, the famed economist:** "Return of the Bond Market Vigilantes," *Wall Street Journal*, 29 May 2008, https://www.wsj.com.

226 **Orszag prepared to battle the bond vigilantes:** Ron Suskind, *Confidence Men: Wall Street, Washington and the Education of a President* (New York: Harper Collins, 2012).

226 **Only the assault never came:** I have drawn from, and am heavily indebted to, Adam Tooze's work in this section, particularly Adam Tooze, "Notes on the Global Condition: Of Bond Vigilantes, Central Bankers and the Crisis, 2008–2017," 7 November 2017, https://adamtooze.com.

226 **"The banks have accounts with the Fed":** CBS, "Interview with Ben Bernanke," *60 Minutes*, 3 December 2009.

227 **Trichet demanded "large-scale privatizations":** "Trichet e Draghi: Un'azione Pressante per Ristabilire La Fiducia Degli Investitori," *Corriere Della Sera*, https://www.corriere.it, accessed 14 July 2020.

227 **"The role of bond markets in relation to the ECB":** Tooze, "Notes on the Global Condition."

227 **"fiscal policy too will have to change":** Neil Irwin, *The Alchemists: Inside the Secret World of Central Bankers* (London: Headline, 2013), p. 233.

228 **In January 2010, Obama declared:** Adam Tooze, *Crashed: How a Decade of Financial Crises Changed the World* (London: Penguin, 2019), p. 351.

228 **once Wall Street ceased to benefit from quantitative easing:** Juan Antonio Montecino and Gerald Epstein, "The Political Economy of QE and the Fed: Who Gained, Who Lost and Why Did It End?," in *The Political Economy of Central Banking* (Cheltenham: Edward Elgar Publishing, 2019), Chapter 19.

229 **"I think that's a problem that's going to go away":** The White House, "Remarks by President Trump at a Business Roundtable, New Delhi, India," 25 February 2020, https://www.whitehouse.gov. Edward Luce, "Inside Trump's Coronavirus Meltdown," *Financial Times*, 14 May 2020.

229 **"take off its Clark Kent spectacles"**: Boris Johnson, "PM Speech in Greenwich," 3 February 2020, https://www.gov.uk.

230 **"herd immunity, protect the economy and if that means some pensioners die, too bad"**: Caroline Wheeler and Tim Shipman, "Coronavirus: Ten Days That Shook Britain—and Changed the Nation For Ever," *Times*, 22 March 2020, https://www.thetimes.co.uk.

230 **"never catch anything"**: Tom Phillips, "Jair Bolsonaro Claims Brazilians 'Never Catch Anything' as Covid-19 Cases Rise," *Guardian*, 27 March 2020, https://www.theguardian.com.

230 **The Bank of England governor, Andrew Bailey:** Andrew Bailey, "Bank of England Is Not Doing 'Monetary Financing,'" *Financial Times*, 5 April 2020, https://www.ft.com.

231 **"The UK has become the first country"**: Philip Georgiadis and Chris Giles, "Bank of England to Directly Finance UK Government's Extra Spending," *Financial Times*, 9 April 2020, https://www.ft.com.

231 **the Bank of International Settlements reported:** Andreas Schrimph, Hyun Song Shin and Vladyslav Sushko, "Leverage and Margin Spirals in Fixed Income Markets During the Covid-19 Crisis," *BIS Bulletin*, no. 2 (2 April 2020), www.bis.org.

231 **Fed chairman Jerome Powell upgraded:** J. J. Kinahan, "'Whatever We Can, for as Long as It Takes': Fed Committed to Long-Term Economic Support with Low Rates," *Forbes*, 10 June 2020, https://www.forbes.com.

233 **even the IMF was forced to admit:** Chris Giles, "IMF Says Austerity Is Not Inevitable to Ease Pandemic Impact on Public Finances," *Financial Times*, 14 October 2020, https://www.ft.com.

233 **He launched a PR campaign instructing unemployed ballet dancers:** "Dying Swan or Lame Duck? Why 'Fatima' the Ballerina's Next Job Was Tripping Up the Government," *Guardian*, 13 October 2020, http://www.theguardian.com.

233 **He was forced to reverse course days later:** Chris Giles, "Rishi Sunak Steps Up Efforts to Avert Mass Unemployment," *Financial Times*, 22 October 2020, https://www.ft.com.

233 **"If we think borrowing is the answer to everything"**: Fraser Nelson and Katy Balls, "'It's Not Morally Right to Keep Borrowing at These Levels': Rishi Sunak's Plan to Fix the UK Economy," *Spectator*, 19 December 2020, https://www.spectator.co.uk.

233 **"sacred duty"**: "Rishi Sunak Vows to 'Balance Books' Despite Pandemic," BBC News, 5 October 2020, https://www.bbc.com.

233 **"I promise you over our dead bodies"**: Kayla Epstein, "'Over Our Dead Bodies': Lindsey Graham Vows Congress Won't Extend Additional $600 Coronavirus-Related Unemployment Benefits, as US Death Toll Crosses the 60,000 Mark," *Business Insider*, 30 April 2020.

233 **"I would rather die than kill the country"**: Chauncey Devega, "Trump's Death Cult Finally Says It: Time to Kill the 'Useless Eaters' for Capitalism," *Salon*, 27 March 2020, https://www.salon.com.

233 **"turn to cannibalism"**: "Rush Limbaugh: Americans Should 'Adapt' to Coro-

navirus, like Famous Pioneers Who 'Had to Turn to Cannibalism,'" *Media Matters for America*, 14 July 2020, https://www.mediamatters.org.

234 **Jerome Powell announced that the Federal Reserve:** Jerome Powell, "New Economic Challenges and the Fed's Monetary Policy Review," 28 August 2020, https://www.fed.gov.

Conclusion: Markets and Madness

237 **The white colonists, he writes, believed:** Peter Worsley, *The Trumpet Shall Sound: A Study of "Cargo" Cults in Melanesia* (2nd edn., London: MacGibbon & Kee, 1968).

Index

About the Author

Rupert Russell is a writer and filmmaker. He has filmed in twenty countries and made two award-winning documentaries. He has a PhD in sociology from Harvard and has published in *The Independent*, *Dazed*, and *Salon*. *Price Wars* is his first book.